Mozart's *La clemenza di Tito*
A Reappraisal

Magnus Tessing Schneider and Ruth Tatlow (eds.)

Published by
Stockholm University Press
Stockholm University
SE-106 91 Stockholm, Sweden
www.stockholmuniversitypress.se

Text © The Author(s) 2018
License CC-BY

Supporting Agency (funding): Performing Premodernity, Stockholm University, The Swedish Foundation for Humanities and Social Sciences

First published 2018
Cover Illustration: P. Travaglia, *Sala ter[r]ena destinata per le pubbliche udienze*, Pietro Travaglia's Sketchbook, f. 11. Published with permission from the Collection of Theatre History at the Hungarian National Széchényi Library, Budapest. Access. Nr. 1955/9645
Cover Copyright: Collection of Theatre History at the Hungarian National Széchényi Library License: CC BY-NC-ND
Cover designed by Karl Edqvist, SUP

Stockholm Studies in Culture and Aesthetics ISSN: 2002-3227

ISBN (Paperback): 978-91-7635-055-3
ISBN (PDF): 978-91-7635-052-2
ISBN (EPUB): 978-91-7635-053-9
ISBN (MOBI): 978-91-7635-054-6

DOI: https://doi.org/10.16993/ban

This work is licensed under the Creative Commons Attribution 4.0 Unported License. To view a copy of this license, visit creativecommons.org/licenses/by/4.0/ or send a letter to Creative Commons, 444 Castro Street, Suite 900, Mountain View, California, 94041, USA. This license allows for copying any part of the work for personal and commercial use, providing author attribution is clearly stated.

Suggested citation:
Tessing Schneider, M. and Tatlow, R. (eds.) 2018 *Mozart's* La clemenza di Tito: *A Reappraisal*. Stockholm: Stockholm University Press. DOI: https://doi.org/10.16993/ban. License: CC-BY 4.0

 To read the free, open access version of this book online, visit https://doi.org/10.16993/ban or scan this QR code with your mobile device.

Stockholm Studies in Culture and Aesthetics

Stockholm Studies in Culture and Aesthetics (SiCA) (ISSN 2002-3227) is a peer-reviewed series of monographs and edited volumes published by Stockholm University Press. SiCA strives to provide a broad forum for research on culture and aesthetics, including the disciplines of Art History, Heritage Studies, Curating Art, History of Ideas, Literary Studies, Musicology, and Performance and Dance Studies.

In terms of subjects and methods, the orientation is wide: critical theory, cultural studies and historiography, modernism and modernity, materiality and mediality, performativity and visual culture, children's literature and children's theatre, queer and gender studies.

It is the ambition of SiCA to place equally high demands on the academic quality of the manuscripts it accepts as those applied by refereed international journals and academic publishers of a similar orientation. SiCA accepts manuscripts in English, Swedish, Danish, and Norwegian.

Editorial Board

Jørgen Bruhn, Professor of Comparative Literature at the Centre for Intermedial and Multimodal Studies at Linnaeus University in Växjö
Karin Dirke, Associate Professor of History of Ideas at the Department of Culture and Aesthetics at Stockholm University
Elina Druker, Associate Professor of Literature at the Department of Culture and Aesthetics at Stockholm University
Johanna Ethnersson Pontara, Associate Professor of Musicology at the Department of Culture and Aesthetics at Stockholm University
Kristina Fjelkestam, Professor of Gender Studies at the Department of Ethnology, History of Religions and Gender Studies at Stockholm University

Malin Hedlin Hayden, Professor of Art History at the Department of Culture and Aesthetics at Stockholm University

Christer Johansson (coordination and communication), PhD Literature, Research Officer at the Department of Culture and Aesthetics at Stockholm University

Jacob Lund, Associate Professor of Aesthetics and Culture at the School of Communication and Culture - Aesthetics and Culture, Aarhus University

Catharina Nolin, Associate Professor of Art History at the Department of Culture and Aesthetics at Stockholm University

Ulf Olsson (chairperson), Professor of Literature at the Department of Culture and Aesthetics at Stockholm University

Meike Wagner, Professor of Theatre Studies at the Department of Culture and Aesthetics at Stockholm University

Titles in the series

1. Rosenberg, T. 2016. *Don't Be Quiet, Start a Riot! Essays on Feminism and Performance.* Stockholm: Stockholm University Press. DOI: https://doi.org/10.16993/baf. License: CC-BY 4.0
2. Lennon, J. & Nilsson, M. (eds.) 2017. *Working-Class Literature(s): Historical and International Perspectives.* Stockholm: Stockholm University Press. DOI: https://doi.org/10.16993/bam. License: CC-BY 4.0
3. Tessing Schneider, M. & Tatlow, R. (eds.) 2018. *Mozart's* La clemenza di Tito: *A Reappraisal.* Stockholm: Stockholm University Press. DOI: https://doi.org/10.16993/ban. License: CC-BY 4.0

Peer Review page

Guidelines for peer review

Stockholm University Press ensures that all book publications are peer-reviewed in two stages. Each book proposal submitted to the Press has been sent to a dedicated Editorial Board of experts in the subject area as well as two independent experts. The full manuscript will be peer reviewed by chapter or as a whole by two independent experts.

A full description of Stockholm University Press' peer-review policies can be found on the website: http://www.stockholmuniversitypress.se/site/peer-review-policies/

Recognition for reviewers

The Editorial Board of Stockholm Studies in Culture and Aesthetics applies single-blind review during proposal and manuscript assessment. We would like to thank all reviewers involved in this process.

Special thanks to the reviewers who have been doing the peer review of the manuscript of this book.

Dedicated to the memory of our dear friend and colleague

Jette Barnholdt Hansen

*7 March 1966 †8 February 2017

Her vil ties, her vil bies,
Her vil bies, o svage Sind!
Vist skal du hente, kun ved at vente,
Kun ved at vente, vor Sommer ind.
Her vil ties, her vil bies,
Her vil bies, o svage Sind!

Contents

Images xi
Preface xiii

La clemenza di Tito: Chronology and Documents 1
Ruth Tatlow and Magnus Tessing Schneider
   I Chronology 2
   II Documents in Parallel Translation 6

Operatic Culture at the Court of Leopold II and Mozart's
La clemenza di Tito 33
John A. Rice

From Metastasio to Mazzolà: Clemency and Pity in
La clemenza di Tito 56
Magnus Tessing Schneider
   From Metastasio to Mozart 60
   The Concept of Pity in Mazzolà's Revision 66
   La clemenza di Tito—A Democratic Opera? 79

Tito's Burden 97
Felicity Baker
   The Operatic Action, Intertext and Context 97
   The Monarch's Need for Truth 102
   Historical Depth in the Character of Tito 107
   From Servilia to Vitellia 109
   The Opera's Burden 113

**Mozart as Epideictic Rhetorician: The Representation of
Vice and Virtue in** *La clemenza di Tito*   120
Jette Barnholdt Hansen
    Theatrum mundi and *fraternité*   121
    The Coronation Opera   124
    Rhetoric and Aesthetics   125
    Opera seria and the *da capo* aria   126
    The Representation of Clemency   129

Stage Directions and Set Design in Mozart's
La clemenza di Tito   134
Sergio Durante
    The Stage Sets and their Importance in Prague 1791   134
    Staging and the Aesthetic of *La clemenza di Tito*   150

Bibliography   159
Index   169
Editors of *La clemenza di Tito*   177

Images

5.1 'Vivat Leopoldus Secundus', coronation of Emperor Leopold II. Engraving by I. C. Berndt, 1790. Reproduced with kind permission from the copyright owner/holder, the Historisches Museum Frankfurt, N42672. On permanent loan from the Städel Museum Frankfurt. Photo: Horst Ziegenfusz. Licence: CC BY-NC-ND 4.0 International use.   122

6.1 P. Travaglia, *Sala ter[r]ena destinata per le pubbliche udienze*, Pietro Travaglia's Sketchbook, f. 11. Published with permission from the copyright owner/holder, the Collection of Theatre History at the Hungarian National Széchényi Library, Budapest. Access. Nr. 1955/9645. Licence: CC BY-NC-ND 4.0 International use.   136

6.2 Symmetrical duplication of the design in Image 1 (with corrected shadows). Designed by Paolo Kirschner and Silvia Tinazzo. Reproduced with permission from the copyright owners/holders, Paolo Kirschner and Silvia Tinazzo. Licence: CC BY-NC-ND 4.0 International use.   138

6.3 Hypothetical realisation of the scenographic elements. Designed by Paolo Kirschner and Silvia Tinazzo. Reproduced with permission from the copyright owners/holders, Paolo Kirschner and Silvia Tinazzo. Licence: CC BY-NC-ND 4.0 International use.   139

6.4 Detail of the set design, showing the rear of the stage. Designed by Paolo Kirschner and Silvia Tinazzo. Reproduced with permission from the copyright owners/holders Paolo Kirschner and Silvia Tinazzo. Licence: CC BY-NC-ND 4.0 International use.   140

6.5 Hypothetical realisation of the long set. Designed by Paolo Kirschner and Silvia Tinazzo. Reproduced with permission from the copyright owners/holders, Paolo Kirschner and Silvia Tinazzo. Licence: CC BY-NC-ND 4.0 International use.   141

6.6 Section and plan of Count Nostitz's National Theatre, Prague, 1793. Copper plate engraving by Johann Berka, after Philipp and Franz Heger. Reproduced with permission from the copyright owner/holder, AKG images / TT Nyhetsbyrån. Licence: CC BY-NC-ND 4.0 International use.   143

6.7 P. Travaglia, [parte del foro romano (…) Campidoglio]. Pietro Travaglia's Sketchbook, f. 12. Published with permission from the copyright owners/holders the Collection of Theatre History at the Hungarian National Széchényi Library, Budapest. Access. Nr. 1955/9645. Licence: CC BY-NC-ND 4.0 International use.   144

6.8 P. Travaglia, [parte del foro romano (…)], symmetrically expanded. Designed by Paolo Kirschner and Silvia Tinazzo. Reproduced with permission from the copyright owners/holders Paolo Kirschner and Silvia Tinazzo. Licence: CC BY-NC-ND 4.0 International use.   146

6.9 Hypothetical realisation of the scenographic elements. Designed by Paolo Kirschner and Silvia Tinazzo. Reproduced with permission from the copyright owners/holders Paolo Kirschner and Silvia Tinazzo. Licence: CC BY-NC-ND 4.0 International use.   147

6.10 A rendering of the scenographic elements placed above the map of Count Nostitz's National Theatre. Designed by Paolo Kirschner and Silvia Tinazzo. Reproduced with permission from the copyright owners/holders Paolo Kirschner and Silvia Tinazzo. Licence: CC BY-NC-ND 4.0 International use.   148

Preface

In the two centuries since Mozart's *La clemenza di Tito* was first performed, and the almost three centuries since Metastasio created the libretto, many rumours, myths and prejudiced opinions have gathered around the work, creating a narrative that Mozart, Mazzolà and their contemporaries would scarcely recognise. Our aim in selecting the essays for this book is to contribute ideas, facts and images that will draw the twenty-first-century reader closer to the events of Central Europe in the late eighteenth century, and through new facts and ideas, to peel off some of the transmitted accretions that may hinder a modern listener from enjoying and understanding the opera in all its fullness. In this sense the essays present the reappraisal promised in the title.

The stripping-down process of this volume begins immediately in chapter one, with a political and operatic chronology aimed to help readers appreciate aspects of the context in which *La clemenza di Tito* was conceived, created and first heard. Although there was no 'breaking news' app to alert travelling musicians and artists to imminent political troubles, there were sufficiently reliable information channels to strike unease in the hearts of the informed. We cannot know how the political unrest affected those who focused their energies on directing and producing the coronation opera for the performance on 6 September 1791, nor how the audience—the royal families, nobility, those with judicial and social power, and the common man in Prague—responded to rumours of troubles on their borders, nor how these affected their prospect of the coronation of Leopold II, who would hopefully lead them into the new century.

We hope that the chronology and the selected documents will greatly enrich the reader's understanding and appreciation of the five essays. The essays represent a cross section of perspectives and disciplines. Their common theme is the desire to move beyond denigrations of the work that have persisted since the premiere of *La clemenza di Tito* in 1791, and that still live on in much current critical literature.

Chapter two is an essay by John A. Rice, leading specialist of Viennese opera at the end of the eighteenth century, whose 1991 Cambridge Opera Handbook on *La clemenza di Tito* established the historical ground on which all studies build today. Here he elaborates on the operatic culture at the court of Leopold II, placing Mozart's opera in the context of the emperor's attempt to promote *opera seria*. Chapter three is by Magnus Tessing Schneider, theatre scholar, co-editor of this volume and founding member of the Performing Premodernity research project. His essay is a close textual reading of Mazzolà's revision of Metastasio's libretto, with a particular focus on the evolving meaning of 'pity' as an indication of commitment to principles of enlightened humanism. In chapter four Felicity Baker, eminent specialist of French and Italian Enlightenment literature, offers a close political reading of the Metastasio-Mazzolà libretto, suggesting that the work questions the very foundations of the institution of monarchy. Chapter five is an amalgamation by Magnus Tessing Schneider from three separate sources by Jette Barnholdt Hansen, two of which were originally published in Danish. As a rhetorician and musicologist Jette was able to bring her unique viewpoint to bear on the symbolic and representational aspects of Mozart's opera. The final chapter is written by Mozart specialist Sergio Durante, who has made *La clemenza di Tito* an important part of his life's work, beginning with his doctoral dissertation in 1993, and more recently collaborating on the publication of the facsimile of the autograph score. His essay focuses on the stage design for the original production, which leads to a broader discussion of the dramaturgy of the opera.

The relationship between the 1791 setting of Metastasio's libretto and the Viennese court of the Habsburgs, the Prague coronation of

Leopold II as king of Bohemia, and the ongoing Revolution in France is highly complex. The extent to which *La clemenza di Tito* was propagandistic, progressive, or even radical, and to which it points towards the emergence of modern democracy and a new aesthetic sensibility, will always remain a subject of discussion and interpretation. Each of the authors provides different answers, while proceeding from the united conviction that it is eminently fruitful to study the music and the poetry in their broader historical, political, cultural, intellectual and artistic contexts.

This book began life within the Performing Premodernity research project, funded by the Swedish Foundation for Humanities and Social Sciences and based at the department of theatre studies of Stockholm University. It took shape during a conference at the historic Royal Coin Cabinet in Stockholm opposite the Royal Palace, the excited buzz of conversations between papers complementing the inspiring surroundings. And it became clear that its continued growth to independence and international influence would best be achieved through facilitating a platform as an open access book, with all the benefits of a Creative Commons license. The added beauty of free, electronic publication is that it allows rare images to be seen and appreciated in high resolution. Gracing this volume are an early image of Prague's National Theatre (today the Estates Theatre), two plates from Pietro Travaglia's sketchbook, and I. C. Berndt's iconic engraving 'Vivat Leopoldus Secundus'.

We would like to thank our authors John A. Rice, Felicity Baker and Sergio Durante for allowing us to include their essays in our volume. Together with the enthusiasm and support of the entire Performing Premodernity team—Willmar Sauter, Meike Wagner, Mark Tatlow, Maria Gullstam, Petra Dotlačilová—it was working alongside the authors that made this book a joy to produce. We would also like to thank Christina Lenz at Stockholm University Press and Tim Wakeford and Paige MacKay at Ubiquity Press for their flexibility and help in enabling us to achieve the production styles we envisaged.

As this book makes its way into the world, we release it with the natural pride and joy of parents, wishing it every success on its journey as we hand over to the reader, performer, opera lover or researcher the task of continuing the reappraisal of *La clemenza di Tito*. We hope that the part we have played will help deepen the reader's intellectual, cultural, musical, and ethical understanding of the work.

Our joy in completing this task is dampened by our sadness that Jette Barnholdt Hansen is no longer with us. We will miss Jette's smiles and encouraging words at our meetings and in our discussions. We nonetheless remember her with deep gratitude for the many loving memories she has left in our hearts, and it is in this spirit that we dedicate *Mozart's* La clemenza di Tito: *A Reappraisal* to Jette.

Ruth Tatlow and Magnus Tessing Schneider

1 *La clemenza di Tito*: Chronology and Documents

Ruth Tatlow and Magnus Tessing Schneider

This chapter begins with a political and operatic chronology aimed to help readers appreciate at-a-glance aspects of the context in which *La clemenza di Tito* was conceived, created and first heard. It is followed by a selection of original documents. Although many of the twenty-four documents are published elsewhere, this is the first time they have appeared side by side with parallel English translations. Some of the translations are entirely new, while the remainder are freshened up from existing versions. These particular sources were selected to create a documentary context for *La clemenza di Tito,* bringing together contemporary responses to the original production, as well as to the circumstances surrounding its genesis. We hope this will help the reader to appreciate the essays that follow, and that many will download and use this chapter as a basic documentary reference tool to gain a deeper understanding of Mozart's opera.

How to cite this book chapter:
Tatlow, R. and Tessing Schneider, M. 2018. *La clemenza di Tito*: Chronology and Documents. In: Tessing Schneider, M. and Tatlow, R. (eds.) *Mozart's* La clemenza di Tito*: A Reappraisal*. Pp. 1–32. Stockholm: Stockholm University Press. DOI: https://doi.org/10.16993/ban.a. License: CC-BY NC-ND 4.0

I Chronology

Prepared by John A. Rice and Magnus Tessing Schneider

Dates and text in italics indicate a political event in France.
The premiere of *La clemenza di Tito* on 6 September 1791 is marked in bold.

	1734
4 November	First performance of *La clemenza di Tito*—libretto by Pietro Metastasio, music by Antonio Caldara—at the Kärntnertortheater in Vienna.

	1789
January	Rebellion against the reforms of Joseph II breaks out in the Austrian Netherlands.
14 July	*Fall of the Bastille; beginning of the French Revolution.*
26 August	*Publication of the* Declaration of the Rights of Man and the Citizen.
5 October	*A mob forces the royal family to move from Versailles to Paris. Marie Antoinette declares 'J'ai tout vu, j'ai tout su, et j'ai tout oublié', a paraphrase of Pierre Corneille's* Cinna *and Metastasio's* La clemenza di Tito.
27 October	Rebel army in the Netherlands defeats the Austrians at Turnhout.
November	Anti-Austrian rioting in Ghent.
2 November	*Church property nationalised.*

	1790
11 January	Rebels in the Austrian Netherlands form the United States of Belgium.
26 January	Premiere of Mozart's *Così fan tutte*.
30 January	Joseph II withdraws almost all his reforms in Hungary.
20 February	Death of Joseph II.
6 April	Oath of allegiance (*Huldigung*) to Leopold as archduke of Austria.
9 May	Many Bohemian serfs, freed by Joseph, forced back into servitude by Leopold.
19 May	*National Assembly abolishes nobility.*
12 July	*Civil Constitution of Clergy requires priests to take an oath of loyalty to the state.*
12 July	Representatives of the Bohemian Estates convene the so-called 'Big Bohemian Diet' of 1790–91 in Prague, to formulate grievances addressed to Leopold.
25 July	Treaty of Reichenbach between Austria and Prussia.
15 September	Premiere of Joseph Weigl's *La caffettiera bizzarra* in celebration of the arrival in Vienna of King Ferdinand and Queen Maria Carolina of Naples.
19 September	Triple Marriage: Archduke Francis to Princess Maria Theresa of Naples, and marriages between four of their younger siblings.
20 September	Antonio Salieri's *Axur re d'Ormus* performed before the Austrian and Neapolitan royal families.
9 October	Coronation of Leopold in Frankfurt as emperor of the Holy Roman Empire. Associated events include performances of Carl Ditters von Dittersdorf's *Der Apotheker und der Doktor* and *Betrug durch Aberglauben*, Salieri's *Axur* and *Il talismano*, Georg Benda's *Romeo und Julie*, and Paul Wranitzky's *Oberon*.
11 November	Coronation of Leopold in Bratislava as king of Hungary.
December	Rebellion in the Austrian Netherlands suppressed.

(Continued)

	1791
1 January	Joseph Haydn arrives in England.
29 January	'Big Bohemian Diet' adjourned.
9 February	King and Queen of Naples attend performance of Mozart's *Le nozze di Figaro* at Schönbrunn.
March	End of Viennese tenure of Adriana Ferrarese, the first Fiordiligi.
1 March	*Opera seria* soprano Cecilia Giuliani begins tenure at the Viennese Court Theatres: start of Leopold's transformation of the Viennese theatre.
2 March	Announcement in Vienna of plans for celebrations of the Prague coronation of Emperor Leopold II as king of Bohemia.
9 March	The Emperor dismisses Lorenzo Da Ponte as imperial court theatre poet.
14 March	The Emperor leaves Vienna for a trip to Italy.
9 April	While away in Venice, the Emperor announces that Giovanni Bertati will succeed Da Ponte as court theatre poet.
29 April	A committee under the Bohemian Estates decides that the Prague coronation celebrations will include Italian opera.
Mid-May	Invited by the director of the Court Theatre, Count Johann Wenzel Ugarte, Saxon court theatre poet Caterino Mazzolà arrives in Vienna to serve as temporary replacement for Da Ponte.
1 June	*Opera seria* tenor Vincenzo Maffoli begins tenure at Viennese Court Theatres.
10 June	Opera impresario Domenico Guardasoni and his company return to Prague after two years in Warsaw.
20 *June*	*Flight to Varennes: Louis XVI and Marie Antoinette's failed attempt to flee.*
8 July	Guardasoni signs a contract with the Bohemian Estates, agreeing to both commission and put on a coronation opera—either an entirely new opera, or a new musical setting of Metastasio's *La clemenza di Tito*.
c.14–31 July	Guardasoni arrives in Vienna. He asks first Salieri, then Mozart to compose the coronation opera. Mazzolà asked (presumably by Guadarsoni) to revise Metastasio's libretto. Guardasoni travels to Bologna to hire principal singers.
Late July	Mazzolà, dismissed by the Emperor, returns to Dresden.
2–4 August	Installation of Anton Esterházy as prince at Eszterháza. Premiere of Weigl's *Venere e Adone* at Eszterháza with Cecilia Giuliani in the role of Venere.
4 August	Treaty of Sistova establishes peace between Austria and Turkey.

c. 15 August	Guardasoni returns to Vienna. Maria Marchetti Fantozzi and Domenico Bedini, the two principal singers, arrive in Vienna around now. Presumably, Mozart works with them.
19 August	Possible date Mozart begins to compose *La clemenza di Tito*, after Niemetschek's 1798 claim that Mozart composed it in 19 days. Mozart begins by composing the ensembles and choruses, and arias for Antonio Baglioni, for whom he had written Don Ottavio in *Don Giovanni* four years earlier.
25 August	Declaration of Pillnitz, in which Leopold and King Frederick William II of Prussia declare their readiness to intervene militarily in France. Mozart leaves Vienna for Prague by mail coach with his wife and his pupil Franz Xaver Süssmayr, who probably composes the *secco* recitatives of the opera.
28 August	The party arrives in Prague. Mozart meets the remaining singers. Mazzolà arrives in Prague around now to assist in text revisions and to direct production.
5 September	Score completed with composition of Tito's second aria, the march, the accompanied recitatives and the overture.
6 September	**Coronation of Leopold as King of Bohemia.** **Premiere of Mozart's *La clemenza di Tito* at the National Theatre**, scheduled for 7pm, but delayed until 7.30 or 8pm due to late arrival of the imperial family. Mozart conducts the performance.
13 September	*Louis XVI formally accepts the Constitution.*
Mid-September	The Mozarts travel back from Prague to Vienna.
20 September	*Louis XVI and Marie Antoinette attend a performance of Rameau's* Castor et Pollux *in celebration of the Fête de la Constitution.*
30 September	Final performance of *La clemenza di Tito* in Prague. Premiere of Mozart's *Die Zauberflöte* in Vienna.
1 October	The *musico* (castrato) Angelo Testori and the ballet master Antonio Muzzarelli begin their tenures at the Viennese Court Theatres.
15 November	Leopold's ballet troupe makes its debut in *Il Capitano Cook agli Ottaiti* in celebration of his name day.
24 November	Leopold's *opera seria* troupe makes its debut with the Viennese premiere of Sebastiano Nasolini's *Teseo a Stige* in celebration of Empress Maria Luisa's birthday.
5 December	Mozart's death.

(Continued)

	1792
6 January	Viennese premiere of Alessio Prati's *La vendetta di Nino*.
7 February	Premiere of Domenico Cimarosa's *Il matrimonio segreto* in Vienna.
1 March	Death of Leopold II, succeeded by his son Francis.
20 April	*War declared against Austria.*
29 July	Haydn arrives in Vienna after his first visit to London.
22 September	*France declared a republic.*

	1793
21 January	*Louis XVI executed.*
11 March	*Monarchist rebellion in the Vendée begins.*
13 July	*Assassination of Jean-Paul Marat.*
27 July	*Maximilien Robespierre elected to the Committee of Public Safety.*
September	*Reign of Terror begins.*
16 October	*Marie Antoinette executed.*

	1794
3 December	Revival of *La clemenza di Tito* by Guardasoni's company in Prague. Teresa Strinasacchi sings Sesto, presumably Baglioni as Tito, and Antonina Campi (formerly Antonina Miklaszewicz) as Vitellia.

	1807
24 April	*La clemenza di Tito* is chosen by the company formerly managed by Guardasoni for their final performance before closing down.

II Documents in Parallel Translation

Selected by Magnus Tessing Schneider

All translations are by Magnus Tessing Schneider, unless based on a published source cited in a footnote. The documents, copied from published sources, are ordered chronologically, numbered and linked electronically to their occurrence in the essay texts.

Document 1. Baron Wilhelm Hugo MacNeven. Draft of the Prague coronation commission.¹

1791, 29 April	
Es dürfte daher durch die drei Täge des Einzuges, der Huldigung und der Krönung mit vorzüglich guten Teutschen Schauspielen und wälschen Singspielen, dann großen Balletten abwechselt werden. Hiezu wären die vornehmste Subjeckte so weit es die Zeit zuläßt herbei zuschaf[f]en, und sich hierwegen mit verschiedenen Impressen [sic] in Korrespondenz und Behandlung zu setzen.	During the three days of the processional entry, the oath of allegiance, and the coronation, there should be an alternation primarily of good German plays and Italian operas, and then of grand ballets. To this end, as far as time permits, the most distinguished persons [i.e. performers] should be put into contact and negotiate with various impresarios.

Document 2. Contract between Domenico Guardasoni and the Bohemian Estates, Prague.²

1791, 8 July	
Specificazione de' punti, ch'io qui sottoscritto mi obligo di mantenere agli Eccelsi Stati di Boemia, ed esigo dalle prefate loro Eccellenze toccante una grand'Opera Seria da rappresentarsi in questo Nazional Teatro in occasione dell'Incoronazione di Sua Maestà Imperiale dentro lo spazio de~~lla metà~~ * principio del prossimo mese di Settembre, qualora mi venghino graziati ed accordati seimila fiorini, o seimilacinquecento, qualora vi fosse il Musico Marchesi.	List of points which the undersigned is obliged to observe vis-à-vis the High Bohemian Estates, and to which he expects the aforementioned Excellencies to adhere, with regard to a grand *opera seria* which is to be performed in the local National Theatre on the occasion of the coronation of His Imperial Majesty ~~in the middle~~ * at the beginning of the next month of September, insofar as the six thousand gulden are paid to me as per agreement, or six thousand five hundred if the singer [Luigi] Marchesi is involved.
1mo mi obligo, di darli un Primo Musico, di prima sfera, come per esempio, o il Marchesini, o il Rubinelli, o il Crescentini, o il Violani, od altro, ma sempre che sia di prima sfera. Come pure mi obligo di darli una prima donna, mede[si]mamente di prima sfera, e di certo la meglio di tal rango che sarà in libertà e di impiegare il resto occorrente di mia compagnia per tale opera.	1. I shall undertake to engage a *primo musico* of the first calibre, such as [Luigi] Marchesini or [Giovanni Battista] Rubinelli or [Girolamo] Crescentini or [Violano] Violani, or someone else, but always of the first calibre. I further agree to engage a *prima donna*, likewise of the first calibre, or in any case the best available in this category; for the other participants I shall engage my own opera company.

(Continued)

	1791, 8 July
2do Mi obligo di far comporre la Poesia del Libro, a norma dei due sogetti datimi da Sua Eccellenza gran Burgravio e di farlo porre in Musica <u>da un celebre Maestro</u>, in caso però che non fosse affatto possibile di ciò effettuare per la strettezza del tempo, mi obligo di procurar un'Opera nuovamente composta sul sogetto del Tito di Metastasio o ~~sia un'altro eguale~~.*	2. I shall undertake to have the libretto written in accordance with the two subjects given to me by his Excellency the Burgrave [Heinrich Franz von Rottenhan], and to have it set to music *by a famous composer*; if this should not be possible owing to the shortness of time available, I shall rearrange to acquire a new opera composed on the basis of [Pietro] Metastasio's *Tito* ~~or a similar subject~~.*
3zo Mi obligo di fare espressamente per tale spettacolo <u>due Decorazioni nuove</u>. Come pure mi obligo di far fare il Vestiario nuovo, ed in specie alle prime parti per tal opera.	3. I shall undertake to prepare *two new stage sets* expressly for this performance. I shall likewise undertake to make new costumes, especially for the opera's main roles.
4to Mi obligo di Illuminare e far parare il Teatro con Festoni e montare di tutto detta opera e darla gratis per una sera a Disposizione dei sudetti Eccelsi Stati, dentro lo spazio sudetto.	4. I shall undertake to illuminate the theatre, to decorate it with garlands, and to equip the entire opera house with everything, as well as to give a performance free of charge for the aforementioned High Estates within the specified period of time.
Punti esigenti.	**Claims.**
1mo Che mi sia improntato <u>Seicento fiorini</u> per il mio Viaggio a Vienna, e in Italia, con un ordine qui da un Banchiere per Vienna, e Italia, che mi sia dato occorrendo <u>un paio di mille fiorini colà</u>, in caso che li sogetti cercassero denari anticipati.	1. I shall be given an advance payment of *six hundred gulden* for my journey to Vienna and Italy, with a payment order prepared here for a banker in Vienna and Italy, so that there I shall be given, if necessary, *one thousand gulden* in case the persons [i.e. performers] should demand payment in advance.
2do Che il resto del pagamento mi sia fatto pagare il giorno dell'esecuzione di detta Opera.	2. The remainder of my fee is to be paid to me on the day on which the said opera is performed.
3zo Se in spazio di 14. giorni dal giorno di mia partenza per Italia fosse difesa l'Opera, allora si pagaranno solamente le spese del Viaggio.	3. If the opera shall be cancelled or prevented within the space of fourteen days after my departure for Italy, I shall be compensated only for my travel expenses.
4to Guardasoni aviserà subito il giorno, nel quale ha impegnato un Virtuoso, da questo giorno, se non fosse Opera, questo Virtuoso avrà una Bonificazione, se sarà già partito d'Italia.	4. Once Guardasoni has engaged a singer, he shall inform us on the same day; should the opera not be given, the singer shall receive compensation from this day on, provided he has already left Italy.

1791, 8 July	

5to Le cose comprate per il denaro speso si devano rendere in natura e quello che non è ancor fermato, contro manderà[.] In caso de la difesa Opera si darà una remunerazione al Guardasoni se Lei proverà, aver avuto più grandi spese nel Viaggio che importerà l'anticipazione.
 	
Praga li 8 luglio 1791.
 	
Enrico Conte di Rottenhan
Casparo Ermanno Conte Kinigl
Giuseppe Conte di Sweerth
Giovanni Conte Unwerth
Giovanni Baron d'Hennet
 	
     Domenico Guardasoni
       Impresario
	5. Objects purchased and paid for are to be returned in kind, and that which has not yet arrived shall be forwarded. If the opera is cancelled [i.e. prevented or hindered], Guardasoni shall receive a credit note, provided that he can prove that he had greater expenses on his journey than were covered by the advance payment.
	
	Prague, 8 July 1791.
	
	Heinrich Graf von Rottenhan
	Kasper Hermann Graf Kinigl
	Joseph Graf von Sweerth
	Johannes Graf Unwerth
	Johannes Baron von Hennet
	
	     Domenico Guardasoni
	       Impresario

* The struck-through words were crossed out in the original document

Document 3. Letter from Antonio Salieri to Prince Paul Anton Esterházy, Vienna.[3]

1791, August	
[...] senza pentirmene però, ho ricusato di scriver l'opera che si prepara per l'incoronazione di Boemio [sic], per la qual'opera l'Impressario di Praga è stato cinque volte da me per pregarmi di ametterne l'impiego coll esibizione [sic] di duecento zecchini, impegno ch'io non potei assumere perchè mi trovavo solo a servire il teatro imperiale.	[...] without regretting it however, I had to decline to write the opera which is being prepared for the coronation in Bohemia, for which opera the Prague impresario [i.e. Guardasoni] came to me five times to press the commission on me to the point of showing me 200 zecchini, a commission which I could not accept since I alone was attending to the affairs of the Court Theatre.

Document 4. Announcement from the Royal Provincial Presidency, Prague.[4]

1791, 3 September

---

1. Am Dienstage den 6ten September wird im Altstädter Nazionaltheater eine große Opera seria [footnote: 'Die Stände wählten die von Abbe Metastasio unter dem Titel: La clemenza di Tito, verfaßte Oper; die Musik hiezu liessen sie eigends von dem Kompositor am k. k. Hofe, Herrn Wolfgang Mozart verfertigen.'] von den Ständen des Königreichs Böhmen gegeben, um den festlichen Tag der Krönung Sr. Majestät des Kaisers, Königs und Landesfürsten zu feiern.

2. Um hiebei alle Unordnung zu vermeiden, werden Billete, ohne welche niemand eingelassen wird, ausgetheilt werden.

3. Bei Austheilung dieser Billete wird man zuvorderst auf die k. k. Hofsuite und auf den fremden Adel, sodann erst auf den hiesigen innländischen Adel, weiters auf die Fremden, und endlich auf die innländischen Honorazioren Bedacht nehmen.

4. Man versieht sich daher zu der bekannten Gefälligkeit des prager [sic] Publikums, daß es so billig denken, und den Fremden im Theater die ersten Plätze überlassen werde.

1. On Tuesday 6 September a grand opera will be given at the National Theatre in the Old Town [footnote: 'The Estates chose the opera known as *La clemenza di Tito* by Abbé Metastasio; they let the composer Herr Wolfgang Mozart from the imperial court provide the music expressly for it.'] by the Estates of the Kingdom of Bohemia, to celebrate the solemn day of the coronation of His Majesty the Emperor, King and Prince of the Land.

2. In order to avoid any confusion, the tickets will be distributed, without which no one will be admitted.

3. In the distribution of these tickets, consideration will be given first to the imperial entourage and the foreign nobility, then to the local nobility, then to foreigners, and finally to local dignitaries.

4. Therefore, one relies on the well-known courtesy of the Prague audience, expecting them to be as fair as to leave the first seats in the theatre to the foreigners.

1791, 3 September

5. Die Kavaliere und Damen, welche am 1. dieses in dem Appartement bei Hofe erschienen sind, und alle landständischen Mitglieder des geistlichen, Herren- und Ritterstandes, so, wie die in Aemtern stehenden Fremden und fremden Offiziere, die nicht bei Hofe erschienen sind, dann die fremden Gelehrten und Negozianten werden ersucht, ihre Billete in der Präsidialkanzlei im Gubernialhause abholen zu lassen, ihre Bedienten aber, welche dahin abgeschickt werden, mit einer schriftlichen Anzeige ihres Namens, und mit ihrem Petschaft zu legitimiren. Man wird am 5ten von 8 Uhr früh bis 1 Uhr Mittags, dann von 3 Uhr Nachmittags bis 6 Uhr Abends, und endlich am 6ten von 8 Uhr früh bis 11 Uhr Vormittags in der Präsidialkanzlei Beamte finden, die eigends mit Vertheilung der Billete sich beschäftigen.	5. The gentlemen and the ladies who appeared in the chambers of the court ['Appartement'] on the first of this month, and all clerical, noble and knightly members of the Estates, as well as the foreign officials and officers who have not appeared at court, and then foreign scholars and merchants, are requested to collect their tickets at the Provincial Presidency in the Gubernatorial House. Their servants who are sent there, however, are requested to prove their identity with a written announcement containing their name and a signet. On the 5th, from 8 a.m. until 1 p.m., then from 3 p.m. until 6 p.m., and finally on the 6th, from 8 a.m. until 11 a.m., officials in the Provincial Presidency will be specially occupied with the distribution of the tickets.
6. Die Dikasterialbeamten aller Stellen und Aemter aber, so, wie die Magistratualmitglieder, der Handelstand, die vier Fakultäten, und andere Honorazioren werden ihre Billete (so weit solche zulangen) bei ihren Präsidenten, Amts- und anderen Vorstehern erhalten.	6. However, the dicasterial [of the Holy Roman Empire] officials of all estates and offices, as well as the members of the municipal administration, the merchant class, the four faculties and other dignitaries will receive their tickets (if such are still available) from their presidents, head officials and other superintendents.
Da es der Raum, und die Aufmerksamkeit, die man dem Hofe schuldig ist, nicht zuläßt, so viele Billete, als man wünschte, auszutheilen, so werden unter die obangeführten Kategorien die sämmtlichen k. k. Räthe, und Amtsvorsteher, die Herren Stadtpfarrer und Dekane, die Sekretäre bei allen k. k. Stellen, die Magistratsräthe der Stadt Prag, die Deputirten der drei privilegirten königl. Städte, die ersten Amtsvorsteher bei den Magistratskanzleien, die Doktoren aller 4 Fakultäten, das Collegium Advocatorum, der höhere Handelstand, als: Banquiers, und Großhändler, dann die Offiziere, Unteroffiziere, und 4 Gemeine von einer jeden Bürgerkompagnie, nebst ihren Gemahlinnen und einer erwachsenen Tochter, gerechnet.	Since the space and the attention owed to the court do not permit the distribution of as many tickets as one would wish, the above-mentioned categories will include all imperial councillors and head officials, the city pastors and deans, the secretaries of all imperial offices, the municipal councillors of the City of Prague, the principal head officials of the municipal chanceries, the doctors of all four faculties, the Collegium Advocatorum, the upper merchant class (such as bankers and wholesale traders), and then the officers, corporals and four common soldiers from each civil regiment, along with their spouses and one grown-up daughter.

(Continued)

1791, 3 September	
7. Um die vergeblichen Anfragen zu vermeiden, wird jedermann, der nach dieser Ankündigung nicht berechtigt ist, ein Billet zu verlangen, ersucht, sich genau an diese Vorschrift zu halten.	7. To avoid futile requests, anyone who, according to this announcement, is not entitled to claim a ticket is asked to pay close attention to this instruction.
8. Die Fahrordnung ist besonders abgedruckt.	8. The driving rules will be printed separately. [See Document 5]
Prag am 3ten September 1791.	Prague, 3 September 1791.

Document 5. Notice from the Royal Provincial Presidency, Prague.[5]

1791, 3 September	
Nachricht, wie man sich den 6ten Sept. bei der Zu- und Abfahrt zur Opera im Nazionaltheater, verhalten solle.	*Information on how to conduct oneself when travelling to and from the opera at the National Theatre on 6 September.*
Da die Opera mit Schlag 7 Uhr anfangen solle, so werden alle in das Nazionaltheater Fahrenden ersuchet, sich zeitlich da einzufinden, damit sowohl ein jeder gemächlich seinen Platz einnehmen könne, als auch die Ankunft Sr. Majestät, und der höchsten Herrschaften durch die spätere Zufuhr nicht beirret werde. Der Zug der Wägen hatte also schon um 5 Uhre anzufangen. […] [133] […]	Since the opera is to begin on the stroke of 7, everyone driving to the National Theatre is requested to be present on time, so that each may take his seat at his leisure, and so that the arrival of His Majesty and Their Highest Lordships is not deterred by late arrivals. Therefore, the train of wagons should start already at 5 o'clock. […]
Prag am 3ten September 1791	Prague, 3 September 1791

Document 6. Wolfgang Amadeus Mozart's catalogue of works.[6]

1791, 5 September	
Den 5: September.—aufgeführt in <u>Prag den 6. September</u>. La Clemenza di Tito, opera Seria in Due Atti, per l'incoronazione di sua Maestà l'imperatore Leopoldo II.—ridotta à vera opera dal Sig:^{re} Mazzolà, Poeta di sua A: S: l'Elettore di Sassonia.—<u>Attrici</u>:—Sig:^{ra} <u>Marchetti Fanto[z]zi</u>.—<u>Sig:^{ra} Antonini</u>.—<u>Attori</u>. <u>Sig:^{re} Bedini</u>. Sig:^{ra} <u>Carolina Perini</u> /da uomo/ <u>Sig:^{re} Baglioni</u>. <u>Sig:^{re} Campi</u>.—e Cori.—24 <u>Pezzi</u>.	5 September. – Performed in *Prague on 6 September*: *La clemenza di Tito*, opera seria in two Acts for the coronation of His Majesty Emperor Leopold II. – reduced to a true opera by Signore [Caterino] Mazzolà, poet to His Serene Highness the Elector of Saxony. *Actresses: Signora [Maria] Marchetti Fantoz[z]i. Signora [Anna] Antonini.* – Actors: *Signore [Domenico] Bedini. Signora Carolina Perini* (as a man). *Signore [Antonio] Baglioni. Signore [Gaetano] Campi.* – and choruses. 24 numbers.

Document 7. From the printed libretto for *La clemenza di Tito*, Prague.[7]

1791, September	
La musica è tutta nuova, composta dal celebre Sig. Wolfgango Amadeo Mozart, maestro di capella in attuale servizio di sua Maestà imperiale.	The music is entirely new, composed by the celebrated Signor Wolfgang Amadeus Mozart, Kapellmeister currently in the service of His Imperial Majesty.
Le tre prime Decorazioni sono d'invenzione del Sig. Pietro Travaglia, all'attual servizio di S. A. il Principe Esterazi.	The three first decorations are the invention of Signor Pietro Travaglia, currently in the service of His Highness Prince Esterházy.
La quarta Decorazione è del Sig. Preisig di Coblenz. Il vestiario tutto nuovo di ricca e vaga invenzione del Sig. Cherubino Babbini di Mantova.	The fourth decoration is by Signor [Johann Adam] Breysig from Koblenz. The costumes, entirely new, are the rich and charming invention of Signor Cherubino Babbini from Mantua.

Document 8. Diary of Count Karl von Zinzendorf, Prague.[8]

1791, 6 September

6.Septembre. […] A 5ʰ au <u>Théatre de la vieille ville</u>. a ce Spectacle que donnent les Etats, on m'introduisit dans une loge au premier, ou etoient Mᵉ de Braun sa niéce Mᵉˡˡᵉ de Staray, Mᵉˡˡᵉ de Klebersberg et Mᵉ Tourinette, le Cᵗᵉ Wallis et l'amb. de Venise. Je fus voir de mes connoissances dans leurs loges, je vis dans celle de Collorado la Pᵉˢˢᵉ Hohenlohe de Breslau, née hoymb. La Cour n'arriva qu'a 7ʰ 1/2 passé on nous regala du plus ennuyeux Spectacle <u>La Clemenza di Tito</u>. Rotenhan en frac dans la loge de l'Empereur avec une canne qu'il a pourtant laissé dehors je crois. La Marchetti chante fort bien, l'Empereur en est entousiasmé. On eut beaucoup de peine a sortir de ce theatre.	6 September. […] At 5 o'clock to the theatre in the Old Town, to the performance given by the Estates. I was shown into a box on the first tier where I found Madame [Louisa Christiana von?] Braun, her niece Mlle. de Staray [i.e. Sztáray], Mlle. von Klebersberg and Madame Tourinette [La Tournelle?], Count [Stephan Olivier von?] Wallis and the Venetian ambassador [i.e. Daniele Andrea Dolfin]. I saw my acquaintances in their boxes. In that of [Prince Franz von] Collarado [i.e. Colloredo] I saw Princess [Amalie Henriette] Hohenlohe of Breslau *née* Hoymb. [Solms-Baruth?]. The court did not arrive before after 7.30. They treated us to the most boring spectacle, *La clemenza di Tito*. [Count] Rot[t]enhan was in the emperor's box, in a coat and with a cane that he nevertheless left outside, I think. Marchetti sings very well; the emperor is enthusiastic about her. It was very difficult to get out of this theatre.

Document 9. Letter from Empress Maria Luisa in Prague to her daughter, Archduchess Maria Theresa.[9]

1791, 7 September

---

au soir au Theatre la grande opera n'est pas grande chose et la musique très mauvaise ainsi nous y avons presque tous dormi. Le Couronnement est allé a merveille.	In the evening at the theatre: the grand opera is not so grand, and the music very bad, so that almost all of us went to sleep. The coronation went marvellously.

Document 10. Entry in the *Diary of the Bohemian Coronation*.[10]

1791, 7 September	
Abends war Freyopera, in welche sich Sr. Majestät mit der durchlauchtigsten Familie, und dem Hofstaate in die für höchstdieselben zubereiteten Logen nach 8 Uhr begeben, wohin höchstdieselben ein allgemeines freudiges Vivatrufen durch allen Gässen begleitete, mit welchem höchstdieselben auch im Theater empfangen wurden.	It was free opera [i.e. no entrance fee] in the evening, in which His Majesty with His Most Serene family and the court arrived at the boxes prepared for them after 8 o'clock. Along the whole route, they were accompanied by general and joyful *vivat* calls, with which Their High Selves were also received in the theatre.

Document 11. Notice in the *Prager Oberpostamtszeitung*.[11]

1791, 8 September	
Vorgestern Abends war freye Opera im altstädter Nazionaltheater, welches größtentheils von dem hier gegenwärtig sehr zahlreichen hohen Adel bese[t]zt war. Die allerhöchsten Herrschaften fanden sich um 8 Uhr gleich falls ein, und wurden im Hin- und Zurückfahren von vielen tausend frohlockenden Menschen begleitet.	The evening before last there was free opera [i.e. no entrance fee] at the National Theatre in the Old Town, which was mainly occupied by the very numerous high nobility that are currently here. Their Supreme Lordships also came at around 8 o'clock, and were accompanied on their way to and from the theatre by several thousand, rejoicing people.

Document 12. Johann Friedrich Ernst Albrecht, *Coronation Journal for Prague.*[12]

1791, 6 September

Festivitäten der Herren Stände.

Am 6ten als am Krönungstage gaben die Herren Stände, um diesen Tag Sr. Majestät zu verherrlichen eine ganz neue [sic] komponirte Oper, deren Text zwar nach dem Italiänischen des Metastasio, von Hrn. Mazzola [sic] aber, Theaterdichter in Dresden[,] verändert worden. Die Komposition ist von dem berühmten Mozart, und macht demselben Ehre, ob er gleich nicht viel Zeit dazu gehabt, und ihn noch dazu eine Krankheit überfiel, in welcher er den letzten Theil derselben verfertigen mußte.

An die Aufführung derselben hatten die Herren Stände alles gewandt, sie hatten den Entrepreneur nach Italien gesandt, der eine *prima donna* und einen ersten Sänger mit sich gebracht. Der Titel der [383] Oper selbst war: *la Clemenza di Tito*. Der Eintritt war frey, und viele Billets waren ausgetheilt. Das Haus fasset eine große Anzahl Menschen, dennoch aber kan[n] man sich denken, daß bei einer solchen Gelegenheit der Zulauf nach den Billets so groß ist, daß sie endlich ein Ende nehmen, daher auch manche Einheimische und Fremde[,] selbst Personen vom Stande[,] wieder weggehen mußte, weil sie sich nicht mit Billets versehen hatte.

Sr. Majestät erschienen um halb acht Uhr, und wurden mit lautem Zujauchzen der Anwesenden empfangen. Der Herren Stände Mitglieder nahmen selbst die Billets ein, und sahen auf die gehörige Ordnung, damit niemand auf sein Billet zurükgewiesen werden, und keiner ohne Billet eindrängen sich mögte. [384]

Festivities of the Noble Estates.

On the 6th, Coronation Day, the Noble Estates, in order to glorify His Majesty on this day, gave a newly composed opera on an Italian text by Metastasio, changed however by Herr Mazzola [sic], theatrical poet in Dresden. The composition is by the famous Mozart, and is an honour to him, although he had not much time for writing it, and moreover fell ill as he was in the process of finishing the last part.

The Noble Estates lavished everything on the performance; they had sent the entrepreneur [i.e. Guardasoni] to Italy in order to bring back a *prima donna* and a leading male singer. The title of the opera itself was *La clemenza di Tito*. The entrance was free of charge, and many tickets were distributed. The house is capable of holding a large number of persons, but one can imagine that on such an occasion, the request for tickets was so great that finally there were none, so that some local citizens and foreigners, even members of the nobility, had to leave because there were no tickets for them.

His Majesty appeared at 7:30 pm and was greeted with loud cries by the audience. Members of the Noble Estates themselves took in the tickets and saw that proper order was kept, so that no one with a ticket was refused and no one without a ticket could enter.

1791, 6 September

Von den Schauspielen. [...]	*On the theatrical performances* [...]
[386] Indessen sind die Schauspiele nicht sehr bese[t]zt. Sind die übrigen Ergötzlichkeiten daran schuld, oder es ist der hohen Preis, der die Liebhaber abschre[c]kt. Weder die zum zweitenmal aufgeführte Oper der Herren Stände, noch das Haus auf der kleinen Seite hatten viel Zuschauer.	Meanwhile the plays are not very full. This is either caused by other entertainments or it is the high price of the tickets that drives the enthusiasts away. Neither the second performance of the opera given by the Noble Estates, nor the house in the Lesser Town had many spectators.

Document 13. Franz Alexander von Kleist, *Daydreams on a Journey to Prague.*[13]

1791, 6 September

Königskrönung. [...]	*Royal coronation.* [...]
[119] Am Abend ward eine sehr schöne neue Oper[,] la Clemenza di Tito[,] frey von den Ständen gegeben. Die Musik ist von *Mozart*, und ganz ihres Meisters würdig, besonders gefällt er hier in dem Andante, wo seine Melodien schön genug sind, die Himmlischen herabzulocken. Kritisch mich darüber auszulassen, ist unmöglich, da ich die Oper nur einmal, in großem Gedränge, gehört habe.	In the evening a most beautiful new opera, *La clemenza di Tito*, was given free of charge by the Estates. The music is by Mozart and quite worthy of its master. Here he especially pleases in the andante where his melodies are sufficiently beautiful to entice heavenly beings to earth. It is impossible for me to pass any critical comment on it, since I only heard the opera once, and in the middle of a great crowd.

Document 14. Johann Debrois, *Record of the Complete Coronation of His Majesty King Leopold II of Bohemia.*[14]

1791, 6 September

Um 7 Uhr gieng die Aufführung dieses ernsthaften italienischen Singspiels vor sich. Die gewöhnliche Theaterwache war verdoppelt, eine Division Karabiniers besetzte die angemessenen Posten, und die Feuerlöschanstalten waren vermehret. Ihre Majestäten der König und die Königinn sammt der k. Familie beehrten das Nazionaltheater, das bis zur Vermeidung eines Gedränges ganz angefüllt war, und wo man aus Prag's bekannter Gefälligkeit, den Fremden die ersten Plätze überliess, mit Ihrer Gegenwart, und wurden mit Jubel empfangen. Das Singspiel selbst ward mit dem Beifalle, welchen Verfasser, Kompositor, und die Singstimmen, besonders die rühmlich bekannte *Todi* [sic], aus vollem Grunde verdienten, aufgenommen, und es schien, dass Ihre Majestäten mit Zufriedenheit das Schauspielhaus verlassen haben.

The performance of this serious Italian opera took place at 7 o'clock. The usual theatre guard had been doubled; a division of *caribiniers* occupied the appropriate places, and the fire extinguishing measures were reinforced. Their Majesties the King and the Queen honoured the National Theatre together with the royal family and were received with cheering. The theatre was full to the point of avoiding a crush, and in accordance with Prague's well-known courtesy, the first seats were left to the foreigners. The opera itself was received with the applause that the poet, the composer and the singing voices—especially the well-known [Luísa] Todi [sic]—fully deserved, and it seemed that Their Majesties left the theatre satisfied.

Document 15. Letter from Wolfgang Amadeus Mozart in Vienna to his wife, Constanze Mozart in Baden.[15]

1791, 7 October

---

in dieser zwischenzeit kam ein brief von Prag vom Stadler; […] – das[s] sonderbareste dabei ist, das den abend als meine neue Oper mit so vielen beifall zum erstenmale aufgeführt wurde, am nemlichen abend in Prag der *Tito* zum leztenmale auch mit ausserordentlichen beifall aufgeführet worden. – alle Stücke sind *applaudirt* worden. – der *Bedini* sang besser als allezeit. – das *Duett*chen *ex A* von die 2 Mädchens wurde wiederhollet – und gerne – hätte man nicht die *Marchetti* geschonet – hätte man auch das *Rondó repetirt*. – dem Stodla wurde |: O böhmisches wunder! – schreibt er :| aus dem Parterre und so gar aus dem *Orchestre bravo* zugerufen. ich hab mich aber auch recht angesetzt, schreibt er […].

Meanwhile I have had a letter which [Anton] Stadler has sent me from Prague. […] And the strangest thing of all is that on the very evening when my new opera [i.e. *Die Zauberflöte*] was performed for the first time with such success [i.e. 30 September], *Tito* was given in Prague for the last time with tremendous applause. All the numbers were *applauded*. Bedini sang better than ever. The little duet in A major which the two maidens [i.e. Perini and Antonini] sing [i.e. duet 7. 'Ah perdona al primo affetto'] was repeated; and had not the audience wished to spare Marchetti, a *repetition* of the rondò [i.e. rondo 23. 'Non più di fiori'] would have been very welcome. Cries of 'Bravo' were shouted at Stodla [i.e. Stadler] from the parterre and even from the orchestra – 'What a miracle for Bohemia!' he writes, 'but indeed I *did my very best*'.

Document 16. Count Heinrich Franz von Rottenhan to the preparation committee, Prague.[16]

1791, 29 October

Guardasoni hat schon von mehrern Wochen ein ähnliches Gesuch mit den anliegenden 2 Berechnungen dem Praesidio übergeben; die eine, die die Verfertigung zweyer nicht in dem Contract bedungener neuen Decorationen betrifft, wird salva moderatione keinem Zweifel unterliegen, weilen diese 2 Decorationen und viele Ausbesserungen wirklich verfertigt worden sind, da das alte Scenarium gar zu sehr abgenu[t]zt war, um zur neuen opera dienen zu können; was der Entschädigungsbitte für die Aufwand der Oper selbst betrifft, das ist blos eine Gnaden Sache, weil dieser Gegenstand durch einen formlichen [sic] Contract seine Bestim[m]ung erhalten hat. Allein es ist allgemein bekannt, daß wegen der vielen Hof Fest[e] und der Balle und Gesellschaften, die in den Privat Haysern gegeben wurden beyde Theater Entreprenneurs sehr wenig zulauf gehabt haben, zeigte sich auch bey Hof wider Mozarts Composition eine vorgefas[s]te Abneigung, allso da die Oper nach der ersten feyerlichen Vorstellung fast gar nicht mehr besucht ward, die ganze Speculation des Entreprenneurs war darauf gebaut, das nebst der bewilligten Gaabe der H. Stände auch die Entrée einen beträchtlichen Beytrag abwerfen wurde, und das hat gänzlich fehlgeschlagen.	Guardasoni already submitted a similar petition to the Presidency several weeks ago, along with the two enclosed invoices. Of the first of these, which regards two new decorations that are not stipulated in the contract, there can be no doubt *salva moderatione** [*shorthand for '*salva moderatione consilii generalis*' i.e. while safeguarding the general direction of the plan], since these two decorations and many rectifications indeed were produced, the old scenery being far too worn to serve for the new opera. As for the request for compensation for the expenditure relating to the opera itself, this is a mere question of grace, since this matter was provided with a clause in a formal contract. However, it is generally known that both theatre entrepreneurs had very little intake due to the many courtly festivities and balls and parties that were given in private houses. Furthermore, a preconceived aversion to Mozart's composition was apparent at court, and thus the opera was barely attended after the first celebratory performance. In addition to the endowment granted by the Noble Estates, the entire venture of the entrepreneur relied on the entrance fees yielding a substantial contribution, and this has failed completely.

Document 17. Anonymous letter report from Prague.[17]

1791, 12 December

Bei der hiesigen Krönung waren zwei musikalischen Arbeiten merkwürdig. Die eine bestand in einer grossen—oder vielmehr mittler—ernsthaften Oper, *einer abermals* komponirten *Clemenza di Tito*, die aber, wiewohl die Musik von Mozart war, nicht gefiel. Dieser sonst grosser Komponist schien dasmal [sic] des Wahlspruchs vom Oktavius: *Festina lente!* vergessen zu haben. Auch waren nur die Arien und Chöre von seiner, die Recitative von einer andern Hand. Die zweite bestand in einer grossen, von Kozeluch gesetzten Kantate. Der Text dazu war auf Verlangen der Stände von Meis[s]ner verfertigt. Diese Tonsetzung fand Beifall, so übelgewählt Ort und Zeit waren, wo sie gegeben ward.	At the coronation in this city two musical works were notable. One was a grand, or rather, semi-serious opera, *another* setting of *La clemenza di Tito*, which, however, although the music was by Mozart, did not find favour. This normally great composer seems to have forgotten Octavius's motto: *Festina lente* [i.e. 'Make haste slowly']! Also, only the arias and choruses were from his hand, the recitatives by another. The second [work] was a grand cantata composed by [Leopold] Koželuch. The text for it was written by [August Gottlieb] Meissner at the request of the Estates. This composition met with applause despite the unpropitious time and place chosen for the performance.

Document 18. Index of the performances of Guardasoni's company.[18]

Early 1792
PRAGA / PRAGUE

Nel Teatro nazionale di Sua Eccellenza il Sig. Conte Nostiz si rappresentò il Dramma Serio intitolato / In the National Theatre of His Excellency Count Nostitz was performed the serious drama with the title

La Clemenza di Tito

Musica nuova del Sig. Maestro Wolfgango Amadeo Mozzart / New music by Sig[nor] Maestro Wolfgang Amadeus Mozart

SIGNORI ATTORI / THE ACTORS

Primo soprano	*Prima Donna*
Domenico Bedini	Maria Marchetti Fantozzi

Primo Tenore

Antonio Baglioni

Ed altri Suggetti, che cantano nelle opere buffe qui sotto descritti / And other persons who sing in the comic operas listed below

SIGNORI ATTORI / THE ACTORS

Antonio Baglioni	Carolina Perini
Felice Ponziani	Luigi Bassi
Gaetano Campi	Giuseppe Lolli
Angiola Perini	Caterina Micelli
Anna Antonini	Caterina Perini

Titoli delle Opere / Titles of the operas

IL Dissoluto punito Axur Re d'Ormus

Document 19. Heinrich August Ottokar Reichard's report on Guardasoni's opera company, Leipzig.[19]

1792, autumn

Im Jahr 1789 bewog ihn der pohlnische Landtag nach Warschau zu gehen. Hier blieb er, bis die Herren Stände des Königreichs Böhmen ihn zur Feyerlichkeit der Krönung des nun verewigten Kaiser Leopolds im vorigen Jahre nach [144] Prag zurückruften. Da aber der öffentlichen Lustbarkeiten zu viel waren und sich auch daselbst mehrere Schauspielergesellschaften befanden, so war das Publikum getheilt, und er fand daher auch seine Rechnung nicht. Guardasoni schloß daher seine Oper zu Ende der Krönung, entließ einige Mitglieder und behielt nur die vorzüglichsten von seiner Gesellschaft bey sich, mit welchen er den Winter hindurch ruhte.

In 1789, the Polish parliament induced him [Guardasoni] to go to Warsaw. There he remained until last year the Noble Estates of the Kingdom of Bohemia called him back to Prague for the festivities for the coronation of the now deceased Emperor Leopold. But since there were too many public entertainments and also several theatrical companies there, the public was divided and he did not even cover his expenses. Guardasoni therefore closed his opera company at the end of the coronation, dismissed several performers and retained only the most excellent members, with whom he rested throughout the winter.

Document 20. 'Some News on the State of the Prague Theatre'. Attributed to Franz Xaver Niemetschek.[20]

1794, December

Endlich muß man noch mit Dank und Lob der Vorstellung der *Clemenzza [sic] di Tito*, von Mozart, Erwähnung [569] machen. Dieses letzte Werk [Footnote: 'Die Zauberflöte war schon fertig, als Mozart bei der Krönung Leopolds in Prag den Titus schrieb, wenigstens spielte er die meisten Stücke daraus seinen Freunden am Klavier. Man irrt also, wenn man die Zauberflöte den Schwanengesang Mozarts nennt.'] der dramatischen Musik Mozarts, welches er zu dem Krönungsfeste des höchstsel. Kaisers Leopold II. in Prag schrieb, gehört unter seine größten Meisterstücke. Es wurde zur Krönungszeit als Freioper und dann einigemal noch gegeben; aber da es das Ungefähr so haben wollte, daß ein elender Kastrat und eine mehr mit den Händen als der Kehle singende Primadonna,

Finally, I do feel obliged to mention the production of *La clemenza di Tito* by Mozart with thanks and praise. Mozart's last work of dramatic music [Footnote: '*Die Zauberflöte* was already finished when Mozart wrote *La clemenza di Tito* for Leopold's coronation in Prague; at least he played most of its numbers on the clavier for his friends. It is therefore wrong to call *Die Zauberflöte* Mozart's swansong.'], which he wrote for the coronation festivity of the late Emperor Leopold II in Prague, belongs among his greatest masterpieces. At the time of the coronation, it was given once free of charge and then a few times more. But since fate decreed that a miserable castrato [i.e. Bedini] and a *prima donna* who sang more with her hands than with her throat, and whom one was

| 1794, December |

| die man für eine Besessene halten mußte, die Hauptparten hatten; da der Stoff zu simpel ist, als daß er eine mit Krönungsfeierlichkeiten, Bällen und Illuminazionen beschäftigte Volksmenge hätte interessiren können, und da es endlich—(Schande unserm Zeitalter)—eine ernsthafte Oper ist, so gefiel sie minder im Allgemeinen, als sie es vermög ihrer wahrhaft himmlischen Musik verdiente. Es ist eine gewisse griechische Simplizität, eine stille Erhabenheit in der ganzen Musik, die das fühlende Herz leise, aber desto tiefer trifft; die zu dem Karakter des Titus, den Zeiten und ganzen Sujet so richtig paßt, und dem feinen Geschmacke Mozarts, so wie seinem Beobachtungsgeiste, Ehre macht. Dabei ist der Gesang durchgängig, vorzüglich aber im Andante, himmlischsüß, voll Empfindung und Ausdruck, die Chöre pompös und erhaben; kurz, Glucks Erhabenheit ist darin mit Mozarts origineller Kunst, seinem strömenden Gefühle und seiner ganzen hinreissenden Harmonie vereinigt. Unübertreffbar, und vielleicht ein *non plus ultra* der Musik, ist das letzte Terzett und Finale des ersten Akts. Die Kenner sind im Zweifel, ob Titus nicht noch sogar den *Don Giovanni* übertreffe. Dieses göttliche Werk des unsterblichen Geistes gab uns Hr. Guardasoni am 3ten Dezember d. J. bei gedrängtvollem Hause und unter dem ungetheiltestem Beifalle des Publikums; er hat dadurch die langen Wünsche aller Kenner und Schätzer des wahren Schönen erfüllt, und ihren vollkommensten Beifall erhalten. Möchte er doch reichlich für dieses Vergnügen unterstützt, und seine Kasse gefüllt werden! Die Sängerin Strenasachi [sic], welche die Part des Kastraten in der Rolle des [570] Sesto als Mann singt, zeichnet sich am meisten durch guten Gesang und ein ächtes Spiel aus, und kein Anwesender wird anstehen, ihr den Vorzug vor dem verstümmelten Menschen zu geben, dessen unförmliche Fleischmasse uns, so oft er auftrat, erschreckte, und zu seiner Bastardstimme sich so komisch verhielt! | obliged to take for a madwoman [i.e. Marchetti Fantozzi], had the principal roles; since the subject matter is too simple to be able to interest a crowd preoccupied with coronation festivities, balls and illuminations; and finally since (shame on our age!) it is a serious opera, it generally pleased less than it deserved by dint of its truly heavenly music. There is a certain Greek simplicity, a quiet grandeur in the entire music, which affects the sensitive heart gently but so much the deeper, and which suits Tito's character, the period and the entire subject so correctly, and which does honour to Mozart's fine taste as well as to his keen observation. In addition, the songs are of heavenly sweetness and full of feeling and expression throughout, but especially in the andantes, and the choruses are magnificient and exultant. In short, [Christoph Willibald] Gluck's grandeur is here united with Mozart's artistic originality, his pouring emotion and all his ravishing harmony. The last trio [10. 'Vengo … aspetatte …'] and finale in Act I [quintet with chorus 12. 'Deh conservate, o Dei'] are unsurpassable and perhaps a *non plus ultra* of music. The connoisseurs are in doubt whether *La clemenza di Tito* might not even surpass *Don Giovanni*. On 3 December this year Herr Guardasoni gave us this divine work of his immortal genius before a crowded house and to the most unanimous applause of the audience. He thus fulfilled the long wishes of all connoisseurs and cherishers of true beauty and received their most complete applause. May he be generously supported for this entertainment, and his coffers filled! The female singer [Teresa] Strinasacchi, who sings the castrato's part in the male role of Sesto, especially distinguished herself with her good singing and genuine acting, and no one present would hesitate to give her preference over the mutilated person whose shapeless mass of flesh frightened us whenever he appeared and was so odd in relation to his bastard voice! |

Document 21. Niemetschek, *Life of the Imperial Kapellmeister Wolfgang Gottlieb Mozart*, Prague.[21]

1798

---

[32] Die Musik zu der Oper *La Clemenza di Tito* war von den böhmischen Ständen zu der Krönung des Kaisers Leopold bestellt. Diese letzte begann er in seinem Reisewagen auf dem Wege von Wien, und vollendete sie in dem kurzen Zeitraume von 18 Tagen in Prag. […]

[47] […] die Meisterstücke der Römer und Griechen gefallen bey fortgesetzter Lektüre und je reifer der Geschmack wird, immer mehr und mehr—das nemliche widerfährt dem Kenner und Nichtkenner bey der Anhörung Mozartischer Musik, besonders der dramatischen Werke. So gieng es uns bey der ersten Vorstellung des Don Juan und insbesondere bey der *Clemenza di Tito*!

Nebst den oben anführten Eigenheiten und Vorzügen des Mozartischen Kunsttalentes, beobachtet an ihm der aufmerksamen Schätzer seiner Werke einen gewissen feinen Sinn, den Charakter jeder Person, Lage und Empfindung aufs genaueste treffen;

reddere convenientia cuique.

The music for the opera *La clemenza di Tito* had been commissioned by the Bohemian Estates for the coronation of Emperor Leopold. [Mozart] began the latter in his travelling coach on the way from Vienna, and he finished it in the short space of eighteen days in Prague. […]

The masterpieces of Rome and Greece are appreciated the more often they are read and the more mature our taste becomes. This applies to connoisseurs as well as non-connoisseurs when listening to Mozart's music, particularly to his dramatic works. Those were our feelings at the first performance of *Don Giovanni* and especially at *La clemenza di Tito*!

In addition to the qualities and superiority of Mozart's style just mentioned, the attentive praiser of his works will notice how with a certain fine perception, the character of each person, situation and emotion is most accurately drawn;

reddere convenientia cuique [a reference to Horace, *The Art of Poetry*'. Line 316 'Reddere personae scit convenientia cuique': 'Each actor must have manners agreeable to the Character']

	1798	
	Diese Eigenschaft war sein wahrer Beruf zum dramatischen Komponisten, und ist zugleich der Erklärungsgrund des Zaubers und der großen Wirkung seiner Werke. Daher hat jede seiner Kompositionen einen bestimmten eigenthümlichen Charakter, den selbst die Wahl der Tonart nicht verläugnet. Kenner seiner Werke bedürfen keiner besondern Beyspiele, da alle Opern von seiner Komposition diese Eigenschaft im hohen Grade an sich haben; aber das schönste Muster davon ist [omitted in 1808 edition: 'die ganze'] Clemenza di Tito.—Wie ganz anders bey den gewöhnlichen Kompositionen? Es sind größtentheils Gesänge von so unbestimmter Charakter, daß sie eben so gut zu einer Messe, als *Opera buffa* taugen. […]	This characteristic showed the real vocation he possessed for dramatic composition and is at the same time an explanation of his magic, and of the great effect of his works. In consequence, each composition has a very distinct character of its own, which is even shown by the choice of key. Connoisseurs of his works will not require any specific examples of this, as all the operas composed by him have this characteristic to a high degree. This is best exemplified in [omitted in 1808 edition: 'the whole of'] *La clemenza di Tito*. How different are ordinary compositions! There the songs are of so indeterminate a character that they would do equally well for a Mass or an *opera buffa*. […]
	[67] Wenn man seine Werke[,] besonders die theatralischen[,] nach der Zeitfolge ihrer Entstehung betrachtet, so merkt man deutlich den Gang seines zur Vollkommenheit schreitenden Geistes. In den frühern, z. B. in der Oper *Idomeneo* und der Entführung aus dem Serail, auch noch zum Theil in Figaro[,] strömt das ganze Feuer einer jugendlichen Phantasie und eine Fülle üppiger Empfindung ohne Gränzen. Es ist mehr Wärme als Licht darinn—die Massen des Gesanges und der Harmonie sind nicht so bestimmt, wie in den spätern Werken, in welchen dieser Strom der Empfindung im[68]mer sanfter sich in sein Bett zurückziehet; alles leichter, einfacher und korrekter wird. Nirgends ist diese Reife des Geschmackes sichtbarer, als in der *Clemenza di Tito*. Daraus läßt es sich schließen, was man noch von Mozart zu erwarten berichtiget war. […]	If we regard his works, particularly his dramatic ones, in the order of their appearance, we clearly recognise his rapid strides to perfection. A whole torrent of youthful imagination gushes forth and never-ending expressions of tenderness pervade his earlier works, such as the opera *Idomeneo* and *Die Entführung aus dem Serail*, and to some extent in *Figaro* as well. There is more warmth than light—the mass of song and harmony is not so distinct, as in his later works, in which this storm of feeling ever gentler is laid to rest; everything becomes lighter, simpler and more correct. Nowhere is this maturing of taste more obvious than in *La clemenza di Tito*. From this, one can judge what might still justifiably have been expected of Mozart. […]

(Continued)

1798

[73] *La Clemenza di Tito* wird in ästhetischer Hinsicht als schönes Kunstwerk, für die vollendeteste Arbeit Mozarts gehalten. Mit einem feinen Sinne faßte Mozart die Einfachheit, die stille Erhabenheit des Charakters des Titus, und der ganzen Handlung auf, und übertrug sie ganz in seine Komposition. Jeder Theil, selbst die gemäßigte Instrumentalparthie trägt dieses Gepräge an sich, und vereinigt sich zu der schönsten Einheit des Ganzen. Da sie für ein Krönungsfest, und für zwey ganz eigends dazu angenommene Sänger aus Italien geschrieben war, so mußte er nothwendig brillante Arien für diese zwey Rollen schreiben. Aber welche Arien sind das? Wie hoch stehen sie über dem gewöhnlichen Troß der Bravour-Gesänge?

Die übrigen Stücke verrathen überall den großen Geist aus dem sie geflossen. Die letzte Scene oder das Finale des 1ten Aktes ist gewiß die vollkommenste [*In the 1808 edition*: 'gelungenste'] Arbeit Mozarts; Ausdruck, Charakter, Empfindung, wetteifern darinn den größten Effekt hervorzubringen. Der Gesang, die Instrumentation, die Abwechslung der Töne, der Wiederhall der fernen Chöre—bewirkten bey jeder Aufführung eine Rührung und Täuschung, die bey Opern eine so seltene Erscheinung ist. Unter allen Chören, die ich gehört habe, ist keiner so fließend, [74] so erhaben und ausdrucksvoll, als der Schlußchor im 2ten Akte; unter allen Arien, keine so lieblich, so voll süßer Schwermuth, so reich an musikalischen Schönheiten, als das vollkommene Rondo in F, mit dem oblig: Baßethorne; *Non piu [sic] di Fiori* im 2ten Akte. Die wenigen instrumentirten Rezitative sind von Mozart, die übrigen alle—was sehr zu bedauern ist,—von einer Schülerhand.

Die Oper, die jetzt noch immer mit Entzücken gehört wird, gefiel das erstemal bey der Krönung nicht so sehr, als sie es verdiente. Ein Publikum, das vom Tanz, von Bällen und Vergnügungen trunken war, in dem Geräusche eines Krönungsfestes, konnte freylich an den einfachen Schönheiten Mozartscher Kunst wenig Geschmack finden!

La clemenza di Tito, considered from an aesthetic standpoint as a fine work of art, is thought to be the most polished. With his fine sensitivity, Mozart comprehended the simplicity, the calm grandeur of the character of Tito and the whole plot, and conveyed this throughout his composition. Every part, even the smallest instrumental part, bears his stamp, and combines to form a beautifully united whole. As it was written for a coronation and for two singers specially engaged from Italy [i.e. Bedini and Marchetti Fantozzi], he was compelled to write brilliant arias for these two roles. But what arias these were! Far above the usual supply of bravura songs.

The remaining numbers betray through and through the great genius from which they stem. The last scene or finale of the first Act is certainly the most perfect [*In the 1808 edition*: 'felicitous'] among Mozart's compositions; expression, character, feeling, all compete with one another to produce the greatest effect. The singing, instrumentation, variety of tone and echo of distant choruses—at each performance these created such emotion and illusion as is seldom apparent at operas. Among all the choruses I have heard, there is none which is so flowing, so magnificent and expressive as the final chorus of Act II [chorus 26. 'Tu è ver, m'assolvi, Augusto']; among all the arias, none so charming, so filled with sweet melancholy, with such a wealth of musical beauty as the perfect rondo [23.] in F, with the basset horn obbligato, 'Non più di fiori' in Act II. The few accompanied recitatives are by Mozart; the rest—much to be regretted—are all in a pupil's hand.

The opera, which is still heard with delight, was not liked as much as it deserved to be at its first performance at the coronation. A public which was surfeited with dances, balls and amusements, in the bustle of coronation festivities, certainly did not find the simple beauties of Mozart's art much to its taste!

Document 22. Johann Friedrich Rochlitz, 'Authentic Anecdotes from the Life of Wolfgang Gottlieb Mozart', Leipzig.[22]

1798, 5 December

Indess nahete sich die Abreise *Leopolds* nach Prag zur Krönung. Die Operndirektion, welche erst spät daran dachte, mit einer neuen Oper den Ueberfluss der Feyerlichkeiten und Feste noch mehr zu überfüllen— wendete sich deshalb an *Mozart*. Seiner Gattin und seinen Freunden war dies angenehm, weil es ihn zu anderer Arbeit und zu Zerstreuungen *zwang*. Auf deren Zuredung, und weil es seinem Ehrgefühl schmeichelte, übernahm er die Komposition der vorgeschlagenen Oper: *Clemenza di Tito*, von *Metastasio*. Der Text war von den böhmischen Ständen erwählt. Die Zeit war aber so kurz, dass er die unbegleiteten Recitative nicht selbst schreiben, auch jeden gelieferten Sa[t]z, sobald er fertig war, sogleich in Stimmen aussetzen lassen musste, und also nicht einmal revidieren konnte. Er sahe sich mithin gezwungen, da er kein Gott war, entweder ein ganz mittelmässiges Werk zu liefern, oder nur die Hauptsätze sehr gut, die minder interessanten ganz leicht hin und blos dem Zeitgeschmack des grossen Haufens gemäss zu bearbeiten. Er erwählte mit Recht das Le[t]zte. Einen Beweiss für die Richtigkeit seines Geschmacks und für seine Theater- und Publikumskenntnis legte er hierbey dadurch ab, dass er die in die Ewigkeit gedehnte Verwechselung, welche bey *Metastasio* ziemlich den ganzen mittlern Akt füllet, wegschnitt, woraus die Handlung einen raschern Gang bekömmt, das Ganze mehr concentriert, dadurch weit interessanter, und in zwey mässiglangen Akten vollendet wird; dass er auch, um mehr Mannigfaltigkeit in die einförmige stete

However, Leopold's departure for his coronation in Prague was approaching. The opera management, who at a late point thought of overfilling the abundance of festivities and celebrations even more with a new opera, therefore turned to Mozart. This appealed to his wife and his friends because it *forced* him to engage in other work and distractions. Due to their persuasion, and because it flattered his sense of honour, he undertook the composition of the suggested opera, *La clemenza di Tito* by Metastasio. The text had been chosen by the Bohemian Estates. The time was so short, however, that he was unable to write the unaccompanied recitatives himself, and as soon as a number was finished he was obliged to let it be written out in parts, not even being able to revise it. Since he was no god, he therefore felt compelled either to deliver a quite mediocre work, or only to produce the main numbers very well, while producing the less interesting ones quite easily and merely according to the fashionable taste of the big crowd. He rightly chose the latter. In so doing, he gave proof of the correctness of his taste and of his knowledge of theatre and the audience, pruning away the mistaken identities that are stretched out perpetually and take up more or less the entire second Act in Metastasio. Thereby, the action acquires a faster pace and is completed in two moderately long Acts, and the whole becomes more concentrated and thereby far more interesting. Furthermore, in order to introduce more variety into the perpetual monotonous alternation of arias and recitatives, he melted together several such numbers towards the end of the first Act.

(Continued)

1798, 5 December	
Abwechselung von Arien und Recitativen zu bringen, mehrere dergleichen Sätze gegen das Ende des ersten Akts zusammenschmolz, und [152] daraus das grosse Meisterstück, das Finale des ersten Akts, bildete— eine Komposition, die, wie schon bemerkt worden, im Ganzen zwar nach einer Scene seines *Idomeneo* angelegt ist, aber *Mozarts shakespear'sche*, allmächtige Kraft im Grossen, Prachtvollen, Schrecklichen, Furchtbaren, Erschütternden so unverkennbar, und so bis zum Haaremportreiben darlegt, als kaum das berühmte Finale des ersten Akts seines D. Giovanni.	He thus formed that great masterstroke, the Act I finale [quintet with chorus 12. 'Deh conservate, oh Dei']: a composition that, as a whole, is structured on a scene from his *Idomeneo*, as already mentioned [in *Allgemeine musikalische Zeitung* I/4 (24 October 1798), 54]. However, it exhibits Mozart's almighty Shakespearean force in the field of the grand, the magnificent, the horrific, the terrifying and the harrowing so unmistakably—to the extent of making the hairs stand on end—as barely even the famous Act I [sic] finale of his *Don Giovanni*.

Document 23. Passage added in the second edition of Niemetschek's Mozart biography, Prague.[23]

1808	
Die Gestalt, in welcher die alte *Opera seria* von Metastasio *La Clemenza di Tito* bey seiner Musik erscheint, ist das Werk seines richtigen Urtheiles und Geschmackes. Und ein solcher Kompositeur, der den Geist des Textes, das eigene der Situation so faßte und verstand—ihn oft verbesserte noch öfter erhob, soll keine höhere Bildung besessen haben?	The form in which Metastasio's old opera seria *La clemenza di Tito* is made to appear through [Mozart's] music is the result of his correct judgement and taste. And such a composer, who grasped and understood the spirit of the text and the individuality of the situation in this way—often improving it, and more often elevating it—should he not have been in possession of first-rate culture?

Document 24. Giuseppe Siboni's recollections, Copenhagen.[24]

1821, 18 January

Ich kam erst 1810 nach Wien, und fing erst nach dieser Zeit an den Titus mit den darin vorgefundenen Veränderungen zu singen, nachdem ich ihn vier oder fünf Jahre hindurch in Prag nach der ursprünglichen Composition vorgetragen hatte. […] Der Verfasser jener Anzeige hat nicht gewußt, daß die Prager Theater-Direktion, als dieselbe beschlossen [160] hatte, zur Krönungs-Feier des Kaisers Leopold eines der schönsten Dramas des unsterblichen Metastasio durch den großen Mozart componiren zu lassen, sich genöthigt sah eine Menge Veränderungen mit dem Stücke vorzunehmen, um es den Umständen angemessener zu machen. Vor fünfzig Jahren, hatte man nicht geglaubt, daß Jemand den Muth haben würde, die Hand an die schönsten Werke eines der größten dramatischen Dichter zu legen, um Veränderungen darin zu machen; dennoch aber geschah es auf Mozarts eigenes Verlangen; und wir besäßen sonst vielleicht nicht dieses herrliche Werk des großen Componisten. Zur Besetzung desselben ließ man aus Italien den damals berühmten Soprano Bedini für die Rolle des Sextus kommen, Mad. Marchetti sang die Vitellia und Hr. B……i den Titus. Da die Direction die Bemerkung machte, das[s] Mozart die Rolle des Titus (obwohl dieses die Hauptrolle und der Protagonist ist) mit weniger Interesse behandelt habe, als die beiden übrigen Hauptrollen, so beklagte sie sich darüber bei Mozart, und verlangte daß er die Musik verändern sollte; dieser aber verweigerte es, und sagte, daß sie einen andern Tenor hätten aus Italien verschreiben sollen, er habe das Kleid für den Körper dessen gemacht, der es tragen sollte; man hätte ihm einen andern Titus vorstellen sollen, so würde er auch eine andere Musik gemacht haben. Mozart hatte ausserdem noch andere Ursachen, welche nicht hierher gehören, denn Hr. B……i war doch, wie ich gehört habe, als Sänger nicht ohne Verdienst. Von der Wahrheit des von mir Angeführten kann der Herr Verfasser sich überzeugen, wenn er sich bei denjenigen Personen erkundigen will, welche damals in Prag mit der Theater-Direction zu thun hatten.	I did not come to Vienna before 1810, and only then did I begin to sing Tito with the modifications that I encountered there, having performed it according to the original composition in Prague [with Guardasoni's company] for four or five years [from 1800 to 1805]. […] The author of that report [in *Originalien aus dem Gebiete der Wahrheit, Kunst, Laune und Phantasie* IV/153 (1820), 1095-96] was unaware that when the Prague theatre management decided to let the great Mozart set one of the most beautiful dramas by the immortal Metastasio to music for the coronation festivities of Emperor Leopold, they felt obliged to make a lot of changes in the piece to make it more appropriate to the circumstances. Fifty years ago, it was inconceivable for anyone to have the courage to lay their hands on the most beautiful works by one of the greatest dramatic poets in order to modify them. However, it happened on Mozart's own demand, and otherwise we would perhaps not possess this wonderful work by the great composer. For the cast, the once famous soprano Bedini was got from Italy for the role of Sesto; Mad. Marchetti sang Vitellia, and Herr B[aglion]i Tito. When the management noted that Mozart had treated the role of Tito with less interest than the two other principal roles (although he is the principal role and the protagonist), they complained to Mozart and demanded that he change the music. He refused to do this, however, and said they should have engaged another tenor from Italy: he had made the suit for the body of the person who was to wear it. If they had presented him with a different Tito, then he would also have composed different music. Mozart had some other reasons, too, which are not relevant in this context, for as I have heard, Herr B[aglion]i was not without merit. The author may convince himself of the truthfulness of this story if he makes an inquiry to the people who were involved with the theatre management in Prague at that time.

(Continued)

1821, 18 January

Auch wird man überall, wo Mozart Opern componirt hat, hören, daß derselbe sich jenen Ideen immer nur insofern überließ, als dieselben mit den Kräften derer übereinstimmten, welche sie ausführen sollten, daß er sie erst dann völlig entwickelte und vollendete, wenn er sich mit den Mitteln und der Art des Gesanges eines jeden der Hauptpersonen genau bekannt gemacht hatte. So haben allen großen und genialen Componisten gehandelt, so handeln sie noch, und so werden alle diejenigen handeln, welche gewissenhaft zu Erfüllung desjenigen Zweckes beitragen wollen, für welchen sie als Componisten von den Directionen bezahlt werden, nämlich dem Publikum zu gefallen, und dadurch der Kasse, aus welcher ihr Verdienst herrührt, Vortheile zu verschaffen.

But anywhere where Mozart composed operas, one will hear that he only surrendered to these ideas to the extent that they matched those who were to execute them, and that he would only develop and perfect them when he had acquainted himself thoroughly with the vocal means and style of each of the principal roles. Great and brilliant composers have always acted this way; they still act this way, and those will always act thus who want to contribute diligently to the one aim for which they are paid as composers by the managements, viz. pleasing the audience and thereby gain benefits for the box office from which their earnings proceed.

Notes

1. Státní Ústřední Archiv, fond Zemský výbor (Central State Archive in Prague, Provincial Committee), department 84/1, Karton 1176. Tomislav Volek, 'Über den Ursprung von Mozarts Oper *La clemenza di Tito*', *Mozart-Jahrbuch 1959* (Salzburg, 1960), 280.

2. Státní Ústřední Archiv, fond Zemský výbor (Central State Archive in Prague, Provincial Committee), department 84/42, Karton 1188, No. 864. Sergio Durante, 'The Chronology of Mozart's *La clemenza di Tito* Reconsidered', *Music & Letters* LXXX/4 (November 1999), 591. Translation based on J. Bradford Robinson, in Wolfgang Amadeus Mozart, *La clemenza di Tito K. 621: Facsimile of the Autograph Score* (Los Altos CA: The Packard Humanities Institute, 2008), 31–2.

3. Országos Széchényi Könyvtár (Széchényi National Library in Budapest). Reproduced from H. C. Robbins Landon, 'Acta Musicalia No. 141', *The Haydn Yearbook* XV (1984), 154.

4. Johann Debrois (ed.), *Aktenmässige Krönungsgeschichte des Königs von Böhmen Leopold des Zweiten und Marie Louisens* (Prague, 1792) I, viii–ix, 128–31.

5. Debrois, *Aktenmässige Krönungsgeschichte*, I, ix, 131–33.

6. Wolfgang Amadé Mozart, *Verzeichnüß aller meiner Werke vom Monath febrario 1784 bis Monath [November] 1[791]*. London, British Library: Zweig MS 63, ff. 28v.

7. *La clemenza di Tito, dramma serio per musica in due atti da rappresentarsi nel Teatro Nazionale di Praga nel settembre 1791. In occasione di sollenizzare il giorno dell'incoronazione di Sua Maestà l'Imperatore Leopoldo II* (Prague: Schönfeld, 1791).

8. Haus-, Hof- und Staatsarchiv in Vienna. Dorothea Link, *The National Court Theatre in Mozart's Vienna: Sources and Documents 1783–1792* (Oxford: Clarendon Press, 1998), 382.

9. Haus-, Hof- und Staatsarchiv in Vienna, Sammelbände, Karton 52. John Rice, *Emperor and Impresario: Leopold II and the Transformation of Viennese Musical Theater 1790–1792* (Berkeley: University of California 1987), 352.

10. *Tagebuch der böhmischen Königskrönung* (Prague: Joseph Walenta, Kunst- und Buchhändler, 1792), 223, 225.

11. *Prager Oberpostamtszeitung*, 10 September 1791. Otto Erich Deutsch, *Mozart: Die Dokumente seines Lebens* (Kassel, Basel: Bärenreiter, 1961), 525.

12. [Johann Friedrich Ernst] Albrecht, *Krönungsjournal für Prag* (Prague: 1791) VI, 382–83, 386. Translation based on H. C. Robbins Landon, *1791: Mozart's Last Year* (New York: Schirmer Books, 1988), 115–16.

13. [Franz Alexander von Kleist:] *Fantasien auf einer Reise nach Prag* (Dresden & Leipzig: Richterschen Buchhandlung, 1792), 112, 119.

14. Johann Debrois, *Urkunde über die vollzogene Krönung Seiner Majestät des Königs von Böhmen Leopold des Zweiten und Ihrer Majestät der Gemahlinn des Königs Maria Louise, gebornen Infantinn von Spanien* (Prague: Gottlieb Haase, 1808), 110.

15. *Mozart Briefe und Dokumente*. Online Edition. http://dme.mozarteum.at/DME/briefe/letter.php?mid=1764&cat=3 Accessed 11 December 2017. Translation based on Emily Anderson, *The Letters of Mozart & His Family*, III (London: Macmillan, 1938), 1437.

16. Státní Ústřední Archiv, fond Zemský výbor (Central State Archive in Prague, Provincial Committee), department. 84/12, Karton 84. Volek, 'Über den Ursprung', 284.

17. F[riedrich] Ae[milius] Kunzen & J[ohann] F[riedrich] Reichardt (eds.), *Studien für Tonkünstler und Musikfreunde: Eine historisch-kritische Zeitschrift fürs Jahr 1792* (Berlin, Verlage der neuen Musikhandlung, 1793) I, 'Nachrichten aus Briefen', in *Musikalisches Wochenblatt* xii, 94. Translation based on Sergio Durante and J. Bradford Robinson, Wolfgang Amadeus Mozart, *La clemenza di Tito K. 621: Facsimile of the Autograph Score*, 24

18. *Indice de' teatrali spettacoli 1791–92*. Ian Woodfield in *Performing Operas for Mozart: Impresarios, Singers and Troupes* (Cambridge: Cambridge University Press, 2012), 172.

19. [Heinrich August Ottokar] Reichard, *Taschenbuch für die Schaubühne, auf das Jahr 1793* (Gotha: Carl Wilhelm Ettinger, [1792]), 143–4. Translation based on Ian Woodfield, *Performing Operas for Mozart*, 170, 176.

20. [Franz Xaver Niemetsche]k, 'Einige Nachrichten über den Zustand des Theaters in Prag. Im Dezember 1794', *Allgemeines europäisches Journal* II/3 (Brno, December 1794), 568–70.

21. Franz [Xaver] Niem[e]tschek, *Leben des K. K. Kapellmeisters Wolfgang Gottlieb Mozart, nach Originalquellen beschrieben* (Prague: Herrlischen Buchhandlung, 1798), 32, 47, 67–8, 73–4. Translation based on Franz Niemetschek, *Mozart: The First Biography*, tr. Helen Mautner (New York, Oxford: Berghahn Books, 2006), 31, 45–6, 66, 71–2.

22. [Johann] Friedrich Rochlitz, 'Verbürgte Anekdoten aus *Wolfgang Gottlieb Mozarts* Leben, ein Beytrag zur richtigern Kenntnis dieses Mannes, als Mensch und Künstler', *Allgemeine musikalische Zeitung*, I/10 (Leipzig, 5 December 1798), 151–2.

23. Franz Xav[er] Němetschek, *Lebensbeschreibung des K. K. Kapellmeisters Wolfgang Amadeus Mozart, aus Originalquellen, Zweite vermehrte Auflage* (Prague: Herrlischen Buchhandlung, 1808). http://mozartsocietyofamerica.org/embp/Niemetschek-1808.pdf Accessed 11 December 2017. The passage is missing in Helen Mautner's translation.

24. J[oseph] Siboni, 'Berichtigung', in *Originalien aus dem Gebiete der Wahrheit, Kunst, Laune und Phantasie* V/20 (Hamburg, 1821), 159–60.

2 Operatic Culture at the Court of Leopold II and Mozart's *La clemenza di Tito*

John A. Rice

On 5 October 1789 a mob, consisting mostly of women, marched from Paris to Versailles, attacked the palace, and forced King Louis XVI and Queen Marie Antoinette to return with them to Paris. Later, Marie Antoinette, putting the best face she could on the unspeakable outrage that had just occurred, expressed royal magnanimity to the judges who came to take her deposition against the mob: 'J'ai tout vu, j'ai tout su, et j'ai tout oublié' (I have seen everything, I have known everything, and I have forgotten everything).[1] Her words echoed those of Emperor Augustus at the end of Pierre Corneille's *Cinna ou la Clémence d'Auguste* (1643): 'Auguste a tout apris & veut tout oublier' ('Augustus has learned everything and will forget everything').[2] She came even closer to Pietro Metastasio's libretto *La clemenza di Tito*—a libretto written for her grandfather, Emperor Charles VI—and the final words of Tito's final monologue: 'Sia noto a Roma / Ch'io son l'istesso; e ch'io / Tutto so, tutti assolvo, e tutto obblio' (Let it be known in Rome that I am the same, and that I know everything, absolve everyone, and forget everything).[3]

The queen's patently theatrical gesture—we might call it 'La clemenza di Maria Antonietta'—reminds us that Mozart's *La clemenza di Tito* was a product of a time in European history dominated by a single event: the French Revolution. Marie Antoinette's words also remind us of the pervasiveness of theatre in the everyday life of eighteenth-century Europe. For both the queen and her subjects, the

---

How to cite this book chapter:
Rice, J. A. 2018. Operatic Culture at the Court of Leopold II and Mozart's *La clemenza di Tito*. In: Tessing Schneider, M. and Tatlow, R. (eds.) *Mozart's* La clemenza di Tito: *A Reappraisal*. Pp. 33–55. Stockholm: Stockholm University Press. DOI: https://doi.org/10.16993/ban.b. License: CC-BY NC-ND 4.0

theatre helped to shape their understanding of themselves, of their place in society, and of contemporary events; those events in turn helped to shape theatre, including opera. This was as true in Vienna as it was in Paris, and it helps to explain why so much thought, money, and energy was put into opera during a period of such momentous political change. A little less than two years after the queen paraphrased Tito's declaration of clemency, while the Revolution continued to unfold, Mozart was to conduct the first performance of his setting of *La clemenza di Tito* for the coronation of Leopold II, Marie Antoinette's brother, as king of Bohemia, on 6 September 1791.

Five months after the death of Emperor Joseph II on 20 February 1790, an anonymous critic, writing for a German journal, evaluated musical life in Vienna during his reign. Turning to Joseph's successor, Leopold, he continued:

> The present king has not been in the theatre, nor has he had his music in private, nor has he shown any other sign of being a music-lover. *Malum signum*, cry our pseudo-prophets. But I believe that once the enormous burdens of statesmanship that lie on his shoulders are reduced to minor difficulties, once he has bestowed golden peace on his dominions, then too will we have a new Golden Age of music.[4]

The writer's hopes were not fulfilled. Emperor Leopold II died in March 1792 after a reign of only two years, and it can hardly be called a golden age of music. Yet his reign deserves study as a period of intense musical activity and change—much of it initiated by Leopold himself as part of a reorganisation of the court theatres' personnel and repertory that he oversaw in 1791. That reorganisation is an important part of the context of Mozart's last two operas, *Die Zauberflöte* and *La clemenza di Tito*.[5]

Leopold's reign fell between two periods of relative stability in the evolution of Viennese musical life. The 1780s, when Joseph II ruled alone after the death in 1780 of Maria Theresa, were shaped by his artistic direction, which favoured the hegemony of a particularly complex and sophisticated kind of *opera buffa*, the virtual absence of *opera seria* and ballet, a turning-away from church music by the best composers, and the cultivation of a rich and highly developed language of instrumental music. The years following Leopold's reign present a very different picture. The brilliant comic operas of Mozart were absent from the court theatres for most of the 1790s, replaced by Italian works of a simpler kind. Comic opera, instead of dominating the stage, shared it with other genres, such as Italian serious opera and ballet, which enjoyed the prestige it had won during the days of Gasparo Angiolini and Jean-Georges Noverre. Outside the theatre, church music regained its former attraction to composers.

In short, Viennese musical life was transformed, and much of the transformation took place during Leopold's reign. The departure from Vienna in early 1791 of Lorenzo Da Ponte signalled the end of an era in Viennese comic opera; Mozart's death later that year removed from the scene the author of the greatest musical achievements of the Josephinian decade. The debuts of Leopold's Italian ballet and *opera seria* troupes less than a month before Mozart's death reintroduced the Viennese to genres with which they had grown unfamiliar. A decree promulgated by Leopold in March 1791 sanctioning the performance of orchestrally accompanied music in churches contributed to a revival of church music, of which Mozart's Requiem, commissioned a few months later, was but one product. 1792, the year of Leopold's death, saw the arrival in Vienna of two musicians who would do more to shape Viennese music during the next decade than any others: Joseph Haydn, still to write his late masses and oratorios, returning from his first trip to London, and Ludwig van Beethoven arriving from Bonn.

Emperor Leopold II, fully aware of the theatre's symbolic power, used it skilfully. During the first year of his reign he pointedly ignored the theatre, successfully projecting the image of a sovereign too busy with the affairs of government to dabble in such trivial matters. Then, in 1791, he initiated and supervised a theatrical reorganisation the lavishness of which Vienna had not experienced since the days of Maria Theresa—a reorganisation that featured the return to Vienna of genres for which it had once been famous; one of those genres being *opera seria*.

Coming to the throne of the Habsburg monarchy at a time of crisis, Leopold faced threats both external (the French Revolution, and war with Turkey) and internal (rebellion in the Austrian Netherlands, the nobility of Bohemia and Hungary pushing back against Joseph's reforms). With a mixture of concessions and firmness he divided and weakened opposing groups. At the same time, he began an ideological offensive against the French Revolution and its sympathisers within the Habsburg monarchy.

Leopold consolidated power slowly—a process manifested in a series of coronations and other similar ceremonies. The first of these ceremonies was the oath of allegiance (*Huldigung*) to Leopold as archduke of Austria, on 6 April 1790; this ritual and its surrounding festivities is particularly well documented in a series of coloured prints by Hieronymus Löschenkohl.[6] The *Huldigung* was celebrated with a procession through the Graben to St. Stephen's Cathedral, a specially constructed 'Freuden-Gerüst' (stage of joy), and an orchestrally accompanied Te Deum in the Court Chapel (Hofkapelle). Then followed the coronations: in October 1790 Leopold was crowned emperor of the Holy Roman Empire in Frankfurt, a month later (in November 1790) king of Hungary in Bratislava, and in September 1791 king of Bohemia. The *Huldigung* and the coronations that followed were opportunities to affirm, through the powerful symbolism of ancient rituals, the strength and resilience of enlightened absolutism. Leopold basked in the warmth of pomp and applause, celebrating and renewing the traditions of the political system that kept him in power. His subjects not only applauded their new ruler but displayed their own traditions, demonstrating that they consented freely to be ruled by Leopold but that such consent came in exchange for his recognition of their rights and privileges.

Like most eighteenth-century coronations, Leopold's were patently theatrical. They were dramas whose casts included the Habsburg monarchy's richest and most powerful actors, the sovereign himself playing the leading role. In keeping with that theatrical quality, the production of plays and operas was an essential part of most of the festivities surrounding Leopold's coronations. The *Huldigung* of April 1790 took place while the theatres were still closed in mourning for Joseph II, so opera could not be a part of that celebration. In Frankfurt, though, performances included several operas and plays, and in Prague, at least three operas were performed in the days before and after Leopold's coronation as king of Bohemia. But the main theatrical event in Prague was the premiere of a new serious opera on the evening of the coronation day: Mozart's *La clemenza di Tito*, a setting of Metastasio's libretto heavily revised by Caterino Mazzolà.

The opera had been conceived and executed in great haste, in a process well documented by Sergio Durante.[7] In this paper I will focus on the genre of Mozart's opera, a choice made by the Bohemian noblemen who commissioned the opera in consultation with the impresario Domenico Guardasoni, considering their choice within the context of contemporary theatrical practices, Leopold's theatrical reorganisation in Vienna, and precedents set by previous coronations.

Although *opera seria* was, along with *tragédie lyrique*, the most prestigious and expensive of eighteenth-century operatic genres, it was not necessarily the automatic choice for a coronation in Central Europe in the early 1790s. Vienna, the city that Metastasio made his home and that honoured him with the title of Court Poet, rejected the kind of opera that he had played so crucial a role in shaping. *Opera seria* maintained its fascination for Italian composers and audiences through the eighteenth century and into the nineteenth. It enjoyed favour in some of the musical centres of northern Europe as well, including London and Berlin. But in Vienna, where many of Metastasio's dramas were first performed, *opera seria* was largely absent during the 1770s and 1780s.

This was partly a matter of the taste of Emperor Joseph II. In preparation for the visit of the Grand Duke and Duchess of Russia in 1781, Prince Wenzel Anton von Kaunitz, as minister of state, urged Joseph to arrange for the performance of *opera seria* and ballet. This, according to Kaunitz, would be an effective means of impressing the Russian visitors with the 'power of this monarchy'.[8] But Joseph rejected the idea of an *opera seria*, and in doing so he made his opinion of the genre clear: 'In regard to *opera seria* from Italy it is too late to arrange something good; and anyway, it is such a boring spectacle that I do not think I will ever use it.'[9] During the 1780s *opera buffa* and *Singspiel* flourished in Vienna. (I use the term *opera buffa* here loosely to refer to the wide spectrum of operas with comic situations and characters, many ensembles, including finales, which make use of singers who specialised in comic opera, but which also incorporate music and dramatic situations characteristic of *opera seria*.)

The dominance of *opera buffa* in Vienna's Burgtheater was reflected in its use in celebrating important dynastic events—not only in Vienna, but also in Prague, whose operatic repertory imitated that of Vienna. When the emperor's niece, Leopold's daughter Archduchess Maria Theresa, married a prince of Saxony in 1787, the bride's journey to Dresden was marked by operas. Her arrival in Vienna was celebrated by the premiere of Vicente Martín y Soler's *L'arbore di Diana*. Mozart intended the premiere of *Don Giovanni* to celebrate the archduchess's visit to Prague in October 1787; a delay in the production of that opera, however, meant that it had to be replaced by a gala performance of *Le nozze di Figaro*. But the most important dynastic event of the 1780s was the marriage in Vienna in January 1788 of Joseph's nephew, Leopold's son Archduke Francis, to Elisabeth of Württemberg. To celebrate that event, the Viennese *opera buffa* troupe presented the first performance of Antonio Salieri's *Axur re d'Ormus*, a *dramma tragicomico* that became Emperor Joseph's favourite opera. All these operas have librettos by Lorenzo Da Ponte, whose success in Vienna was a direct result of Joseph's operatic tastes and policies.

The use of *opera buffa* on occasions of state set a precedent that survived Joseph. 19 September 1790 was the day of the triple marriage that Leopold had arranged with his sister, Queen Maria Carolina of Naples: Archduke Francis, whose wife Elisabeth had died earlier in the year, was to marry Princess Maria Theresa of Naples, while two of Francis's younger siblings were to marry two of Maria Theresa's younger siblings. The whole Neapolitan royal family came to Vienna to witness the ceremony, and they stayed in Vienna for several months, enjoying with Leopold and his family a splendid succession of theatrical performances, concerts, banquets, and balls.[10]

The arrival of the Neapolitans was celebrated by the premiere of Joseph Weigl's *La caffettiera bizzarra* (libretto by Da Ponte) on 15 September. Looking back from a time when operatic aesthetics differed greatly from those of the Josephinian decade, Weigl later blamed the failure of *La caffettiera bizzarra* on its belonging to the wrong genre for the occasion:

> In the meantime I wrote another comic opera, *La caffettiera*, which takes place in the Prater. Because no other score was available, it was chosen for performance on the arrival of His Majesty the king of Naples, and it was a complete flop. How could a Prater story be of interest in the presence of such distinguished guests? I must openly admit that neither the book nor the music deserved a better fate, and I still cannot understand how a beginner (which I truly still was) could have been permitted to present such a plot on such a festive occasion.[11]

Salieri's *Axur*, revived five days later, was evidently deemed more appropriate for this kind of celebration (*Feyerlichkeit*), probably at least in part on account of its having originally served to celebrate Francis's first wedding in 1788. Count Karl von Zinzendorf, the Austrian bureaucrat whose diary serves as a crucial source of information about Viennese opera, had dismissed *La caffettiera bizzarra* as 'un tres sot opera'.[12] But at the performance of *Axur* his attention was drawn less to the opera itself than to the very first appearance in the Burgtheater of Joseph's successor, Leopold, writing 'To the theatre. *Axur re d'Ormus*. The entire Neapolitan royal family. Our king arrived when Axur is on his throne and was strongly applauded.'[13] (Leopold here was 'our king' rather than 'our emperor' because he had not yet been crowned emperor). Salieri's Axur is wicked, and at the end of the opera he prefers to commit suicide to being deposed. Leopold had no wish to be likened to Axur. But in one important respect they were the same: they were both kings. That was presumably enough for Zinzendorf to feel the appropriateness of Leopold's arrival in the royal box while Axur (probably portrayed by the great *buffo* Francesco Benucci, who had created the role in 1788) sat in royal splendour on the stage.

Emperor Joseph's operatic tastes and policies also influenced the choice of operas performed at the election and coronation in Frankfurt—an extremely Vienna-centric repertory that included Carl Ditters von Dittersdorf's *Der Apotheker und der Doktor*, Salieri's *Axur*, and Paul Wranitzky's *Oberon*.[14]

Viennese opera of the 1780s was still dominating the repertory of the court theatres in early 1791, a year after Joseph's death. On a festive day in February on which Leopold evidently pulled out all the stops to impress the king and queen of Naples, the opera clearly represented Josephinian values. The *Gazzetta universale* printed a report from Vienna dated 10 February:

> Yesterday, in honour of Their Sicilian Majesties, the court gave a magnificent sleigh ride to Schönbrunn, where there was a splendid dinner attended by many members of the high nobility. On their return, the same procession passed through the principal streets and squares of this city, after which they attended the opera *Le nozze di Figaro* at the Italian Theatre; then they went to the Redoutensaal, where the quality of the assembled guests made this one of the most beautiful spectacles ever seen.[15]

Yet seven months later, for the coronation opera in Prague, the Bohemian nobility that commissioned *La clemenza di Tito* conspicuously turned away from the precedent established by Joseph II, with his preference for *opera buffa* and *Singspiel*, specifying instead a genre that Joseph had said he would never use.

In turning to *opera seria*, the Bohemian nobility probably took account of earlier Habsburg coronations in Prague. In 1723, for example, the coronation of Charles VI as king of Bohemia had been celebrated with the splendid production of Johann Joseph Fux's *Costanza e fortezza* on an outdoor stage erected for the occasion just outside Prague Castle. Twenty years later, in May 1743, a setting of Metastasio's libretto *Semiramide* was performed as part of the festivities at the coronation of Maria Theresa as queen of Bohemia. The libretto printed for the occasion mentions no composer; it was probably a *pasticcio*.[16] As an *opera seria*, Leopold's coronation opera represented the continuation of a tradition to which both his grandfather and his mother had contributed.

The Bohemian nobility had yet another reason to celebrate Leopold's coronation with an *opera seria*. Before succeeding his brother in 1790, Leopold had spent twenty-five years in Florence as grand duke of Tuscany. When he and his wife Maria Luisa came to Vienna, they brought with them operatic tastes very different from those of Joseph II. *Opera seria* was an essential part of the theatrical repertory in Florence, as in the rest of Italy: an average of just under four *opere serie* were performed each year in Florence during the 1780s. So it is not really surprising that the transformation of the Viennese theatrical personnel and repertory launched by Leopold in early 1791 was shaped by his Italianate tastes and experience, and included the formation of an *opera seria* troupe. Leopold engaged two of Italy's leading *opera seria* singers, the soprano Cecilia Giuliani and the tenor Vincenzo Maffoli, and he chose the operas in which they were to make their Viennese debuts.[17] A review of the careers of Giuliani and Maffoli shows that they had reached the pinnacle of Italy's operatic hierarchy, and suggests that Leopold himself was familiar with their singing from their performances in Florence and (in the case of Maffoli) other Tuscan cities.

Cecilia Giuliani trained and began her career at the Ospedale dei Mendicanti in Venice. After singing Latin oratorios for almost a decade in Venice, she entered the secular world of *opera seria* in Florence in 1785, in Angelo Tarchi's *Virginia*. Also in Florence, Giuliani achieved one of her biggest early successes as Semiramide in Alessio Prati's *La vendetta di Nino*, a *melodramma tragico* in which she is struck dead by her son in one of the horrifying final scenes. During the next few years her engagements brought her to the theatres of Venice, Milan, and London, as well as Florence, where she made a triumphant return during Carnival 1791 in Sebastiano Nasolini's *Teseo a Stige* and a revival of *La vendetta di Nino*.

Vincenzo Maffoli had achieved equal fame by the time Leopold engaged him to sing in Vienna. He made his debut in Rome in 1781 and remained a favourite there, returning in 1787 and 1790. But he was also known in Florence and elsewhere in Tuscany; he sang in Florence 1788 and 1791, and in Livorno, Pisa, and Siena. His appearance in Pietro Guglielmi's *Debora e Sisara* in Florence during Lent 1791 was praised in the *Gazzetta toscana*.[18]

Maffoli was to sing the role of Sisara once more at least. In the audience in Florence was Emperor Leopold, in Tuscany to supervise the installation of his son Ferdinand as grand duke. Leopold must have been pleased with what he heard in *Debora e Sisara*. Maffoli entered imperial service in Vienna on 1 June 1791. He portrayed Sisara when Guglielmi's *dramma sacro* was presented in Vienna during Lent 1792, the last production before Leopold's death on 1 March of that year.

The third crucial member of Leopold's *opera seria* troupe was Angelo Testori, a *musico* (the most common contemporary term for castrato) who differed from Giuliani and Maffoli in having enjoyed only a short career before singing in Vienna. Evidently he was very young, and unable to command the huge salaries demanded by leading *musici* such as Luigi Marchesi and Gasparo Pacchierotti. Testori did not join the troupe until October 1791, suggesting that Leopold had trouble finding a first-rate *musico* who was both affordable *and* willing to move to Vienna.

Leopold's *opera seria* singers made their Viennese debut in the two operas in which Giuliani had starred just a few months earlier in Florence. They celebrated the birthday of Empress Maria Luisa, on 24 November 1791, with a performance of Nasolini's *Teseo a Stige*, followed a few weeks later with Prati's *La vendetta di Nino*.

Although these performances did not take place until more than two months after the coronation in Prague, the preparations for the re-establishment of *opera seria* had begun much earlier in the year. The Bohemian nobility, many of whom had residences in Vienna, and Guardasoni must have been aware of them.

After hiring Giuliani, Maffoli, and Testori, Leopold filled out his *opera seria* troupe with singers from the *opera buffa* troupe already established in the court theatres. Guardasoni did exactly the same in preparation for *La clemenza di Tito*. His contract (carefully analysed by Durante) required him to engage a first rate *musico* and *prima donna* (see Chapter 1, II Document 2). Honouring this stipulation, he brought to Prague the *musico* Domenico Bedini (who portrayed Sesto), and Maria Marchetti Fantozzi (who portrayed Vitellia). But for the rest of the cast the contract allowed him to use singers from his own troupe (including the tenor Antonio Baglioni, who portrayed Tito). Although those singers were most experienced in *opera buffa*—a repertory similar to that of the court theatres in Vienna—they did have some experience with *opera seria*. During the years 1789–91 they were resident in Warsaw, where the repertory included several serious operas.[19]

La clemenza di Tito was not the first musical event to take account of and pay tribute to the Italianate tastes of Leopold and his family.

Concerts given in Vienna in April 1791 included excerpts from an *opera seria*. And a celebration that occurred a month before the coronation in Prague also included a staged cantata. Both the concerts in April and the cantata in August anticipated the inauguration of Leopold's *opera seria* troupe; in doing so, they also anticipated certain aspects of Mozart's coronation opera.

On 16 and 17 April 1791 Vienna's Tonkünstler-Societät (Society of Musicians) presented excerpts from Giovanni Paisiello's *Fedra* as part of the regular concerts given near the end of Advent and Lent for the benefit of musicians' widows and orphans. Paisiello wrote *Fedra* for Naples, where it was first performed in 1788. It is based on the same story—the Greek tragedy of Phaedra as recast by Jean Racine—as Nasolini's *Teseo a Stige*, the opera with which Leopold's *opera seria* troupe was to make its debut later in 1791.

The playbill for the Lenten concerts lists three soloists and mentions that one of the arias to be sung was by Mozart:

> An excerpt from the opera *Fedra*.
>   The singers will be:
>   In the role of Aricia . . . . . Mad. Lange. [Aloisia Lange]
>   In the role of Ippolito . . . . Herr Kalvesi. [Vincenzo Calvesi]
>   In the role of Teseo . . . . . . Herr Nenzini. [Santi Nencini]
>   Chorus
> The music is by Johann Paisiello, with the exception of the aria sung by Mad. Lange, which is by Mozart.[20]

A manuscript collection of music from *Fedra* preserved in the Gesellschaft der Musikfreunde probably represents the opera as it was performed in the Burgtheater in April 1791: the one aria for Aricia in this collection is Mozart's 'No, che non sei capace', K. 419, written in 1783 for Aloisia Lange to sing in Pasquale Anfossi's *Il curioso indiscreto*.[21]

Surprisingly the poster does not mention the title role of *Fedra*, and the collection of excerpts that includes 'No, che non sei capace' does not include any of Fedra's music. This suggests the possibility that whoever came up with the idea of performing extracts from *Fedra* originally intended for Cecilia Giuliani to sing the role that she had sung in Nasolini's opera in Florence a few months earlier. She started receiving a salary from the Burgtheater on 1 March 1791, so it would have been reasonable to expect her to be available to sing in Vienna a month and a half later. But perhaps she arrived in Vienna later than expected. Her earliest known performance in imperial employ was in a concert at Laxenburg on 23 June 1791. With Adriana Ferrarese's departure from Vienna at the end of the previous theatrical season, there may have been no singer available in April 1791 who could perform the role of Fedra with the virtuosity and dramatic power that it must have required.

As for the *primo uomo* role of Ippolito, the assignment to Vincenzo Calvesi of this role followed what seems to have been a common practice—where *opera seria* was performed but where *musici*, for one reason or another, were not employed—of entrusting *primo uomo* roles to tenors. Leopold's late engagement of Testori meant that a tenor had to take the role that Paisiello had written for the young, but soon to be famous *musico*, Girolamo Crescentini.

We do not know how or why it was decided to perform excerpts from *Fedra* as part of the Tonkünstler-Societät a few months before *Teseo a Stige* came to the stage of the Burgtheater, but the performances may have served as a kind of trial. Two important questions needed to be answered in view of Leopold's intentions of reintroducing *opera seria* to Vienna. First, how would the Viennese public react to a genre with which it had become unfamiliar? If *Fedra* pleased, *Teseo* was likely to please as well. Second, to which extent was the current opera troupe, basically a comic troupe, capable of performing *opera seria*? Were the voices of Lange, Calvesi, and Nencini big enough, and was their stage presence strong enough to bring them success in *opera seria*? Preliminary answers to these questions might have been provided by the concerts of April 1791, well before Cecilia Giuliani, Vincenzo Maffoli, and Angelo Testori made their Viennese debuts.

The contract that Guardasoni signed on 8 July 1791 (see Chapter 1, II Document 2) required that he find 'a famous composer' to write the opera to celebrate Leopold's coronation in Prague. Travelling quickly to Vienna, he first offered the commission to the Hofkapellmeister Salieri, but he turned it down. It was evidently only after Salieri declined the commission that Guardasoni turned to Mozart.[22]

Salieri later explained, in a letter to Prince Anton Esterházy (see Chapter 1, II Document 3), that he was exceptionally busy during the summer of 1791 attending to the day-to-day affairs of the court theatres, because his protégé Joseph Weigl, who normally attended to such matters, was occupied in the composition of a cantata for the prince. It was Salieri's activities in the court theatres that forced him to refuse to compose the coronation opera for Prague. The only reason that Prince Esterházy commissioned Weigl to write a cantata was that the prince's Kapellmeister, Haydn, was in London. Haydn's absence was thus indirectly responsible for Mozart's receiving the commission for *La clemenza di Tito*.

The cantata that Weigl wrote for Prince Esterházy, *Venere e Adone*, was performed on 3 August 1791, as part of a three-day series of festivities celebrating the installation of Anton Esterházy as the new prince—the successor to Prince Nicholas, who had died the previous year. This installation was the princely equivalent to a coronation, and the festivities surrounding it analogous to those surrounding a coronation.[23] Such festivities demanded opera, which put the new prince in a difficult position, since he had dismissed his father's opera troupe soon after Nicholas's death. He turned, in response, to the Viennese court opera—not only for a composer, but also for singers.

The libretto booklet printed for the occasion emphasised the presence of the imperial court in the full title: *Venere e Adone, cantata da rappresentarsi alla presenza dell'imperial corte*. Furthermore, it names not only Weigl as composer, and Giovanni Battista Casti as librettist, but also Pietro Travaglia as stage designer. Although Weigl, in describing the occasion, mentioned Archduke Francis, Emperor Leopold's oldest son, as the only member of the imperial family to be invited, other accounts make it clear that Prince Esterházy had hoped to entertain the entire imperial family, but that the emperor himself had declined the invitation. Yet Weigl must have welcomed this opportunity to redeem himself before the court after the failure of *La caffettiera bizzarra* less than twelve months earlier:

> Francis, at that time crown prince, was invited to a great celebration given at Esterháza by Prince Anton Esterházy. I had received a commission from the prince to write the grand cantata *Venere ed Adone* and to supervise the entire production, since Kapellmeister Haydn was at that time in London. I took care of everything—the singers, the chorus, the ballet troupe—and the cantata was performed at Esterháza with great splendour and to the satisfaction of the members of the imperial family; and we were all generously rewarded by the prince.[24]

From a report in the *Wiener Zeitung* we learn that all four soloists belonged to the court theatre in Vienna. So did the three singers who participated in the performance of extracts from Paisiello's *Fedra* a few months earlier, as did Cecilia Giuliani, who instead of being conspicuously absent, was now part of the cast:

> Regarding the recent celebration at Esterháza, all accounts agree that in the series of amusements that distinguished themselves in organisation, taste, and beauty and competed with one another to delight those attending, the cantata performed on this occasion, *Venus and Adonis* (*Venere e Adone*), won first prize. The libretto is by Herr Abate Casti, the music by Herr Joseph Weigl, in the service of the National Court Theatre—music honoured by Their Highnesses the archdukes as well as by the high nobility and other guests with the loudest applause, which it also received from connoisseurs of music. The cast consisted of four members of the Viennese court theatre: Demoiselle [Cecilia]

Giuliani, Madame [Dorothea] Bussani, and Herrn [Vincenzo] Calvesi and [Valentin] Adamberger.[25]

Note that the cast (like that of *Fedra* in Vienna) did not include a *musico*. The two male characters in *Venere e Adone* are Adone (Venere's young lover) and Marte (Venere's older husband). Calvesi presumably created the *primo uomo* role of Adone (taking the place of the *musico* for whom this role seems appropriate); the older singer Adamberger presumably sang the *secondo uomo* role of Marte. That a tenor took the role designed for a castrated singer reflects the continued absence of a *musico* from the Viennese troupe.

Another report, in the *Gazzetta universale* of Florence, contains more information about the staging of *Venere e Adone*, its reception, and the rewards received by some of the participants. We learn that this was Giuliani's debut 'on these stages', presumably meaning theatres in and near Vienna. The *Gazzetta universale* also emphasises the importance of Travaglia's scenery: this cantata was obviously no mere concert piece (and in this regard greatly differed from the performance of excerpts from *Fedra* earlier in the year):

> It is worth reporting the contents of a letter from Esterháza in Hungary, dated 8 August, which mentions the splendid festivities given by Prince Esterházy [starting] on 2 August to celebrate the sacred memory of the favours granted by Leopold II. Although His Majesty, due to his pressing occupations, was unable to attend, the festivities were attended by the whole royal family, accompanied by one hundred members of the Viennese nobility, as well as by 600 members of the Hungarian nobility, who enjoyed three days of continuous entertainment. On the first day, shortly after the arrival of the court, a cantata entitled *Venere e Adone* was given in the theatre. The poetry by Signor Abate Casti and the wonderful music by the young Signor Giuseppe Weigl, presently in the service of the theatre of His Imperial Majesty, earned unanimous applause. Signora Giuliani, appearing for the first time on these stages, met the expectations with which she had been justifiably acclaimed. She lacked none of those things that one expects in a great singer. After the first performance, she was immediately rewarded with a gorgeous

diamond ring and 500 zecchini, and all the others who contributed to the success of the festivity received equal recompense. The scenery, the costumes, and the machines all worked together, because everything was under the excellent direction of Signora Giuliani's brother. In the final scene, several of these machines lowered various clouds, which the characters enter; rising again in view of the audience, the clouds reveal the stage, transformed into a ballroom. The royal court and the other spectators applauded this transformation, whose inventor received as a gift a snuffbox with 200 zecchini.[26]

Although this account names Giuliani's brother Francesco as having supervised the entire production, the 'inventor' of the stunning scene change at the end of *Venere e Adone* was, according to the libretto booklet, Travaglia. He must have left Esterháza shortly after pocketing this reward as a month later he was supervising the scenery for *La clemenza di Tito* in Prague.

Venere e Adone is a large-scale, elaborately staged music drama in two parts that might take ninety minutes in performance. It differs from an *opera seria* only in being slightly shorter than a typical late eighteenth-century *dramma per musica*, in having a cast of four, instead of the six or seven soloists demanded by most *drammi per musica*, and in lacking a part for a *musico*. With an audience made up of members of the imperial family and the Viennese and Hungarian aristocracy, its performance near Vienna must have been understood as a response to Leopold's ongoing preparations for the restoration of *opera seria* to the Viennese court theatres. It was a kind of preview of the performances that the imperial troupe would begin later in 1791. *La clemenza di Tito* could have been interpreted along the same lines.

Since the first performances of *Venere e Adone* and *La clemenza di Tito* took place only a little more than a month apart, it is not too surprising that only a single person—Travaglia—contributed to both productions. But that should not prevent us from thinking of both of these works as responses to Leopold's reorganisation of the court theatres, and in particular of his reintroduction of *opera seria* to Vienna.

Thinking of them in this way suggests the possibility that Weigl and Mozart as composers, Casti and Mazzolà as librettists, and Travaglia as stage designer shared some of the same motivations in contributing to these works. All of them stood to benefit from demonstrating to Leopold their abilities to contribute effectively to his *opera seria* troupe.

Let us conclude by returning to where we started, Paris, and with yet another operatic performance in 1791—a performance that reminds us once again of the political context in which *La clemenza di Tito* was conceived and performed, and that can give us insights into the thoughts and feelings with which its first audience perceived it. About two and a half months before Mozart's opera was first performed on Leopold's coronation day, King Louis XVI and Marie Antoinette had fled Paris, but had been stopped at Varennes and returned to virtual imprisonment in the Tuileries Palace. On 20 September, two weeks after Leopold and his family attended *La clemenza di Tito* in Prague, Louis and Marie Antoinette attended a performance of Jean-Philippe Rameau's *Castor et Pollux*, heavily revised by Pierre-Joseph Candeille, to mark the proclamation of the new French Constitution. According to a royalist newspaper, 'The king was deeply moved by the welcome given him by the people, previously depicted to him as a mass of savages and regicides'.[27] An Englishman in the audience noted: 'One verse, *Régnez sur un peuple fidèle* [Reign over a faithful people], was encored, and amazingly clapped'.[28]

Fire plays as important a role in *Castor et Pollux* as in *La clemenza di Tito*. Madame de Staël wrote of that evening in her *Considérations sur la Révolution française*: 'When the furies were dancing and shaking their torches, and the brilliance of the fire illuminated the whole auditorium, I saw the face of the king and queen in the dim glow of this imitation of the inferno, and I was seized by melancholy forebodings of the future'.[29] This was the last time the royal family attended the Opéra. A year later the National Assembly abolished the constitutional monarchy and ordered the king to be arrested. Found guilty of high treason, he was executed in January 1793. Nine months later, Marie Antoinette followed him to the guillotine.

Notes

1. Louise-Élisabeth Vigée-Lebrun, *Souvenirs*, 3 vols. (Paris: H. Fournier, 1835–7) I, 194.

2. [Pierre] Corneille, *Cinna ou la Clémence d'Auguste, tragédie* (Paris: Toussainct Quinet, 1643), Act V, scene 3.

3. Pietro Metastasio, *La clemenza di Tito, dramma per musica, da rappresentarsi nella cesarea corte* (Vienna: Gio. Pietro Van Ghelen, 1734), Act III, scene 13.

4. 'Der jetzige König war noch nicht im Theater, hatte noch keine Musik bei sich, noch sonst ein Merkmal von Liebhaberei zur Musik gezeigt. Malum signum schreien unsere Afterpropheten. Allein ich denke, wenn einmal die Riesengebürge von Staatsgeschäften, die auf seinen Schultern liegen, werden zu Sandhügeln abgeebnet seyn, wenn er seinen Staaten den goldnen Frieden wird wieder geschenkt haben, daß alsdann auch das goldene Zeitalter für die Musik eine neue Periode bei uns haben wird' ('Auszug eines Schreibens aus Wien vom 5ten Jul. 1790', *Musikalische Korrespondenz der teutschen filharmonischen Gesellschaft*, 28 July 1790, cols. 27–31; reprinted in Rudolph Angermüller, *Antonio Salieri: Sein Leben und seine Welt unter besonderer Berücksichtigung seiner großen Opern*, 3 vols. (Munich: Katzbichler, 1971–74), III, 55.

5. See John A. Rice, 'Emperor and Impresario: Leopold II and the Transformation of Viennese Theater, 1790–1792', PhD dissertation (Berkeley: University of California, 1987).

6. Hieronymus Löschenkohl, *Beschreibung der Huldigungsfeyerlichkeiten seiner königlichen apostolischen Majestät Leopolds II. Königs von Ungarn und Böheim, Erzherzogs von Österreich, welche von den Nieder-Oesterreichischen Landständen zu Wien am 6ten April 1790 gehalten wurden* (Vienna: Löschenkohl, 1790).

7. Sergio Durante, 'The Chronology of Mozart's *La clemenza di Tito* Reconsidered', *Music and Letters*, LXXX (1999), 560–94. On the

genesis of the opera, see also Chapter 1, II Documents 1–3, 6, 17, 19, 21, 22 and 24.

8. '[…] la puissance de cette monarchie'. (Kaunitz to Joseph, Mariahilf, 22 July 1781, in Adolf Beer, ed., *Joseph II., Leopold II. und Kaunitz: Ihr Briefwechsel* (Vienna: Wilhelm Braumüller, 1873), 91).

9. 'À l'egard de l'Opera serieux d'Italie c'est trop tard de se procurer quelque chose de bon et c'est d'ailleurs un spectacle si ennuyant que je ne crois pas jamais en faire usage'. (Joseph to Kaunitz, Versailles, 31 July 1781, in ibid., 101).

10. Dexter Edge, 'Mozart's Reception in Vienna, 1787–1791', in *Wolfgang Amadeus Mozart: Essays on His Life and His Music*, ed. Stanley Sadie (Oxford: Clarendon Press, 1996), 66–117, esp. 88–93.

11. 'Ich schrieb indessen eine andere comische Oper *La Caffettiera*, welche im Pratter spielte. Sie wurde, weil sonst keine andere Partitur vorhanden war, bey Ankunft S. M. des Königs von Neapel zur Aufführung bestimmt und fiel allgemein durch. Wie konnte auch eine Pratter Geschichte bey Anwesenheit so hoher Gäste interessieren. Ich muß offenherzig gestehen, sowohl Buch als Musick hat kein besseres Schicksal verdient und ich kann noch nicht begreifen, wie man hat gestatten können, eine solche Handlung von einem Anfänger (denn das war ich noch im strengsten Verstande) zu so einer Feyerlichkeit aufzuführen'. (Rudolph Angermüller, 'Zwei Selbstbiographien von Joseph Weigl (1766–1846)', in *Deutsches Jahrbuch der Musikwissenschaft* 16 (1971), 46–85, esp. 55).

12. Dorothea Link, *The National Court Theatre in Mozart's Vienna: Sources and Documents, 1783–1792* (Oxford: Clarendon Press, 1998), 362.

13. 'Au Spectacle. *Axur, Re d'Ormus*. Toute la famille royale et Napolitaine. Notre roi y arriva quand Axur est sur son trone, et fut fortement applaudi'. Ibid., 363.

14. [Heinrich August Ottokar] Reichard, *Theater-Kalender auf das Jahr 1790* (Gotha: Carl Wilhelm Ettinger, [1789]), 276.

15. 'Jeri in contemplazione delle LL. MM. Siciliane la Corte dette una superba corsa di Slitte fino a Schombrun, ove fu gran pranzo con molti

altri Personaggi di questa primaria Nobiltà. Nel ritorno passarono tutti col medesimo treno per le principali strade, e piazze di questa Città, dopo di che si trasferirono all'Opera in Musica le *Nozze di Figarò* al Teatro Italiano; quindi intervennero alla Sala del Ridotto, ove per la scelta delle persone concorse, lo Spettacolo riescì dei più belli, che si potessero mai vedere' (*Gazzetta univerale* XVIII/16 (22 February 1791), published with commentary in Dexter Edge, 'The Habsburg Court and Guests Attend *Le nozze di Figaro*', in *Mozart: New Documents*, ed. Dexter Edge and David Black, first published 12 June 2014, accessed 16 June 2014. https://sites.google.com/site/mozartdocuments/

16. Milada Jonášová, '*Semiramide riconosciuta*—opera k pražské korunovaci Marie Terezie 1743', *Barokní Praha – barokní Čechie 1620–1740: Sborník příspěvků z vědecké konference o fenoménu baroka v Čechách, Praha, Anežský klášter a Clam-Gallasův palác, 24.-27. září 2001* (Prague: Scriptorium, 2004), 19–68.

17. Rice, 'Emperor and Impresario' (1987), 254–304.

18. *Gazzetta toscana* XXVI/16 (1791), 63. Article dated 16 April.

19. See Ian Woodfield, *Performing Operas for Mozart: Impresarios, Singers and Troupes* (Cambridge: Cambridge University Press, 2012), which places the Guardasoni troupe's performances of Mozart's operas within the context of a migratory existence through which it contributed to the operatic life of Leipzig and Warsaw as well as Prague; and John A. Rice, 'Antonio Baglioni, Mozart's First Don Ottavio and Tito, in Italy and Prague', in *Böhmische Aspekte des Lebens und des Werkes von W. A. Mozart*, ed. Milada Jonášová and Tomislav Volek (Prague: Institute of Ethnology of the Czech Academy of Sciences, 2012), 295–321. Anna Ryszka-Komarnicka, 'From Venice to Warsaw: *Zenobia e di Palmira* by Sertor and Anfossi Performed by Guardasoni's Troupe (1791)', in *Mozart in Prague: Essays on Performance, Patronage, Sources and Receptions*, ed. Kathryn L. Libin (Prague: Institute of Ethnology of the Czech Academy of Sciences, 2016), 295–310.

20. The playbill is illustrated in the article 'Vienna' in *The New Grove Dictionary of Music*, Macmillan, London, 1980.

21. Ludwig Köchel, *Chronologisch-thematisches Verzeichnis sämtlicher Tonwerke Wolfgang Amadé Mozarts*, 6th edition (Wiesbaden: Breitkopf und Härtel, 1964), 419.

22. John A. Rice, *Antonio Salieri and Viennese Opera* (Chicago: University of Chicago Press, 1998), 505–7.

23. For an account of the entire series of festivities, see *Wiener Zeitung*, 64 (10 August 1791), 2069–70.

24. 'Der damahlige Kronprinz Erzherzog Franz war zu einem grossen Feste nach Esterhaz zu dem Fürsten Anton Esterhazy eingeladen. Ich hatte von dem Fürsten den Auftrag, eine grosse Cantate *Venere ed Adone* zu schreiben und ganz für die Aufführung alles zu besorgen, da Kapellmeister Haydn zu dieser Zeit in London war. Ich besorgte alles, die Sänger, Chor, Baletgesellschaft, und die Cantate wurde in Esterhaz mit aller Pracht und zur Friedenheit der anwesenden allerhöchsten Herrschaften gegeben und wir alle von dem Fürsten reichlich belohnt'. Angermüller, 'Zwei Selbstbiographien' (1971), 55.

25. 'In Ansehung der zu Esterhaz jüngst gewesenen Freudenfeste stimmen alle darüber eingegangenen Berichte überein, daß, unter der Reihe von abwechselnden Ergötzlichkeiten, welche durch Ordnung, Geschmack und Schönheit sich so vorzüglich auszeichneten, und gleichsam um die Zufriedenheit der Anwesenden wetteiferten, die bey dieser Gelegenheit aufgeführte Cantate: Venus und Adonis, den Preis errungen habe. Die Poesie derselben ist vom Hrn. Abbate Casti, die Musik aber von dem Hrn. Joseph Weigl, in Diensten des Nationalhoftheaters, welche von der Erzherzoge KK. HH. sowohl, als von dem anwesenden hohen Adel und den übrigen Gästen dieses Festes mit dem lautesten Beyfall den sie von Kennern der Tonkunst auch ganz vorzüglich erhielt, beehrt ward. Das spielende Personale bestand aus 4 Mitgliedern des Wiener Hoftheaters, der Demoiselle Giuliani, der Madame Bussani, und den Herren Calvesi und Adamberger'. *Wiener Zeitung*, 65 (13 August 1791), 2102–3.

26. 'Merita di esser riportata una lettera pervenutaci da Esztherazy in Ungheria in data del dì 8. del corrente, in cui si fa menzione delle grandiose feste date da quel Principe Regnante Esztherazy nel dì 2. per solennizzare la fausta memoria delle beneficenze compartite da Leopoldo II. Non potendo intervenirvi la M. S. per le grandi occupazioni vennero esse onorate da tutta la R. Famiglia col seguito di cento Nobili Viennesi, oltre i mille 600. Nobili Ungaresi, i quali passarono tre giorni in continovi divertimenti. Nel primo appena che fu arrivata la Corte, si dette lo

spettacolo al Teatro, ove si rappresentò una Cantata col titolo di *Venere, e Adone*. La poesia del Sig. Abate Casti, e la superba musica del giovine Sig. Giuseppe Weigel all'attual servizio del Teatro di S. M. Cesarea ottenne un generale incontro. La Sig. Giuliani per la prima volta, che si è fatta sentire sopra questi Teatri corrispose a quella espettazione, colla quale viene giustamente decantata, non mancandole cos' alcuna delle molte, che si richiedono in una abilissima Cantatrice. Terminata la prima recita, ebbe subito in dono da quel Principe un superbo anello di brillanti, e 500. zecchini, e tutti gli altri Soggetti, che cooperarono al buon' esito della festa vennero egualmente ricompensati. Le decorazioni, il vestiario, e le macchine erano tutte analoghe, e ben' intese, poichè la direzione del fratello della Sig. Giuliani fu ottima e sorprendente. Nell' ultima scena varie di dette macchine si viddero calare involte in diverse nubi, che riempiendosi dei personaggi, e rimontando in aria a vista del pubblico, rapportarono il palco scenico, e fecero comparire una sala da ballo. La R. Corte, e gli spettatori applaudirono questa trasformazione, e l'inventore ebbe in regalo una tabacchiera d'oro con 200. zecchini'. *Gazzetta universale* XVIII/71 (3 September 1791), 566; article dated Vienna, 22 August.

27. 'Le roi a été pénétré de l'acceuil que le peuple, qu'on lui avoit présenté comme un composé d'hommes féroces et de régicides, lui a fait'. *Chronique de Paris* IV/265 (23 September 1791), 1072.

28. Sir Samuel Romilly, *Memoirs*, 2nd edition, 3 vols. (London: John Murray, 1840), I, 436.

29. 'Au moment où les Furies dansaient en secouant leurs flambeaux, et où cet éclat d'incendie se répandait dans toutes la salle, je vis le visage du roi et de la reine à la pâle lueur de cette imitation des enfers, et des pressentiments funestes sur l'avenir me saisirent'. Madame de Staël, *Considération sur la Révolution Française*, 2 vols. (Paris: Charpentier, 1862), I, 337–8.

3 From Metastasio to Mazzolà: Clemency and Pity in *La clemenza di Tito*

Magnus Tessing Schneider

How to cite this book chapter:
Tessing Schneider, M. 2018. From Metastasio to Mazzolà: Clemency and Pity in *La clemenza di Tito*. In: Tessing Schneider, M. and Tatlow, R. (eds.) *Mozart's* La clemenza di Tito: A Reappraisal. Pp. 56–96. Stockholm: Stockholm University Press. DOI: https://doi.org/10.16993/ban.c. License: CC-BY NC-ND 4.0

Of all Mozart's mature operas, *La clemenza di Tito* has attracted most conflicting critiques, frequently referring to the circumstances of its genesis. Mozart did not himself choose to set an opera to an old libretto by Pietro Metastasio. Commissioned for the coronation of Emperor Leopold II as king of Bohemia, this was stipulated in the contract drawn up barely two months earlier between the Bohemian Estates and Domenico Guardasoni, the manager of Prague's Italian opera company, and before the composer had even been chosen (see Chapter 1, II Document 2). The facts that Metastasio's drama of princely virtue was stipulated, and that Mozart was obliged to write the music in a short time, have been used repeatedly to demonstrate how artistically compromised Mozart's work is. Whether due to the deficiencies of the text or to work pressure, it has been said that Mozart was not inspired to give his best. Daniel E. Freeman, for example, argues that the coronation—and hence probably the choice of libretto—reflected an effort by the Bohemian nobility to resist the progressive reforms introduced by the Habsburg emperors. He concludes that the composer was just a tool in the reactionary political propaganda machine, and he uses this to dismiss the notion that Mozart was an enlightened artist. However, Freeman seems to be basing his arguments on the assumption that the meaning of a work of art is determined entirely by its context, barely discussing the contents of the opera itself beyond repeating the timeworn opinion that the composition shows signs of being written in great haste.[1] The latter verdict was first aired on 12 December 1791, just three months after the premiere, in the Berlin musical publication, *Musikalisches Wochenblatt*, in a report comparing Mozart's opera unfavourably with the coronation cantata by Leopold Koželuch (libretto by August Gottlieb Meissner) (see Chapter 1, II Document 17). It states that Mozart's 'grand, or rather, semi-serious' opera, which had failed to please the audience in Prague, was '*yet another*' setting of Metastasio's *La clemenza di Tito*, and that Mozart had failed to 'make haste slowly' when composing it. However, Sergio Durante suggests that this critique is likely to reflect a cabal against Mozart;[2] Koželuch may have been favoured by Bohemian nationalists, whereas Metastasio (and to a lesser extent, Mozart) was associated with the Viennese court and its depraved Italianate taste. The accusations against the coronation opera were repeated in the *Allgemeine musikalische Zeitung* in 1798, again with a cultural political subtext. This time, though, the views were coloured by a desire to promote Mozart as a champion of German music, the author of the article being the influential Leipzig music critic Friedrich Rochlitz (see Chapter 1, II Document 22). Resenting the fact that Mozart's penultimate opera was a Metastasian *opera seria* for a Habsburg coronation, Rochlitz was keen to emphasise that the composer accepted the commission only because his wife and friends insisted upon it, and because it 'flattered his sense of honour'. Due to time pressure, Mozart allegedly decided to write the most important numbers 'very well', while he wrote the remaining numbers merely according to 'the fashionable taste of the big crowd'. Furthermore, while Rochlitz praised the libretto revisions introduced by the Saxon court poet Caterino Mazzolà, albeit attributing them to Mozart, he depicted them merely as a means of tightening the action, to make the drama 'more concentrated' and 'far more interesting'; and to break the 'perpetual monotonous alternation of arias and recitatives' through the introduction of ensembles.

The impact of Rochlitz's nationalistic narrative on the later reception of the opera can hardly be exaggerated. Though modern scholars may feel less of a need to make excuses for Mozart's acceptance of the commission, the accusations against the work for its hastiness and conventionality linger, as does the implication that the reduction of the textual revisions were solely a question of dramatic expediency, of enhanced 'naturalness', and of offering more opportunities for musical expression. Even commentators who admire *La clemenza di Tito* have tended to underestimate the profound extent to which Mazzolà's revisions transform the drama, although Mozart himself credited the poet for turning the libretto into 'a true opera' (see Chapter 1, II Document 6).[3]

Some early commentators were more willing than Rochlitz to acknowledge the extent of Mazzolà's contribution. As anonymous text revisions were standard procedure in eighteenth-century opera productions, it is remarkable that the *Krönungsjournal für Prag* felt obliged to mention that 'Herr Mazzola [sic], theatrical poet in Dresden', had 'changed' Metastasio's libretto (see Chapter 1, II Document 12). Even more significant is the 1821 testimony of the tenor Giuseppe Siboni. As the lead tenor of Guardasoni's opera company in Prague from 1800 until 1805,[4] Siboni had performed the title role in *La clemenza di Tito* 'for four or five years' according to the 'original composition', i.e. without the extra numbers included in most other nineteenth-century productions (see Chapter 1, II Document 24).[5] Siboni recounted the following story, which he probably heard from Guardasoni:

> [...] when the Prague theatre management decided to let the great Mozart set one of the most beautiful dramas by the immortal Metastasio to music for the coronation festivities of Emperor Leopold, they felt obliged to make a lot of changes in the piece to make it more appropriate to the circumstances. Fifty years ago, it was inconceivable for anyone to have the courage to lay their hands on the most beautiful works by one of the greatest dramatic poets in order to modify them.

However, it happened on Mozart's own demand, and otherwise we would perhaps not possess this wonderful work by the great composer.

The anecdote lends support to suggestions made by John A. Rice, that some of the revisions reflect the political circumstances in the years after the French Revolution,[6] and by Sergio Durante that Mazzolà's employment was effected by Guardasoni rather than by the imperial court.[7] Perhaps most importantly, though, the anecdote indicates that the changes demanded by Mozart were so radical that even thirty years after the event, an Italian singer was sensitive to their controversial implications. The story prompts us to question the lingering view that Mozart and Metastasio held an identical underlying political vision for the work. Indeed, I would argue that Mazzolà's revision is more radical than many scholars seem willing to allow, even to the extent that *La clemenza di Tito* by Mozart and Mazzolà, is no longer really an opera about clemency, despite its title, but rather an opera about compassion (*pietà*). And the differences between these two concepts are the differences that separate 1791 from 1734 politically, theatrically and musically, even though fundamental principles of enlightened thinking and critique were current earlier in the century.[8]

Jessica Waldoff has already discussed the use of the concept of *pietà* in this opera, though without delving into the differences between Metastasio's and Mazzolà's versions, which leads her to a definition that seems to me less appropriate to the late Enlightenment. She takes a far more favourable view of the opera than Freeman, to be sure, yet when she describes *pietà* as 'an enlightened conviction that embodies Christian teachings',[9] she nevertheless seems to agree with him that the moral perspective of the opera is ultimately Catholic.[10] In this essay, I will argue that the moral perspective of the Mozart-Mazzolà opera is defined rather by an enlightened humanism that is entirely secular and entirely egalitarian, an interpretation that is incompatible with the view of the opera as a work of propaganda.

From Metastasio to Mozart

The word *clemenza* (and its adjectival forms *clemente* and *clementissimo*) occurs nine times in Metastasio's original libretto, and all occurrences were retained by Mazzolà. The concept is used either by Sesto and Vitellia to describe Tito's character or conduct, or by the emperor himself when he ponders which strategy to adopt after their betrayal, always speaking of clemency as a path he can choose to follow or not. This use of the word concurs with the definition given in Louis de Jaucourt's 1753 article on *clémence* in the Diderot-d'Alembert *Encyclopédie*, where clemency is defined as 'an act by which the sovereign relaxes the rigour of the law', and 'a virtue that makes the prince inclined towards gentleness, and towards restraining and relaxing, with judgment and discretion, the rigour of justice'.[11] In other words, whether clemency is seen as an act or as a virtue, it is reserved for a sovereign. Jaucourt also quotes the definition of clemency given by Montesquieu in *The Spirit of the Laws* (1748) as 'the distinctive quality of monarchs' less necessary in a republic than in a monarchy 'where one is governed by honour, which often requires what the law forbids'.[12]

The word *pietà* or *pietade* (and its adjectival form *pietoso*), which is much more common in Italian than *clemenza*, occurs twenty-one times in Metastasio's original libretto, although used without the conceptual precision and significance it would acquire later in the century. Metastasio sometimes used the concept of 'pity' in the sense of 'mercy', referring to a clement sovereign's act of pardoning a guilty subject, and sometimes in the sense of 'compassion', referring to a sentiment that all human beings can feel. In his revision of the drama, Mazzolà exploits Metastasio's imprecise use of the word, and introduces a new degree of analytical precision, emphasising the sense of 'compassion', partly by allowing the concept of pity to figure prominently in five of the opera's closed numbers for which he wrote new texts, and partly by omitting eight of the original occurrences of the word. While most of these were cut because the libretto had to be shortened, a few seem to have been cut because their usage clashed with the definition of pity that Mazzolà (and probably Mozart) wished to promote.

One example is the aria in which Annio begs Tito to pardon Sesto. Metastasio's original aria text reads:

> Pietà Signor di lui.
> So che il rigore è giusto:
> Ma norma i falli altrui
> Non son del tuo rigor.
>   Se a prieghi miei non vuoi;
> Se all'error suo non puoi;
> Donalo al cor d'Augusto,
> Donalo a te Signor. (Act III, scene 3)[13]

(Take pity on him, my lord! I know that rigour would be justified, but the faults of others are not the norm of your rigour. If you will not have pity in answer to my prayers, if you cannot pity his error, then feel pity in the emperor's heart; have pity on yourself, my lord.)

Mazzolà replaced this with an entirely new text:

> Tu fosti tradito:
> Ei degno è di morte:
> Ma il core di Tito
> Pur lascia sperar.
>   Deh prendi consiglio,
> Signor, dal tuo core:
> Il nostro dolore
> Ti degna mirar. (Act II, scene 7)[14]

(You were betrayed: he deserves to die, but the heart of Titus still lets us hope. Oh take advice, my lord, from your heart: deign to behold our pain.)

Apart from the fact that Mazzolà's aria text is syntactically simpler and emotionally more direct, his Annio urges Tito to listen to his compassionate heart, whereas Metastasio's Annio reminds Tito of merciful principles.[15]

Another example is Servilia's speech to Vitellia at the end of the opera. Annio leaves to search for Tito, expecting the future Empress Vitellia to follow him and beg him to be merciful to Sesto. Vitellia, however, hesitates. At this point in Metastasio's libretto Servilia says to Vitellia:

> Deh non lasciarlo
> Nel più bel fior degli anni
> Perir così. Sai che finor di Roma
> Fu la speme, e l'amore. Al fiero eccesso
> Chi sa chi l'à sedotto. In te sarebbe
> Obbligo la pietà: quell'infelice
> T'amò più di se stesso: avea fra' labbri
> Sempre il tuo nome: impallidia qualora
> Si parlava di te. Tu piangi! (Act III, scene 10)

(Oh, do not let [Sextus] perish thus in the fairest flower of youth. You know that he was the hope and love of Rome till now. Who knows who enticed him to this cruel excess? To you, pity should be an obligation. That unhappy man loved you more than he loved himself; your name was always on his lips; he turned pale if someone spoke of you. You are weeping!)

This is followed a little later by Servilia's aria, in which she reproaches Vitellia for letting self-interest curb her pity:

> S'altro che lagrime
> Per lui non tenti;
> Tutto il tuo piangere
> Non gioverà[.]
>   A questa inutile
> Pietà, che senti,
> Oh quanto è simile
> La crudeltà. (Act III, scene 9)

(If you attempt nothing but weeping for him, all your tears will be in vain. Oh how similar to cruelty is that futile pity that you feel.)

In his revision, Mazzolà cuts the first lines of Servilia's speech, down to and including the lines 'In te sarebbe / Obbligo la pietà'. Thereby, he not only made Servilia's plea less pointed (i.e. she no longer hints that Vitellia might be responsible for Sesto's misfortune); it also omits the implication that the sentiment of pity can be an obligation, making it clearer that Vitellia is moved to tears not because she *should* take pity on Sesto, but because Servilia reminds her of Sesto's love for her.

In such cases, Mazzolà's revisions support the dramatic function of Mozart's music: the arias of both Annio and Servilia become emotional appeals to the compassion of the onstage audience, which also gives the music a different dramaturgical function, rather than eloquent calls for virtuous conduct.

This change of perspective reflects the fact that the meaning of 'pity' had undergone significant changes since 1734, not least due to the influence of the writings of Jean-Jacques Rousseau. Both original Metastasian passages imply that pity is a Christian moral principle or duty, whereas Rousseau, in his *Discours sur l'origine de l'inégalité* [*Discourse on the origin of inequality*] of 1755, rejects Christian morality as the source of pity. He defined compassion or pity (*pitié*) as 'an innate aversion to the sight of a fellow creature's suffering':[16] i.e. it is the sole natural virtue from which flow all the social virtues. Rousseau asks what are generosity, clemency or humanity, if not compassion applied to the weak, to the guilty, or to mankind in general, writing: 'Kindliness, and even friendship, correctly understood, is only the outcome of an enduring pity for a particular object, for, is wishing a person not to suffer anything other than wishing him to be happy?'[17] The feeling of compassion puts us in the place of those who suffer, and the more the beholder identifies with the pain of the sufferer, the stronger the compassion. Importantly, Rousseau emphasises that compassion comes before any kind of reflection, and although 'it may be the business of Socrates and others of that stamp to acquire virtue through reason, the human race would long ago have ceased to exist if its preservation had depended strictly on the reasoning power of the individuals who make it up'.[18] On the contrary, it is reason 'that breeds vanity and reflection that strengthens it; reason that turns man inward; reason that separates man from everything that troubles or afflicts him'.[19]

Some aspects of Metastasio's moralistic concept of pity must therefore have struck Mozart and Mazzolà as somewhat old-fashioned. Metastasio does not make clear whether Tito's pardoning of Sesto and Vitellia is due to compassion or to moral and political reflection, while Mazzolà's revisions suggest that it is due to compassion. The fact that princely clemency describes a vertical relation between sovereign and subject, in contrast to pity in Rousseau's definition as compassion, which describes a horizontal relation between fellow creatures, helps to explain why the revisions draw out the horizontal relations in the drama: not only the emperor's sympathy for the traitors, but also the sympathy in other characters, and the audience, for the traitors and even for the emperor himself. These revisions touch the very foundations of Metastasio's dramaturgy and imply both a changed theatrical and operatic aesthetic, and a changed view of sovereignty.

Rousseau's ideas greatly influenced the aesthetic thinking of the period, including the theories of the German critic and playwright Gotthold Ephraim Lessing who in 1766 published his own major contribution to Enlightenment aesthetics, the essay *Laocoön, or, On the Limits of Painting and Poetry*. Here he discusses the relationship between the good, the true and the beautiful in the arts, specifically promoting the concept of the beholders' feeling of pity or compassion (*Mitleid*) as a central aim. Lessing mainly uses the Vatican Greek sculpture group *Laocoön and His Sons* to define his concept of compassion in art. Quoting Pliny the Elder, he points out that it originally happened to stand in the palace of the Emperor Titus:

> The master was striving to attain the greatest beauty under the given conditions of bodily pain. Pain, in its disfiguring extreme, was not compatible with beauty, and must therefore be softened. Screams must be reduced to sighs, not because screams would betray weakness, but

because they would deform the countenance to a repulsive degree. Imagine Laocoön's mouth open, and judge. Let him scream, and see. It was, before, a figure to inspire compassion in its beauty and suffering. Now it is ugly, abhorrent, and we gladly avert our eyes from a painful spectacle, destitute of the beauty which alone could turn our pain into the sweet feeling of pity for the suffering object.[20]

These aesthetic ideals—even down to the wording—are echoed in Mozart's famous letter to his father of 26 September 1781, in which he discusses Osmin's aria 3. 'Solche hergelaufne Laffen' in *Die Entführung aus dem Serail*. Mozart writes:

> [...] as Osmin's rage gradually increases, there comes (just when the aria seems to be at an end) the allegro assai, which is in a totally different measure and in a different key; this is bound to be very effective. For just as a man in such a towering rage oversteps all the bounds of order, moderation and propriety and completely forgets himself, so must the music too forget itself. But as passions, whether violent or not, must never be expressed in such a way as to excite disgust, and as music, even in the most terrible situations, must never offend the ear, but must please the hearer, or in other words must never cease to be *music*, I have gone from F (the key in which the aria is written), not into a remote key, but into a related one, not, however, into the nearest relative D minor, but into the more remote A minor.[21]

Although Mozart does not refer to 'pity' here, his aim is clearly to prevent the audience from turning away from Osmin in disgust, just as the ancient Greek artist prevented the spectators from turning away from Laocoön, and just as Mazzolà and Mozart later strove to prevent us from turning away from Sesto and Vitellia. The feeling of disgust (Mozart uses Lessing's term *Ekel*) aroused by an exaggerated expression of pain or rage is both an aesthetic and a moral reaction, in other words, just as its opposite, the beautiful, is an ideal inextricably linked to the good.

In 1767–69, immediately after publishing his *Laocoön*, Lessing wrote the reviews that were later collected under the title *Hamburg*

Dramaturgy in which he reinterpreted Aristotle's ideal of tragic catharsis, the spectators' 'purification' of the passions of pity and terror, along the lines of Enlightenment aesthetics. For Lessing, the purpose of catharsis is to transform the sentiment of pity into virtuous habits. He considers drama the most edifying art form since it is the most cathartic, theatrical pity being closely related to a sense of fear for ourselves, writing:

> [Aristotle] speaks of pity and *fear*, not of pity and *terror*, and his fear is by no means the fear excited in us by misfortune threatening another person. It is the fear which arises for ourselves from the similarity of our position with that of the sufferer; it is the fear that the calamities impending over the sufferer might also befall ourselves; it is the fear that we ourselves might thus become objects of pity. In a word, this fear is compassion referred back to ourselves.[22]

Such thoughts exerted a major influence on Mozart's cultural environment. In Prague, for example, the National Theatre itself had been inaugurated in 1783 with Lessing's tragedy *Emilia Galotti*, and its proscenium arch was adorned with Lessing's medallion portrait.[23]

The Concept of Pity in Mazzolà's Revision

Nearly all the revisions Mazzolà made to the libretto for *La clemenza di Tito* reflect a turning away from Metastasio's absolutist political vision, and a turning towards the egalitarian humanism of Rousseau and Lessing. The concept of pity plays a crucial role in this change of direction. The first reference to pity occurs in duet 1. 'Come ti piace imponi' between Sesto and Vitellia, Mazzolà replacing a recitative dialogue and adding the following concluding lines that have no equivalent in Metastasio's text:

> Fan mille affetti insieme
> Battaglia in me spietata.

Un'alma lacerata
Più della mia non v'è. (Act I, scene 1)

(A thousand emotions are engaged in a pitiless battle against each other. There is no soul more torn than mine.)

The word *spietata* (which occurs only here) is the antonym of *pietosa*, suggesting that the action of the opera is sparked by Vitellia's and Sesto's unresolved and aggressive emotions, which form a contrast in the drama's symmetrical structure to Tito's pitying absolution in the final scene. Furthermore, Mazzolà uses the concept *furore* (rage) as the antithesis of *pietà* throughout Act I, suggesting that Vitellia is driven to attempted murder by an irrational urge for destruction. *Furore* is linked in Mazzolà's libretto metaphorically to the element of fire, establishing a connection between Vitellia's 'burning' rage and the fire that eventually 'rages' at the Capitol. In duet 1. Sesto sings 'Già il tuo furor m'accende' (I am already kindled by your rage), Mazzolà anticipating a hint given by Metastasio in Sesto's next encounter with Vitellia, which contrasts burning rage with chilling horror:

Basta, basta non più, già m'inspirasti,
Vitellia, il tuo furore. Arder vedrai
Fra poco il Campidoglio, e quest'acciaro
Nel sen di Tito - - - (Ah, sommi Dei! qual gelo
Mi ricerca le vene - - -). (Act I, scene 9)

(Enough, enough; no more! Your rage already inspired me. Soon you will see the Capitol burn, and in Titus' breast this dagger... (Ah, gods on high, what chill runs through my veins...)

The third and last mention of *furore* follows in the trio 10. 'Vengo - - - aspettate - - Sesto' of the very next scene, again in contrast to the chill of horror, when Vitellia reacts with consternation to the news that Tito has chosen her as his bride. In Metastasio, the message is communicated to Vitellia only by Publio, after which she expresses her regret in an aria soliloquy, whereas Mazzolà adds Annio to the scene and focusses instead on Vitellia's confusion in an 'action trio', in which her disjointed speech contrasts starkly with her commanding and manipulative presence in the previous scene:

> Oh sdegno mio funesto!
> Oh insano mio furor!
> (Che angustia! che tormento!
> Io gelo oh Dio! d'orror.) (Act I, scene 10)
>
> (Oh my fatal anger! Oh my insane rage! (What anxiety, what torment! Oh God, my blood runs cold with horror!))

As in the first duet, there is no equivalent of the *furore* reference in the Metastasio libretto; it is an image Mazzolà has introduced to suggest the dramatic build-up in Act I.

Although the emotional source of the destructive flames is now cold, Vitellia realises that the fire of her rage threatens to spread to the Capitol. Mazzolà emphasises this pivotal function of the trio by compressing the succeeding seven scenes from Metastasio's Act II into the four breathless scenes acted out at the Capitol, which conclude the new Act I. Mozart linked the last three numbers of the Act musically, in effect turning them into a through-composed Act finale characterised by confusion, desperation and abrupt changes: a musical representation of an emotional and social conflagration, sparked originally in the first duet, rekindled in Sesto's aria 9. 'Parto, ma tu ben mio', running wild into the following trio and into Sesto's accompanied recitative 11. 'Oh Dei, che smania è questa', until it finally reaches its terrifying climax in the closing quintet with chorus 12. 'Deh conservate, o Dei'.

The metaphorical complex that Mazzolà constructs around the word *furore* implicates the motivation of Vitellia's assassination plot. In fact, Metastasio's libretto had already implied that she may be driven less by filial loyalty—or even lust for power—than by a jealous rage caused by thwarted love. In her first two encounters with Sesto in Act I Vitellia suggests, in asides to the audience, that Tito made her fall in love with him. In the opening scene she says:

> [...] e più non pensi
> Che questo eroe clemente un soglio usurpa
> Dal suo tolto al mio padre?
> Che mi ingannò, che mi sedusse, (e questo
> È il suo fallo maggior) quasi ad amarlo. (Act I, scene 1)

(Do you no longer keep in mind that this clement hero usurps the throne that his father stole from my father? That he betrayed me, seduced me (and this is his greatest fault) almost to the point of making me love him?)

And in scene 9 she tells Sesto:

> Sappi, che Tito amai,
> Che del mio cor l'acquisto
> Ei t'impedì: che se rimane in vita,
> Si può pentir: ch'io ritornar potrei
> (Non mi fido di me) forse ad amarlo. (Act I, scene 9)

(Know this, that I loved Titus, that he made it impossible for you to take possession of my heart; that if his life is saved, he may repent; that I may then perhaps (I don't trust myself) start loving him again.)

In the final scene Vitellia then tells Tito that this love originated when she misinterpreted his kindness:

> Credei
> Che questa fosse amor. La destra e'l trono
> Da te sperava in dono, e poi negletta
> Restai più volte, e procurai vendetta. (Act II, scene 17)

(I thought this was love. I hoped to obtain your hand and the throne in return, and when I had been passed by more times, I planned my revenge.)

It hence seems that her two calls for his murder are spawned by her envious jealousy of Berenice and Servilia, Tito's preferred brides.[24]

Sesto perceives this motive in both scenes, but Vitellia manages to persuade him, and even herself, through various diversions, to believe that she is driven by the more honourable motive of avenging her father's dethronement and murder. That the blood vengeance is only a pretext is made apparent by the fact that she would much prefer to marry Tito than to have him murdered. By giving Vitellia the exclamation 'Oh insano mio furor!' Mazzolà shows her horror when she realises that her scheming is backfiring. The adjective *insano*, used only twice in the libretto, occurs first in the opening scene when Vitellia described Tito's love for Berenice as an 'amore insano', but her exclamation in the quintet suggests that it was her own raging madness that was 'insane'.

A relatively inconspicuous feature in Metastasio's text is the complete absence of the word *pietà* from the first half of the drama. Mazzolà takes this and turns it into a key principle of the dramaturgical structure, giving its absence symbolic significance, partly by making the pity-less rage of jealousy and envy the dramatic motor in the first half of the opera, and partly by giving greater prominence to the first occurrence of the word *pietà*. It is uttered by Vitellia in the quintet when she enters the Capitol, realising that she is unable to stop the murderous conflagration she has sparked: 'Chi per pietade oh Dio! / M'addita dov'è Sesto?' (Oh God! For pity's sake, who can show me where Sextus is?) (Act I, scene 13). This seemingly casual reference to the concept of pity, rescued from Metastasio's recitative dialogue,[25] and inserted into the closed form of the quintet, demands attention, not least because Mazzolà retains very little text from the many scenes he compressed into these tersely worded final scenes. It implies that the pitiless Vitellia is now herself in need of pity, and that the spectators—not just passers-by on the Capitol—are invited to take pity on her. The almost programmatic significance of her appeal is brought out by the fact that the use of the word *pietade* is followed immediately by the opera's only two occurrences of the word *terror*, this time with no equivalent in Metastasio's text. Vitellia continues with the aside: 'In odio a me son'io / Ed ho di me terror' (I hate myself and I fill myself with terror). And when Sesto enters a few moments later, immediately after stabbing who he thinks is Tito, he says: 'Mi fa terror il giorno' (The light of day fills me with terror) (Act I, scene 14). That the concepts of pity and terror make their first appearance in the opera simultaneously is no coincidence, and points to the broader aims, according to the *Poetics* of Aristotle, of tragic drama. The sight of Vitellia and Sesto reduced to a state of misery, terrified at the thought of their wicked actions, ushers in the possibility that the audience may eventually pity them, the 'conflagration' dramaturgy further promoting such a reaction by portraying Vitellia and Sesto in a somewhat redeeming light, as people who act impulsively, and are then terrified by their actions. In accordance with Lessing's interpretation of Aristotle, illustrated by the case of the Laocoön group, tragic events should inspire terror in the characters rather than in the spectators, but their terror should also inspire the fear that the spectators may end up in a similar situation. The final scenes of Act I depict the agonising realisation that one has done something terrible in a fit of insane rage, which could lead to the desperate conclusion that one is forever excluded from the secure embrace of humanity. In the event, however, it is exactly the expression of remorse that shows one's real human dignity, as Tito says to Sesto at the very end of the opera:[26]

> Il vero pentimento,
> Di cui tu sei capace,
> Val più d'una verace
> Costante fedeltà. (Act II, scene 17)

(The true repentance of which you are capable is worth more than a reliable and constant faithfulness.)

Mazzolà's revision of the characters of Annio and Servilia serves to strengthen the effect of Sesto's exclusion from and re-inclusion into human society. In Metastasio's original, Vitellia, Sesto and Servilia have five arias each, Annio has four arias, and Servilia and Annio, designed to take leading roles, serve as positive contrasts to Vitellia and Sesto: Servilia and Annio represent the sincerity, constancy and self-sacrifice that their erring counterparts lack. Mazzolà, however, drastically reduces the size of their roles, using them more as representatives of the society from which Sesto excludes himself, and less as virtuous contrasts to him and Vitellia. In Metastasio's libretto, the first scene with Sesto and Annio concludes with Annio's exit aria, in which he expresses his anxiety that he may not be able to marry Servilia, and Sesto's aria soliloquy, in which he tells of his moral doubts. Mazzolà, in his revised libretto, replaced these introspective arias with the duettino 3. 'Deh prendi un dolce amplesso' in which the two friends pledge eternal friendship, concluding with a 'sweet embrace' (Act I, scene 3), the natural expression and symbol of equality and fraternity in a society. Similarly, Mazzolà emphasises the direct contact between Annio and Servilia in their first scene at the expense of introvert reflection. In the original Metastasio, Annio bids farewell to Servilia in an anguished exit aria, after which Servilia swears fidelity to him in an aria soliloquy. Mazzolà conflates these two speeches into duet 7. 'Ah perdona al primo affetto' in which Servilia rapidly dispels Annio's pain. This love duet is a parallel to the previous friendship duet (3.), showing how love as well as friendship can exemplify compassionate concord among citizens, without gender discrimination. These two duets serve as a contrast to the rage duet (1.) sung by Sesto and Vitellia, thereby suggesting the socially damaging effects when human relations are defined by a lack of mutual acceptance and compassion. With Sesto singing in both the rage duet and the friendship duet Mazzolà and Mozart portray him as a divided person capable of nurturing healthy human relations, but in whom violently passionate love clouds his emotional and social awareness. It is the recognition by Tito and by the audience of Sesto's moral awareness behind his passion, however, which eventually justifies his reintegration into society. Annio predicts this in his aria 13., which has no equivalent in Metastasio. Addressing Sesto, he says:

> Torna di Tito a lato:
> Torna; e l'error passato
> Con replicate emenda
> Prove di fedeltà.
>   L'acerbo tuo dolore
> È segno manifesto
> Che di Virtù nel core
> L'immagine ti stà. (Act II, scene 1)

> (Return to Titus' side: return and amend your past error with repeated proofs of your fidelity. Your bitter pain is a manifest sign that the image of virtue remains in your heart.)

The second and third times that Mazzolà introduces the word *pietà* into the libretto follow immediately, in trio 14. 'Se al volto mai ti senti' (Act II, scene 4), in which Publio comes to arrest Sesto for the attempted assassination, the latter taking leave of Vitellia one last time. In Metastasio, Sesto sings an aria to Vitellia before he is carried off by Publio and the guards, after which Vitellia gives vent to her fear and remorse in an aria soliloquy, but once more Mazzolà replaces two successive exit arias with an ensemble. Mazzolà here allows Vitellia to express her torn feelings, in an aside with Sesto still on stage, while Publio—who remains completely silent in Metastasio—expresses his compassion for Sesto in another aside. In this way Vitellia's evasiveness, her unwillingness to take responsibility for the plot and thereby perhaps save the life of the young man who longs for her love, is thrown into relief by Sesto's loving farewell to her and by Publio's sympathetic concern. This contrast is further highlighted by the fact that Sesto's and Publio's quatrains both end with the word 'pietà': Vitellia's does not. Sesto sings:

> Rammenta chi t'adora
> In questo stato ancora.

> Mercede al mio dolore
> Sia almen la tua pietà.

> (Remember the one who adores you even in this situation. May your pity, at least, be the reward of my pain.)

And Publio sings:

> L'acerbo amaro pianto
> Che da' suoi lumi piove,
> L'anima mi commove,
> Ma vana è la pietà.

> (The painful and bitter tears that rain from his eyes move my soul, but my pity is useless.)

Vitellia, however, sings to herself:

> Mi laceran il core
> Rimorso, orror, spavento.
> Quel che nell'alma io sento
> Di duol morir mi fa.

> (My heart is torn between remorse, horror and fear! That which I feel in my soul makes me die of pain.)

Her conflicting emotions, her concluding focus on her own rather than on Sesto's pain and the conspicuous absence of the word *pietà*—which she has only used so far while begging others to take pity on *her*—imply once more that Vitellia's moral awareness is still lacking.

Vitellia's failure to pity Sesto in this trio seems to have been deliberately constructed by Mazzolà and Mozart to contrast Tito's pity for Sesto in the next trio, 18. 'Quello di Tito è il volto', when the young traitor is called to appear before his sovereign, even though Tito has much less reason to pity him than Vitellia does. At the first sight of Sesto, broken down by shame and remorse, Tito remarks in an aside in the following Metastasian recitative: 'Eppur mi fa pietà' (And yet he inspires pity in me) (Act II, scene 10), words which are then echoed by Sesto in his first address to the emperor: 'se tu veder potessi / Questo misero cor, spergiuro, ingrato, / Pur ti farei pietà' (if you could see my wretched heart, treacherous and ungrateful, I would inspire pity in you even so). The trial scene ends with Sesto's rondo 19. 'Deh per questo instante solo', which contains Mazzolà's next reference to *pietà*. While the rondo draws partly on original Metastasian lines, its second quatrain has no equivalent in the earlier text:

> Di pietade indegno è vero,
> Sol spirar io deggio orror.
> Pur saresti men severo,
> Se vedessi questo cor.
>
> (Unworthy of pity indeed, I must inspire nothing but horror. Even so, you would be less severe if you could see my heart.)

Once more Mazzolà picks up an image in Metastasio's dialogue and develops it into a kind of verbal leitmotif, in this case Sesto's preceding implication that if Tito could see his heart, he might pity him even so, which Mazzolà treats as an anticipation of his lines in the rondo. Sesto's aria in the Metastasio libretto expresses his desperation in the face of death because he has betrayed his friend, whereas in Mazzolà's libretto Sesto's rondo contains an indirect appeal to Tito's compassion.

The spectators, who know that Sesto's heart is not obdurate, though to this point crazed by passion, may be able to absolve him more easily than Tito. How then does Tito come to absolve him? In Metastasio's original version, the emperor is torn in his subsequent soliloquy between the desire for revenge and the inclination to exonerate him. The lines that Mazzolà cut include:

> Vendetta! Ah! Tito! E tu sarai capace
> D'un sì basso desio: Che rende eguale
> L'offeso, all'offensor! Merita invero
> Gran lode una vendetta, ove non costi

> Più che il volerla. Il torre altrui la vita
> È facoltà comune
> Al più vil della terra: Il darla è solo
> De' Numi e de' regnanti. (Act III, scene 7)

> (Revenge! Ah Titus, and are you capable of so base a desire that makes the offended equal to the offender? That revenge which costs no more than wanting it indeed deserves great praise. The ability to take the life of another is common to the vilest man on earth, but the ability to give it only to gods and rulers.)

Mazzolà replaces these with the following: 'Vendetta! – – – Il cor di Tito / Tali sensi produce? – – Eh viva – – – in vano / Parlan dunque le leggi?' (Revenge! Can such feelings rise in Titus' heart? ... Oh, let him live ... But do the laws speak in vain, then?) (Act II, scene 11). Mazzolà's Tito does not need abstract reasoning to dismiss revenge as an unworthy option: he represses as repulsive his own tendency to vengefulness, and hence his inner conflict is less between clemency and revenge than between pity and respect for the rigour of the law. Here the music acquires a dramatic significance not implied by Metastasio's original text. In Metastasio libretto, Sesto's preceding aria shows the young traitor expressing desperation more to himself than to Tito, which in no way affects the verdict of the emperor who having heard it still feels a desire for revenge. In Mazzolà, however, Sesto's rondo is addressed directly to Tito, and if Tito felt any desire for revenge beforehand, he certainly feels none afterwards. The changed dramatic function of Sesto's solo implies that he is not absolved because of rational or political considerations, but because Tito sympathises with the young traitor whose essentially good character is revealed in the trial scene, through his agonising conflict and broken stage appearance that both Tito and the audience recognise during the trio 18. 'Quello di Tito è il volto', and through the tender expression and inner beauty of Mozart's music in rondo 19. 'Deh per questo instante solo'.

The last occurrence of the word *pietà* that Mazzolà introduced into the libretto is found in Vitellia's rondo 23. 'Non più di fiori', which she sings after finally deciding to confess her crimes to save Sesto's life.[27] Mazzolà wrote an entirely new text for this solo replacing the aria text of Metastasio's original. Metastasio's aria reads:

> Getta il nocchier talora
> Pur que' tesori all'onde,
> Che da remote sponde
> Per tanto mar portò.
>   E giunto al lido amico
> Gli Dei ringrazia ancora,
> Che ritornò mendico,
> Ma salvo ritornò. (Act III, scene 10)

> (Sometimes the helmsman throws to the waves the very treasures he carried over so many seas from faraway coasts. Having reached the friendly shore, he thanks the gods that he returned a beggar, but returned safely.)

It seems obvious why Mazzolà and Mozart found this text unsatisfactory: not only does it employ the maritime imagery for which Metastasio's librettos were frequently ridiculed even in the eighteenth century, but the older poet portrays Vitellia as someone who acquires virtue through reason rather than by innate compassion. The keyword 'salvo' hardly suggests that Vitellia will be 'safe' if she confesses her crimes, but rather that her soul or honour will be 'saved'. Mazzolà reimaged the scene, writing instead:

> Non più di fiori
> Vaghe catene
> Discenda Imene
> Ad intrecciar.
>   Stretta fra barbare
> Aspre ritorte
> Veggo la morte
> Ver me avanzar.

> Infelice! qual orrore!
> Ah, di me che si dirà.
> Chi vedesse il mio dolore,
> Pur avria di me pietà. (Act II, scene 15)

(No more shall Hymen come down to weave lovely chains of flowers. Clutched in barbarous and harsh ropes, I see my death approaching. Unhappy woman! What horror! Oh, what will they say of me? Those who could see my pain would even yet feel pity for me.)

Unlike the Metastasian Vitellia, Mazzolà's Vitellia does not pride herself on having made the right moral choice, which might arouse belated admiration in the audience. Instead she arouses our compassion because for the first time she acts in an unselfish way: she sets herself aside for Sesto's sake at the expense of her future, her freedom, her honour and, finally, her hope of marrying Tito. This last point is much clearer in Mazzolà's text than in Metastasio's where the 'treasures' thrown to the waves refer to the loss of both her 'imperial and [her] nuptial' hopes mentioned in the preceding recitative ('Speranze addio / D'impero e d'imenei', Act II, scene 15). In the new aria text she makes no reference to the imperial throne, but laments only the loss of her nuptial garlands. The word 'pietà', furthermore, not only concludes the rondo but references previous occurrences of the concept, corresponding symmetrically to the use of *furore* and *spietata*, opposites of *pietà* and *pietosa*, in Sesto's and Vitellia's opening rage duet 1. 'Come ti piace imponi'. At the end of the opera Vitellia's rage has cooled and she is even able to forget herself and run to Tito at the end of her solo in order to prevent him from having Sesto killed, just as she ran to Sesto at the end of the trio 10. 'Vengo - - - aspettate - - Sesto' in Act I in order to prevent him from killing Tito. Mozart emphasises the thematic and structural connection between the two numbers through their orchestral postludes, which both function as scene change music, transitioning to the crowd scenes that conclude the two Acts.[28] Apart from referring back to Vitellia's own previous uses or non-uses of the word *pietà*, its occurrence in her rondo also points back to the trial scene and the verbal leitmotif of Mazzolà's formulation in Sesto's rondo 'if you could see my heart, you would even yet feel pity'. The metaphorical connection between the two rondos implies that they serve similar dramatic functions: rather than appealing directly to the audience, Sesto and Vitellia, unaware of the audience, reveal their human dignity as expressed in the beauty and emotional truthfulness of their music.

Vitellia's rondo sums up a further poetic cross-reference. Although the word 'infelice' (unhappy) is not uncommon in the libretto, it occurs in only three of the musical numbers: in Sesto's soliloquy, the accompanied recitative 11. 'Oh Dei, che smania è questa' where, before his attempted murder of Tito, he exclaims: 'Sesto infelice!' (Unhappy Sextus!) (Act I, scene 11). In Tito's soliloquy, the accompanied recitative preceding the trial scene, the emperor exclaims: 'È pur di chi regna / Infelice il destino!' (The destiny of those who rule is also unhappy!) (Act II, scene 8). And in Vitellia's soliloquy, rondo 23. 'Non più di fiori', preceding her confession in the final scene, she exclaims: 'Infelice!' (Unhappy woman!). Each occurrence of the word 'infelice' forms the emotional climax in the three characters' introspective soliloquies that immediately precede their life-determining interventions. Thus an existential link is established between them, the audience recognising the virtually identical feelings of despair and emotional isolation of the exclamations. The characters are, in a sense, interchangeable here, and by recognising their common humanity the audience may intuitively be inspired with pity.

La clemenza di Tito—A Democratic Opera?

In the opera *La clemenza di Tito* by Mazzolà/Mozart the audience is invited to pity the sovereign, an approach that departs from the political ideology of Metastasian dramaturgy, and demonstrates that the concept of sovereignty in 1734 was no longer viable in 1791. Regardless of the religious implications of their coronation ceremonies, emperors no longer ruled by divine right: they were no more than human beings. As in the original Metastasio, Mazzolà's Tito is a solitary figure, but his solitude is different. His dismissal at the beginning of the opera of his beloved Berenice, and his decision at the end of the opera never to marry but to regard Rome as his bride, served in Metastasio's libretto to portray Tito as a kind of political martyr who sublimates the need for close human bonds in favour of his concern for the good of the state. In Mazzolà's revision, however, the ideal ruler seems to be someone capable of sharing close ties with any unhappy subjects because he recognises their sense of isolation as similar to his own. 'Mille diversi affetti / In Tito guerra fanno' (A thousand different emotions battle in Titus), says Publio in an aside in the trio 18. ('Quello di Tito è il volto!') when Sesto enters the throne room: 'S'ei prova un tale affanno, / Lo seguita ad amar' (If he is so troubled, he still loves him) (Act III, scene 10). The audience is invited here to pity the emperor, as we are in Sesto's rondo 19. 'Deh per questo instante solo', where Tito is required to remain silent over his conflict between compassion and indignation. Moreover, by altering the role of the chorus, Mazzolà and Mozart portray Tito as a sovereign in contact with his people. In the original Metastasio the chorus had a purely ceremonial and celebratory function, whereas the choral lament in the quintet with chorus that ends Act I communicates a sense of human loss. Similarly, Tito responds to the new thanksgiving chorus 15. 'Ah grazie si rendano' with the words:

> Ah nò sventurato
> Non sono cotanto,
> Se in Roma il mio fato
> Si trova compianto,
> Se voti per Tito
> Si formano ancor. (Act II, scene 5)

> (Ah no, I am not so unfortunate if my fate finds compassion in Rome, if prayers are still said for Titus.)

One of the subtlest departures from Metastasio's representation of the emperor, however, is found in Mazzolà's treatment, or rather non-treatment, of Tito's arias. Of all the twenty-six arias in the original Metastasio, only half are directly addressed to another character on stage, with nine being soliloquies and a handful of abstract reflections that may, or may not, be addressed to another character. Of the fourteen arias in Mazzolà's revision, on the other hand, ten are directly addressed to another character, just one, Vitellia's rondo, is unambiguously a soliloquy, and Tito's three arias, which all retain the original Metastasian texts, are abstract moral reflections with no precise addressee on stage, even though sung in the presence of other characters. In a staging of Metastasio's original drama, with its abundance of soliloquies addressed to the audience, this is unlikely to strike an audience as departing from the norm. On the other hand, in Mazzolà's revised version, in which Diderot's fourth wall has been raised between the stage and the auditorium, Tito's arias stand out as exceptions that imply an altogether different mode of theatrical communication. The audience, having been detached beholders, and passively admiring subjects of a clement monarch by the grace of God in Metastasio, is invited by the emperor (and Mazzolà) to step into the drama and act as members of his Privy Council, allowed to ponder on whether they would do as Tito and pardon Sesto and Vitellia, or whether they would rather have them thrown to the lions. This representation of the ruler ultimately points beyond monarchy as a form of government, gazing into the modern age.[29]

Those who describe Mozart's *La clemenza di Tito* as a propaganda work invariably fail to take account of its early reception. Since propaganda is not meant to generate independent emotional and intellectual responses, it eschews aesthetic complexity, yet it is exactly this complexity that explains the opera's initial lack of success. The official accounts of the premiere on 6 September 1791 conspicuously omit any reference to the music or its reception, focusing instead on the gleeful greeting of the imperial family when they entered the auditorium (see Chapter 1, II Documents 10-12).[30] The young Franz Alexander von Kleist, a member of the Prussian delegation, found the opera 'quite worthy' of Mozart whose andante melodies were 'sufficiently beautiful to entice heavenly beings to earth', but since he only heard the opera once, and in a crowded theatre, he did not feel able to offer a more extensive critique (see Chapter 1, II Document 13). Notably, even though poorly attended from the second performance (see Chapter 1, II Document 12), at its last performance on 30 September, the opera was finally received with 'tremendous applause', and 'all the numbers were *applauded*', as Mozart heard from Anton Stadler (see Chapter 1, II Document 15). Three years later, the local critic Franz Xaver Niemetschek observed that *La clemenza di Tito* had failed to please at the premiere despite its 'truly heavenly music' because its serious mood and simple subject matter were unable to interest a crowd occupied with coronation festivities, balls and illuminations; but he wrote that its triumphant revival on 3 December 1794 greatly pleased 'all connoisseurs and cherishers of true beauty' (see Chapter 1, II Document 20). He later repeated some of these observations in his biography of the composer,[31] noting that the fun-craving crowd at the coronation had been unable to appreciate 'the simple beauties of Mozart's art' (see Chapter 1, II Document 21):

> The masterpieces of Rome and Greece are appreciated the more often they are read and the more mature our taste becomes. This applies to the connoisseur as well as non-connoisseurs when listening to Mozart's music, particularly to his dramatic works. Those were our feelings at the first performance of *Don Giovanni* and especially *La clemenza di Tito*!

Indeed, after its revival, *La clemenza di Tito* remained one of the most enduring successes of the Italian opera company in Prague: it seems to have been performed virtually every season, Niemetschek mentioning that it was still heard 'with delight' in 1797 (see Chapter 1, II

Document 21), and the company even chose it for their farewell performance on 24 April 1807.³²

This slow process of appreciation is hardly compatible with the aims of propaganda. Furthermore, members of the imperial court were dissatisfied with the work in 1791, the privy finance minister, Count Karl von Zinzendorf, describing the opera as 'the most boring spectacle' (see Chapter 1, II Document 8), and Empress Maria Luisa opining that the 'grand opera is not so grand, and the music very bad, so that almost all of us went to sleep' (see Chapter 1, II Document 9). It is difficult to gauge exactly where, in the words of Count Heinrich Franz von Rottenhan (see Chapter 1, II Document 16), the court's 'preconceived aversion to Mozart's composition' lay, particularly as the frequently cited story about the empress dismissing the opera as a piece of 'porcheria tedesca' (German swinishness) is spurious.³³ But it seems likely that the empress and other members of the court reacted against Mozart's refusal to achieve the 'grandeur' usually associated with coronation operas. If the court or the Bohemian Estates had expected a grand propaganda spectacle, they were clearly disappointed.

Of those spectators in the gala premiere who were familiar with Metastasio's drama, most would have known it from reading the text rather than from hearing it performed in the theatre. No setting of *La clemenza di Tito* had been given in Prague or Vienna for thirty years, nor had it been performed in Florence while Leopold ruled as grand duke.³⁴ However, the foreign visitors would probably have been more familiar with the genre of *opera seria*; the Prague audience had more experience with comic opera. Indeed, much of the local opposition to Mozart's opera seems to reflect a general prejudice against its genre, which perhaps explains the contrasting verdicts on the two guest singers, the *prima donna* Maria Marchetti Fantozzi and the castrato Domenico Bedini, both of whom were 'regular' *seria* performers directly imported from Italy. According to Zinzendorf,

Marchetti sang 'very well', and the emperor was 'enthusiastic about her' (see Chapter 1, II Document 8). Mozart's letter also implies a positive verdict on both her and Bedini (see Chapter 1, II Document 15). In spite of this, Niemetschek placed the blame of the opera's initial lack of success with the local audience partly on the insufficiencies of the two guest stars, whom he compared unfavourably to the singers of the 1794 revival. He described Marchetti as a '*prima donna* who sang more with her hands than with her throat, and whom one was obliged to take for a madwoman', and the 'miserable castrato' Bedini as a 'mutilated person whose shapeless mass of flesh frightened us whenever he appeared and was so odd in relation to his bastard voice' (see Chapter 1, II Document 20). This harsh criticism seems to reflect a more general criticism of the perceived unnaturalness of *opera seria* with its old-fashioned rhetorical acting style and its soprano heroes. Later, in his biography of Mozart, Niemetschek went on to observe that Mozart had been 'compelled to write brilliant arias' for the two singers specifically contracted for the coronation festivities, and that the arias he wrote stood 'far above the usual supply of bravura songs' (see Chapter 1, II Document 21), which again implies a negative attitude towards *opera seria*. Niemetschek does not name the singer of the role of Vitellia in the 1794 revival, but she was almost certainly the twenty-year-old Polish soprano Antonia Campi who, as Antonina Miklaszewicz, had created the role of Servilia in 1791, and had since risen to become the company's *prima donna* in serious roles.[35] In 1811 and 1813 she sang Vitellia in the first German-language production in Vienna, alongside Siboni as Titus, and she also sang the role in Leipzig in 1818.[36] Campi was rarely admired for her acting skills, and was frequently criticised for over-ornamenting Mozart's music. Nonetheless, she was known as an accomplished vocalist, a quality that Niemetschek picks up by inference. Having lambasted the original Vittelia, he writes without naming the singer, that no aria is 'so charming, so filled with sweet melancholy, with such a wealth of musical beauty' as Vitellia's rondo 23.'Non più di fiori' (see Chapter 1, II Document 21), which must reflect Campi's performance. The interpretation he heard clearly lacked the aggressiveness with which it is frequently coloured by singers today.[37] The Sesto of the 1794 revival was the twenty-six-year-old Teresa Strinasacchi who, according to Niemetschek, surpassed Bedini by excelling with 'good singing and genuine acting' (see Chapter 1, II Document 20). A poem written for her benefit performance on 31 March 1797 on the occasion of her departure from the company, indicate the type and degree of emotional involvement on the part of the audience: 'Willst du glühen uns und beben machen: / Tritt als Sesto vor uns hin!' (Will you make us smoulder and shudder, then appear before us as Sesto!)[38]

Since Campi and Strinasacchi were both young performers who had received most of their training in Guardasoni's company, they were seen as more 'local' than Marchetti and Bedini, and they fitted better into Niemetschek's nationalistic narrative. Cultural politics notwithstanding, the early reception of *La clemenza di Tito* in Prague also suggests that the opera simultaneously broke two sets of operatic conventions. Its dramatic and musical simplicity differed from traditional *opera seria*, and its sublime seriousness differed from the Viennese *drammi giocosi* to which the Prague audience was accustomed. The Mazzolà/Mozart *La clemenza di tito* belonged to a new intermediate genre, which can indeed be described as 'semi-serious', the hallmark of which is the appeal to the delicate sensibilities and sympathies of the spectators, hinted at in the references to Campi's and Strinasacchi's portrayals of Vitellia and Sesto.

In light of the preceding analyses of Mazzolà's transformation of Metastasio's original, it is further noteworthy that Niemetschek regarded the numbers surrounding the scene changes at the end of both Acts as the highpoints of the opera, perhaps suggesting that the sense of musical-dramatic build-up and the contrast between the conclusions of the two Acts were central to his emotional experience.

In 1794 he described the trio 10. 'Vengo - - - aspettate - - Sesto' and the 'Act I finale' (i.e. the quintet with chorus 12. 'Deh conservate, o Dei') as 'unsurpassable and perhaps a *non plus ultra* of music' (see Chapter 1, II Document 20), in 1798 describing the finale as 'the most perfect among Mozart's compositions' (see Chapter 1, II Document 21):

> […] expression, character, feeling, all compete with one another to produce the greatest effect. The singing, instrumentation, variety of tone and echo of distant choruses—at each performance these created such emotion and illusion as is seldom apparent at operas.

Niemetschek's other favourite moments were Vitellia's rondo 23. 'Non più di fiori' and the 'final chorus of Act II' (i.e. probably the sextet and chorus 26. 'Tu è ver, m'assolvi, Augusto') about which he wrote that no other chorus was 'so flowing, so magnificent and expressive'. (see Chapter 1, II Document 21).

Perhaps the most significant of Niemetschek's observations regarding the opera's musical dramaturgy, however, is his view that Mozart allows Tito's character to pervade the whole opera: 'There is a certain Greek simplicity, a quiet sublimity in the entire music, which affects the sensitive heart gently but so much the deeper, and which suits Tito's character, the period and the entire subject so correctly' (see Chapter 1, II Document 20): and with his 'fine sensitivity,' Mozart comprehended 'the simplicity, the calm grandeur of the character of Tito and the whole plot, and conveyed this throughout his composition' (see Chapter 1, II Document 21). Indeed Niemetschek later felt compelled to defend Mozart's musical-dramatic conception against its critics (see Chapter 1, II Document 23). There is an interesting correspondence between this perception and that of Søren Kierkegaard concerning *Don Giovanni*, which he heard in Copenhagen in the 1830s, in a production where, significantly, the singers had been coached by Siboni who had sung the roles of both Tito and Don Ottavio in Guardasoni's company in Prague as a young man:[39]

the very secret of this opera is that its hero is also the force animating the other characters. Don Giovanni's own life is the principle of life in them. His passion sets in motion the passions of the others; it resonates everywhere, it resonates in and sustains the Commendatore's earnest, Elvira's anger, Anna's hate, Ottavio's self-importance, Zerlina's anxiety, Masetto's indignation and Leporello's confusion. As the eponymous hero, as a hero in general, he gives the piece its name. But he is more; he is, if I may so put it, the common denominator.[40]

Niemetschek likewise suggests that Tito is the common denominator in *La clemenza di Tito*. If Mozart's music in *Don Giovanni* seduces the audience with the same sensual charm with which the eponymous hero seduces the women on stage, the music of *La clemenza di Tito* touches the audience with the sweetness, emotion and sublimity with which its eponymous hero forgives Vitellia and Sesto. And it is this ethical-aesthetical transformation of the interlocutors-listeners, effected through the emphasis on pity through Mazzolà's text and the liberating force of Mozart's music, that places *La clemenza di Tito* firmly in the vanguard of the late Enlightenment.

Notes

1. Daniel E. Freeman, 'Mozart, *La clemenza di Tito*, and Aristocratic Reaction in Bohemia', *Music in Eighteenth-Century Life: Cities, Courts, Churches*, ed. Mara E. Parker (Ann Arbor: Steglein Publishing, Inc., 2006), 125–41, esp. 136.

2. Sergio Durante, 'Musicological Introduction', in Wolfgang Amadeus Mozart, *La clemenza di Tito, K. 621: Facsimile of the Autograph Score* (Los Altos CA: The Packard Humanities Institute, 2008), 17–34, esp. 26–27.

3. This is the case, for example, with Helga Lühning's meticulous analysis of Mazzolà's revisions. While acknowledging the many formal innovations (which she tends to attribute to Mozart), she implies that the Saxon court poet, with his 'klischeehafte Sprache und seine Unselbständigkeit in der Formulierung der neuen Passagen' (clichéd language and lack of independence in the formulation of the new passages), remains true to Metastasio's dramatic vision; see Titus-*Vertonungen im 18. Jahrhundert:*

Untersuchungen zur Tradition der opera seria *von Hasse bis Mozart* (Volkach: Arno Volk – Laaber Verlag, 1983), 107.

4. Gerhard Schepelern, *Giuseppe Siboni: Sangeren – Syngemesteren: Et Afsnit af Operaens Historie ude og hjemme hovedsagelig paa Grundlag af hidtil ubenyttede trykte og utrykte Kilder*, 2 vols. (Copenhagen: Amadeus, 1989) I, 31, 37.

5. In 1791 the title role in *La clemenza di Tito* was created by Antonio Baglioni, who probably sang it again for the 1794 revival and until he left the company in 1795 or early 1796. See John A. Rice, 'Antonio Baglioni, Mozart's First Don Ottavio and Tito, in Italy and Prague', *Böhmische Aspekte des Lebens und des Werkes von W. A. Mozart*, ed. Milada Jonášová and Tomislav Volek (Prague, 2012), 295–321.

6. John A. Rice, *W. A. Mozart:* La clemenza di Tito (Cambridge: Cambridge University Press, 1991), 40–44.

7. Durante, 'Musicological Introduction' (2008), 18.

8. Felicity Baker adopts a different perspective in her chapter in this book (see Chapter 4, 'Tito's Burden'), arguing that already Metastasio's 1734 libretto could be understood by enlightened spectators as contributing to an undermining of absolutist monarchy as an institution.

9. Jessica Waldoff, *Recognition in Mozart's Operas* (Oxford: Oxford University Press, 2006), 270.

10. Freeman, 'Aristocratic Reaction in Bohemia', (2006), 140–1.

11. 'CLÉMENCE, s. f. (*Droit polit.*) Favorin la définit, *un acte par lequel le souverain se relâche à propos de la rigueur du Droit;* & Charron l'appelle *une vertu* qui fait incliner le prince à la douceur, à remettre, & relâcher la rigueur de la justice avec jugement & discrétion.' *Encyclopédie ou Dictionnaire raisonné des sciences, des arts et des métiers*, III (Paris: Le Breton, Durand, Briasson and Michel-Antoine David, 1753), 521.

12. 'La *clémence* est la qualité distinctive des monarques. Dans la république où l'on a pour principe la vertu, elle est moins nécessaire. [...] Dans les monarchies où l'on est gouverné par l'honneur, qui souvent exige ce que la loi défend, elle est plus nécessaire.' *L'esprit des lois*, quoted from *Encyclopédie* (1753), 521–2. On the association of clemency with

monarchy, see also Sergio Durante's essay in this book (see Chapter 6, 'Staging Problems and Aesthetics in Mozart's *La clemenza di Tito*'.)

13. Quotations from Pietro Metastasio's 1734 libretto are taken from *La clemenza di Tito, dramma per musica, da rappresentarsi nella cesarea corte* (Vienna: Gio. Pietro Van Ghelen, 1734).

14. Quotations from Mazzolà's revision are made from *La clemenza di Tito, dramma serio per musica in due atti da rappresentarsi nel Teatro Nazionale di Praga nel settembre 1791. In occasione di sollenizzare il giorno dell' incoronazione di Sua Maestà l'Imperatore Leopoldo II* (Prague: Schönfeld, 1791).

15. Notably so, according to Lühning, who regards Mazzolà's revisions as strictly formal in nature, there is 'überhaupt kein Grund ersichtlich' (no obvious reason at all) why the original aria text was not used; see *Titus-Vertonungen* (1983), 95.

16. '[...] cet amour tempere l'ardeur qu'il a pour son bien-être par une répugnance innée à voir souffrir son semblable.' Jean-Jacques Rousseau, *Discours sur l'origine et les fondemens de l'inégalité parmi les hommes* (1755), *Collection complète des œuvres* (Genève, 1780–88), I, 74; on-line edition: *Jean-Jacques Rousseau. Collection complète des œvres.* 17 vol. in 4°, Genève, 1780–88. https://www.rousseauonline.ch/tdm.php (accessed 20 April 2017). Translation from *Discourse on the Origin of Inequality*, trans. Franklin Philip (Oxford: Oxford University Press, 1994/2009), 45.

17. Ibid., 76. 'La bienveillance & l'amitié même sont, à le bien prendre, des productions d'une pitié constante, fixée sur un objet particulier: car désirer que quelqu'un ne souffre point, qu'est-ce autre chose que désirer qu'il soit heureux?' Translation Philip (1994/2009), 46.

18. 'Ibid., 78. 'Quoiqu'il puisse appartenir à Socrate, & aux esprits de sa trempe, d'acquérir de la vertu par raison, il y a long-tems que le genre humain ne seroit plus, si sa conservation n'eût dépendu que des raisonnemens de ceux qui le composent.' Translation Philip, *Discourse* (1994/2009), 48.

19. Ibid., 77. 'C'est la raison qui engendre l'amour-propre, & c'est la réflexion qui le fortifie; c'est elle qui replie l'homme sur lui-même; c'est

elle qui le sépare de tout ce qui le gêne & l'afflige.' Translation Philip, *Discourse* (1994/2009), 47.

20. 'Der Meister arbeitete auf die höchste Schönheit, unter den angenommenen Umständen des körperlichen Schmerzes. Dieser, in aller seiner entstellenden Heftigkeit, war mit jener nicht zu verbinden. Er mußte ihn also herab setzen; er mußte Schreyen in Seufzen mildern; nicht weil das Schreyen eine unedle Seele verräth, sondern weil es das Gesicht auf eine ekelhafte Weise verstellet. Denn man reisse dem Laokoon in Gedanken nur den Mund auf, und urtheile. Man lasse ihn schreyen, und sehe. Es war eine Bildung, die Mitleid einflößte, weil sie Schönheit und Schmerz zugleich zeigte; nun ist es eine häßliche, eine abscheuliche Bildung geworden, von der man gern sein Gesicht verwendet, weil der Anblick des Schmerzes Unlust erregt, ohne daß die Schönheit des leidenden Gegenstandes diese Unlust in das süsse Gefühl des Mitleids verwandeln kann.' Gotthold Ephraim Lessing, *Laokoon: oder über die Grenzen der Mahlerey und Poesie. Mit beyläufigen Erläuterungen verschiedener Punkte der alten Kunstgeschichte* (Berlin: Christian Friedrich Voß, 1766), I, 20. Translation by Ellen Frothingham, *Laocoon: An Essay upon the Limits of Painting and Poetry*, (Mineola NY: Dover Publications, Inc., 2005 [1898]), 13–14.

21. '[...] da sein zorn imer wächst, so muß – da man glaubt die *aria* seÿe schon zu Ende – das *allegro assai* – ganz in einem andern zeitmaas, und in einem andern Ton – eben den besten *Effect* machen; den, ein Mensch der sich in einem so heftigen zorn befindet, überschreitet alle ordnung, Maas und Ziel, er kent sich nicht – so muß sich auch die Musick nicht mehr kenen – weil aber die leidenschaften, heftig oder nicht, niemal bis zum Eckel [sic] ausgedrücket seÿn müssen, und die Musick, auch in der schaudervollsten lage, das ohr niemalen beleidigen, sondern doch dabeÿ vergnügen muß, folglich allzeit Musick bleiben Muß, so habe ich keinen fremden ton zum *F* zum ton der *aria* sondern einen befreundten dazu, aber nicht den Nächsten, *D minor*, sondern den weitern, *A minor*, gewählt.' *Mozart Briefe und Dokumente – Online-Edition* (Mozarteum Foundation Salzburg and The Packard Humanities Institute Salzburg); www.dme.mozarteum.at/DME/briefe/letter.php?mid=1195&cat=   (accessed 8 December 2017). Translation from *The Letters of Mozart & His Family: Chronologically Arranged, Translated and Edited with an*

Introduction, Notes and Indices, trans. Emily Anderson, 3 vols. (London: Macmillan & Co., 1938), II, 769.

22. 'Er spricht von Mitleid und Furcht, nicht von Mitleid und Schrecken; und seine Furcht ist durchaus nicht die Furcht, welche uns das bevorstehende Uebel eines Andern, für diesen Andern erweckt, sondern es ist die Furcht, welche aus unserer Aehnlichkeit mit der leidenden Person für uns selbst entspringt; es ist die Furcht, daß die Unglücksfalle, die wir über diese verhängt sehen, uns selbst treffen können; es ist die Furcht, daß wir der bemitleidete Gegenstand selbst werden können. Mit Einem Worte: diese Furcht ist das auf uns selbst bezogene Mitleid.' Gotthold Ephraim Lessing, *Sämmtliche Werke. Dreyzehnter Band. Zweyter Theil. Hamburgische Dramaturgie* (Vienna: Anton Pichler, 1801), LXXV (19 January 1768), 41. Translation from *Sources of Dramatic Theory. Vol. 2: Voltaire to Hugo*, ed. Michael Sidney (Cambridge: Cambridge University Press, 1994), 121.

23. Prague's National Theatre, which saw the world premieres of *Don Giovanni* and *La clemenza di Tito* took its inspiration from Hamburg, where the first national theatre in the German-speaking world was established. The 'national theatre' concept (i.e. a theatre devoted to performance in the national language) was closely associated with Lessing's name.

24. In her chapter in this volume, however, Felicity Baker stresses that Metastasio has left Vitellia's motives open to interpretation; it may also be Vitellia's political ambition that blinds her to her own feelings. See Chapter 4 'Tito's Burden'.

25. 'Chi per pietà m'addita / Sesto dov'è?' Act II, scene 6.

26. It is along these lines that Slavoj Žižek bases his interpretation of the opera in '*La Clemenza di Tito*, or the Ridiculously-Obscene Excess of Mercy' published in 2004 on http://www.lacan.com/zizekopera1.htm (accessed 8 December 2017). According to Žižek, 'the pardon does not really abolish the debt, it rather makes it infinite—we are FOREVER indebted to the person who pardoned us. No wonder Tito prefers repentance to fidelity: in fidelity to the Master, I follow him out of respect, while in repentance, what attached me to the Master is the infinite indelible guilt. In this, Tito is a thoroughly Christian master.' In my view,

however, Žižek does not take the difference between clemency/mercy and the Enlightenment concept of pity sufficiently into account. I would argue that by pitying Sesto, Tito restores Sesto's humanity and thereby relieves him of his debt.

27. I am grateful to John A. Rice for pointing out to me that rondo texts often include the word 'pietà'. Examples from Mozart's operas include Donna Anna's second aria in *Don Giovanni*, which concludes with the lines 'Forse un giorno il cielo ancora / sentirà pietà di me'; Donna Elvira's last aria in the Vienna version of the same opera, which includes the lines 'Ma, tradita e abbandonata, / provo ancor per lui pietà'; and Fiordiligi's final aria in *Così fan tutte*, which opens with the lines 'Per pietà, ben mio, perdona / all'error di un'alma amante'. Notably, all these examples represent emotional climaxes in a final Act, and in the rondos for Donna Anna, Fiordiligi and Vitellia the plea for pity would seem to be addressed indirectly to the audience. Rice suggests that the rondo as an aria-type may have been associated by late eighteenth-century composers (and not only Mozart) with the enlightened concept of pity.

28. The parallel between the two crowd scenes would have been further emphasised with the staging strategies outlined in Sergio Durante's article, Chapter Six 'Staging Problems and Aesthetics in Mozart's *La clemenza di Tito*.

29. For an alternative interpretation of the reliance of Tito's arias on traditional *opera seria* forms see Jette Barnholdt Hansen, 'Mozart as Epideictic Rhetorician', Chapter 5 in this volume.

30. Only Johann Debrois (see Chapter 1, II Document 14) maintains that the opera was received with the 'applause' that the poet, the composer and the singers 'fully deserved', and that the imperial couple seemed to leave the theatre 'satisfied'. However, Debrois also claims that the performance began as scheduled at 7pm (in fact, it was delayed until 7.30 or 8.00, due to the late arrival of the imperial family), and that the *prima donna* was the Portuguese mezzosoprano Luísa Todi (in fact, it was the Italian soprano Maria Marchetti Fantozzi), which suggests that he was neither present in the theatre himself nor relied on oral accounts.

31. Scholars are not agreed on the identity of the unnamed author of the critique of Prague's theatrical scene (including a review of the revival

of *La clemenza di Tito*) published in *Allgemeines europäisches Journal* in 1794/5. It is a two-part review, the first part (1794, see Chapter 1, II Documents 20) signed ***k, and the second part, published as 'Fortsetzung der Nachrichten über das Theater zu Prag', *Allgemeines europäisches Journal*, II/3 (March 1795), 215, signed N.k. The abbreviations suggest that the author's name begins with 'N' and ends with 'k'. Niemetschek is a good fit. Furthermore, stylistic similarities between Niemetschek›s 1798 Mozart biography (see Chapter 1, II Documents 21) and the formulation, opinion and focus of the 1794/5 review further imply, if not confirm, that Niemetschek is the unnamed author.

32. Our knowledge of the Prague repertoire is incomplete, but the *Allgemeines europäisches Journal* included several years' worth of theatre calendars, which have been collected and reproduced in Tomislav Volek (ed.), *Miscellanea musicologica* vol. 16: *Repertoir Nosticovského divadla v Praze z let 1794, 1796–98,* (Prague: Charles University, 1961). After the revival of *La clemenza di Tito* on 3 December 1794, it was performed twice more in the same month. We have no calendar for 1795, but in 1796 it was performed thirteen times; in 1797 four times (and on four evenings, one of the Acts was given in a double bill with a non-operatic show): and in 1798 seven times. On 1 April 1796 *La clemenza di Tito* was performed to the benefit of the entire company, which suggests that it was a great success. Giuseppe Siboni claimed to have sung the title role in Prague for four or five years (see Chapter 1, II Document 24) i.e. between the end of 1800 and late spring 1805, furthermore, and according to the *Indice de' teatrali spettacoli*, it was certainly performed in the 1803-4 season; see Schepelern, *Giuseppe Siboni* (1989), I, 39. It was also performed twice in the 1806-7 season; see *Prager Theater-Almanach auf das Jahr 1808* (Prague: Caltreischen Buchhandlung, 1807), 31–32.

33. For the origin of this anecdote, see Joseph Heinz Eible, 'Una porcheria tedesca'? Zur Uraufführung von Mozarts *La clemenza di Tito*', *Österreichische Musikzeitschrift*, 31 (1976), 329–334. Eible points out that the immediate source is Alfred Meissner's highly unreliable *Rococobilder: Nach den Aufzeichnungen meines Grossvaters* from 1871, although Otto Jahn, in the fourth volume of his *W. A. Mozart* from 1859, had already referred to a Prague tradition, according to which the empress dismissed German music in general as 'porcheria'. On the other hand,

German music critics in the first three decades of the nineteenth century invariably attributed the phrase 'Che porcheria tedesca!' to the elderly Giovanni Paisiello when speaking about a composition by Joseph Haydn. Apparently, Paisiello made this remark when hearing Haydn's cantata *Arianna a Naxos* in Naples; see 'Ueber den gegenwärtigen Zustand der Tonkunst in Italian', *Ephemeriden der italiänischen Litteratur, Gesetz-Gebung und Kunst für Deutschland*, ed. Joseph Wismayr, IV/6 (1804), 301–9, esp. 307, but Carl Friedrich Cramer changed the story, making him refer to *Die Schöpfung* instead, in *Individualitäten aus und über Paris*, 1 (Amsterdam: Kunst- und Industrie-Comptoir, 1806), 134. Later, the phrase seems to have become a proverbial way of illustrating Italians' alleged prejudicial attitude towards German music. For example, the singer Signora Stelle-Numi uses the phrase when dismissing arias from Mozart's *Le nozze di Figaro* and *Don Giovanni* in Julius von Voss' comedy *Berlin im Jahre 1824*, Act II, scene 1, in *Auswahl neuer Lustspiele für das Königliche Hof-Theater in Berlin* (Berlin: Schüppelschen Buchhandlung, 1824). Since the anti-Italian attitudes of German nationalism flourished in Bohemia in the first half of the nineteenth century, Prague traditions surrounding the reception of *La clemenza di Tito* are likely to have been influenced by the earlier tradition, which attributed the infamous phrase to Paisiello. In any case, the empress is more likely to have commented on the opera in French than in Italian.

34. For a list of the settings of Metastasio's libretto, see Lühning, *Titus-Vertonungen* (1983), 504–22.

35. Ian Woodfield has recently questioned whether 'Sig:[ra] Antonini', who created the role of Servilia (see Chapter 1, II Document 6) was really Antonina Miklaszewicz, an identification first suggested by Walter Brauneis in 'Wer war Mozarts "Sig[no]ra Antonini" in der Prager Uraufführung von *La Clemenza di Tito*?', *Mitteilungen der Internationalen Stiftung Mozaerteum*, XLVII (1999), 32–40. Woodfield points out that the singer's first name is elsewhere given as 'Anna' (see Chapter 1, II Document 18); see *Performing Operas for Mozart: Impresarios, Singers and Troupes* (Cambridge: Cambridge University Press, 2012), 172–3. It seems more likely to me, however, that 'Anna Antonini' was the Italian-sounding stage name used by Miklaszewicz before her marriage to Gaetano Campi shortly after the premiere of *La clemenza di Tito*.

36. Antonia Campi left Prague in the summer of 1801 along with her husband. She probably sang Vitellia with Guardasoni's company until then. Her portrayal of the role in Vienna and Leipzig is described in *Allgemeine musikalische Zeitung*, XIII/8 (20 February 1811), 146; XV/11 (17 March 1813), 193; *Der Sammler, ein Unterhaltungsblatt*, V/36 (4 March 1813), 144; *Zeitung für die elegante Welt*, XVIII/215 (2 November 1818), 1739; *Morgenblatt für gebildete Stände*, XII/181 (24 November 1818), 1124; Eduard Genast: *Aus dem Tagebuche eines alten Schauspielers*, 4 vols. (Leipzig: Voigt & Günther, 1862), II, 119–20.

37. The aggression is possibly related to the fact that Vitellia tends to be sung by rather heavy voices today, sometimes even by mezzo-sopranos. However, as suggested by Campi's other Mozart roles in Guardasoni's company (Countess Almaviva in *Le nozze di Figaro*, Donna Anna in *Don Giovanni*, Fiordiligi in *Così fan tutte* and Astrifiammante (the Queen of the Night) in *Il flauto magico*), her voice was probably very far from those of today's dramatic sopranos or mezzo-sopranos; see Woodfield, *Performing Operas for Mozart* (2012), 224, 226. The same seems to have been the case with Luigia Caravoglia (later Sandrini), who succeeded Campi as the last *prima donna* of Guardasoni's company, from 1802 to 1807. When Sandrini-Caravoglia sang Vitellia in the 1815 Dresden premiere, one critic complained that she lacked 'necessary power in the lower notes, which are meant to have such great effect in her arias'. 'Was den Gesang anbetrifft, so vermisste man zwar die nöthige Stärke in den, auf so grosse Wirkung berechneten tiefern Tönen ihrer Arien'. *Allgemeine musikalische Zeitung* XVII/8 (22 February 1815), 132. On Luigia Caravoglia in the Prague production of *La clemenza di Tito*, see Marie Börner-Sandrini, *Erinnerungen einer alten Dresdnerin* (Dresden: Warnatz & Lehmann, 1876), 41–42.

38. The poem is reproduced in 'Strinasacchi, Theresia', in Gottfried Johann Dlabacž (ed.), *Allgemeines historisches Künstler-Lexikon für Böhmen und zum Theil auch für Mähren und Schlesien*, 3 vols. (Prague: Gottlieb Haase, 1815), III. The last time Strinasacchi sang Sesto in Prague was probably on 20 March 1797, when Act II was given in a double bill with another show. The next time *La clemenza di Tito* was given, on 6 and 10 November, the German singer Demoiselle Doliagny was praised for her debut in a male role in the production, suggesting that she had

taken over Sesto. See Volek, *Repertoir Nosticovského divadla* (1961), 116, 135–36.

39. See Tessing Schneider, 'Kierkegaard and the Copenhagen Production of Mozart's *Don Giovanni*', *European Romantic Review*, 29/1 (2018), 43–50.

40. '[...] det er netop Hemmeligheden i denne Opera, at Helten deri tillige er Kraften i de øvrige Personer, *Don Juans* Liv er Livsprincipet i dem. Hans Lidenskab sætter de andres Lidenskab i Bevægelse, hans Lidenskab gjenlyder overalt, den gjenlyder i og bærer *Commandantens* Alvor, *Elvires* Vrede, *Annas* Had, *Ottavios* Vigtighed, *Zerlines* Angst, *Mazettos* Forbittrelse, *Leporellos* Forvirring. Som Helten i Operaen er *Don Juan* Stykkets Nævner, han giver det som Helten i Almindelighed dets Navn, men han er Mere, han er, om jeg saa maa sige, General-Nævner.' Søren Kierkegaard, *Enten–Eller: Et Livs-Fragment*, 2 vols. (1843) I, 121. Quoted from the digital edition of Søren Kierkegaard Forskningscenteret, Copenhagen 2013: www.sks.dk (accessed 20 April 2017). The translation is taken from *Either/Or: A Fragment of Life*, trans. Alastair Hannay (London: Penguin Books, 1992/2004), 121.

4 Tito's Burden
Felicity Baker

The Operatic Action, Intertext and Context

The libretto for *La clemenza di Tito* (by Pietro Metastasio in 1734, revised by Caterino Mazzolà in 1791) dramatises events on the day after Titus renounced his love for the foreign queen Berenice. Even though he was absolute ruler, he renounced his love in compliance with popular demand because he desired the Roman people's consent to his being their emperor. The opera's first scenes recount that agonising renunciation. It was already known to audiences as constituting the entire action of Jean Racine's 1670 tragedy *Bérénice*, during which the two main characters are both close to suicide. The following discussion invites reflection on the context of the times of composition of those two works, Racine's *Bérénice* and the libretto for *La clemenza di Tito*.

Bérénice was written about twenty years after the French royal armies' brutal crushing of the second Fronde—an important revolt of the nobles against the rule of Louis XIV. The 1670 tragedy expresses, in Titus's own disenchanted words, the loss of belief in the value of high status and *gloire*, the fame and grandeur attached to the desire and effort to be the impossible: the perfect ruler. In living memory of the Fronde, Racine's tragedy may have suggested to its first public a political commentary on their present time, as the playwright represents Titus as an absolute monarch, on the model of a French king.[1]

How to cite this book chapter:
Baker, F. 2018. Tito's Burden. In: Tessing Schneider, M. and Tatlow, R. (eds.) *Mozart's* La clemenza di Tito: *A Reappraisal*. Pp. 97–119. Stockholm: Stockholm University Press. DOI: https://doi.org/10.16993/ban.d. License: CC-BY NC-ND 4.0

The choice of the story of Titus's clemency to celebrate the coronation of Leopold II as king of Bohemia in 1791, at a time when Titus was a quasi-mythical figure of benevolent rule for the Enlightenment, can be seen as an expression of love for the reforming monarch, while the Roman ruler himself, in keeping with his earlier representation in Racine's tragedy, enacts his doubts and regrets, and even a distrust of his own royal authority. The confrontation of the subjects' uncritical love for Tito and the latter's self-criticism in Metastasio's libretto adumbrates an Enlightenment critique of monarchy as such.

Mozart was commissioned to produce a new score for the 1734 libretto *La clemenza di Tito* for the festivities accompanying Leopold's coronation on 6 September 1791 (he seems to have attended the premiere without enthusiasm, see Chapter 1, II Documents 9 and 16). Mozart's score entailed some modifications to the libretto. Metastasio's *opera seria* of the early Enlightenment had had many performances through the eighteenth century, with musical scores by a number of different composers. Almost sixty years after its original composition, the poetically powerful text needed the up-to-date revisions effected by Mazzolà without loss of its poetic qualities, to accommodate both Mozart's music and Mazzolà's stagecraft. The large body of Metastasio's writing preserved in the final version suggests that the creators of the new opera held his work in high esteem. At the same time, where certain verses of the original text are excised by the critical artists of 1791, we can discern the uncritical, sometimes self-indulgent character of the earlier era. The text of the Mozart-Mazzolà final version forms the subject of my comments on the libretto.

Anomalously, this demonstrably rich, multi-faceted libretto belongs with a Mozart score that may still be suffering from a lingering prejudice that deems it unequal to his other great operas. Discussion of the music is beyond the scope of my discussion here, but if there still persists any such disparagement of the music, I would be sorry to set the matter aside without first citing the succinct vindication of *La clemenza di Tito* by Stanley Sadie. Many composers were setting Metastasio's classical librettos, adding ensembles and choruses for the tastes of the later times. In *La clemenza di Tito* Mozart cut eighteen arias and added four, with three new duets, three trios, a choral ensemble and two finale ensembles. Sadie points out that the music for this serious opera is necessarily more austere than that of the Mozart-Da Ponte comic operas or *Die Zauberflöte*. The style befits the serious topic, and 'in its reduced form it may be seen as conforming to the neo-classical ideals then rapidly gaining ground in Germany'. He adds: 'Mozart responded with restrained orchestral writing, smooth, broad vocal lines, and relatively brief numbers', and concludes: '*La clemenza di Tito*, compared with the preceding operas, is no less refined in craftsmanship, and it shows Mozart responding with music of restraint, nobility and warmth to a new kind of stimulus'.[2]

John A. Rice has described in detail the construction and the qualities of this *opera seria* that made it the perfect choice for the grand occasion and for the courtly audience of September 1791. It was a drama representing Tito's benign kingship and the judicious governance that peacefully resolves a dangerous day of political turbulence, evocative of the revolutionary events currently unfolding in other lands.[3] Rice's methodical assembling of all the external circumstances and reasons for the choice of that opera, its characters and its topic, facilitates and inspires a closer reading of the libretto, for internal analysis and discussion of the text and the action, which I hope will reveal further details that shed light on different facets of the work's historical context, and its importance for our own time.[4]

La clemenza di Tito celebrates virtuous kingship, while at the same time representing the monarch's role as onerous for him. Tito's generosity, the positive construction of his character, although derided by some critics, becomes credible when we perceive him as a victim of tragic irony, his deep love for Berenice having made him aspire to become the perfect ruler who, for that very reason, must send her away from Rome.

When Leopold came to Bohemia for his coronation, it was the duty of the Bohemian Estates[5] to decide the festivities, which included the choice of the opera (see Chapter 1, II Documents 1 and 2). We can infer that the choice signified simultaneously both their homage to the emperor and their appeal to him to respect an ideal of benevolence and heed their supplications. Bohemia was at that time impoverished by famine and wars, and one of a number of provinces attempting to obstruct the ruler's policies and taxes, the more audaciously just after Joseph's death.[6] Leopold would anticipate a display of such tensions in the welcome extended to him. It was inherent in the situation of benevolent subjection that the subjects would inform the ruler of their needs. The pressure on the monarch of such appeals might account in part for his apparent lack of interest at the opera premiere.

La clemenza di Tito stages that relationship favourably. On stage the Roman people initiate their relationship with Tito with celebrations, but also with their stern demand, made in the republican spirit not forgotten in the era of the Roman Empire, that he should choose a Roman woman as empress. Imperial absolutism entitles Tito to disregard that demand, but he knows better than to do so. The opera powerfully dramatises the simultaneity of loving homage and pressure that so intensely defines the absolute monarch's experience of his closest courtiers' dependence on him. Once Tito concedes the people's demand by sending Berenice away, the people must reciprocate by giving their consent to the emperor's authority. They can henceforth make appeals to his goodwill, but they cannot make demands on him. The rebellion that dominates the opera's central action results from the failure of its instigator, Vitellia, to understand that Tito has already satisfied the popular demand. Vitellia's manipulation of the people's feelings about their ruler has mixed motivations, in which her own political ambition skews her perception of others' actions, and momentarily blinds her to her own feelings—whether love or hate—towards Tito. She is a brilliant, larger-than-life creation. However, the people's generally positive feelings for Tito, their consent to his authority, and their relief when he is known to have survived Sesto's inept attempt on his life, soon prevail over her misjudged leadership.

Thereafter, with Tito's generous and affectionate authority confirmed, Act II can explore and partly resolve the mystery of the loyal Sesto's moment of guilt, and question his refusal to explain why he endangered his beloved monarch's life. This dramatic series of tense confrontations between the two men remains deadlocked, as Sesto would die rather than denounce Vitellia, whom he passionately loves. Heartlessly, she has relied on his helpless love for her, and ordered him to kill his other object of love, Tito, and Sesto's pathetic dilemma leaves him powerless to act on his horror at her criminal plotting. Vitellia is finally wakened from her indifference to Sesto's love by a transforming realisation that he will die without denouncing her. She resolves the deadlock. At the last moment, she rushes on stage with her full confession to Tito, before the whole court, admitting that she instigated the rebellion and compelled Sesto to attempt regicide. That attainment of complete clarification opens the way to the ruler's absolution of the entire Roman people.

In Act II, the hard work of Tito's determination to resolve the crisis ultimately succeeds through the laborious clarification of Sesto's destructive deeds. The extraordinary action of this Act is worthy of comparison with today's practice of *restorative justice*, whereby instead of traditional modes of punishment of an offender, an authorised person assembles all those involved in or affected by the crime so that the event can be excavated in detail and a resolution collectively agreed.[7] But unlike today's procedure, where traditionally imposed penalties give way to collective egalitarian processes that work towards restorative justice, the resolution in *La clemenza di Tito* remains, to the end of the work, the work of Tito alone, as the sole recourse for justice. Tito remains imprisoned under the burden of his power; the operatic action exposes relentlessly that defining injustice of the tradition of absolute monarchy.

In the spirit of its official festive purpose, the opera celebrates good kingship, while maintaining the extreme tension between that celebration and an exploration of a turbulent moment in Europe's gradual falling out of love with absolute monarchy. In *La clemenza di Tito*, the tension is dramatised in the character construction of Tito himself. That tension remains unresolved at the opera's close, even as it remained unresolved in the Europe of 1791.[8]

The Monarch's Need for Truth

In classical tragedy, the central character has a confidant who gives him or her advice and information about the small milieu of the court and the world outside the court. For Tito, the absence of a reliable interlocutor of this kind is a major obstacle towards him developing the non-authoritarian leadership he aspires to. Servilia, perhaps the member of Tito's small inner circle of the court who has the least status, earns his highest praise by disappointing him—telling him that she loves Annio. Tito's abiding ambition to be a perfect emperor puts him at the mercy of even his friends' incapacity to tell him the truth. Their admiring love for the absolute ruler obstructs the feeling of equality that might facilitate truthful exchange. Truth is almost continually inhibited or 'trapped' (cf. Act 1, scene 7, 'L'insidiata verità'). Tito is confident that the subjects closest to him admire and love him, but they respond to his own aspiration to perfection by idealising him and by withholding from him, for more or less innocent reasons, information that may not please him.

Pietro Metastasio is generally appreciated as a warmly lyrical poet, but is thought to have lesser talents for psychological analysis. *La clemenza di Tito* allowed him to display other strengths. His undeniable gift of *political* insight, of which Servilia's scene is a subtle instance, unquestionably prevails in the libretto's brilliantly rich depiction of one turbulent day in the very gradual dismantling of the ancient institution of monarchy. We especially recognise it in the slow processes of change in the personal relationships prevailing at the monarch's court; processes not irrelevant to the demise of the classical tragic genre, structured as it was on the extreme representation of royal grandeur and courtly magnificence. Furthermore, Tito's anxiety about the rarity of truth-telling among members of his closest circle suggests to us the literary-political motivation for discarding the role of the confidant. One day before the action of the *opera seria*, Racine had given Titus a crucially necessary confidant in Paulinus, who told him his absolute power meant he could override Rome's objection to a foreigner and a queen as a choice of empress, but (when pressed by Titus) he admitted that he would then certainly have to deal with the Senate's complaints and the people's entreaties. The next day, in Metastasio's libretto, Tito finds himself with no reliable confidant as he had heeded Paulinus's warning and, to the profound grief of both the lovers, sent Berenice away from Rome—all this in order to be the perfect monarch that Berenice had always wanted him to be. He now has a group of grateful, respectful and affectionate friends who are not frank with him.

Servilia, however, knows from the start how to speak truth to the ruler in her situation of subjection, and in so doing, she enables Tito to express the longing for truth that from the opera's first Act constitutes the imperative of clarification which is catharsis.[9] In a rare reference to Berenice, his sacrificed love, Tito has explained to Sesto and Annio that another love is out of the question for him, but that he will marry a daughter of Rome, and that his friendship for Sesto can determine his choice of Servilia, Sesto's sister, to become his wife that very day (Act I, scene 4). Tito is unaware that Annio and Servilia are promised to each other. Sesto and Annio both instantly despair of the existing love, but they hide their dismay, feigning their joy at his choice of such a woman. Their words seem close to flattery, but they contain none of the flatterer's veiled political cunning. The grieving Annio announces to Servilia her future greatness, but Servilia responds by confronting Tito with the news that her heart belongs to Annio and that her thoughts would always be of him. However, aware that she has no right to oppose the sovereign's will, she concludes by offering him her hand if, knowing of her love for Annio, he still wants her as his spouse. Tito responds with admiration and relief at being told a disappointing truth: his own heart could not bear to thwart their love (Act I, scene 7). At the end of the scene, Tito sings aria 8. 'Ah, se fosse intorno al trono', the words of which define both the opera's dramatic situation and the feelings of the character:

> Ah, se fosse intorno al trono
> Ogni cor così sincero,
> Non tormento un vasto impero,
> Ma saria felicità.
>   Non dovrebbero i regnanti
> Tollerar sì grande affanno
> Per distinguer dall'inganno
> L'insidiata verità.[10]

(Oh, if the throne were surrounded only by such sincere hearts, a vast empire would not be torment, but bliss. Rulers should not tolerate the anguish of having to distinguish deceit from inhibited veracity.)

When Tito later decides in solitude (Act II, scene 11), after great inner conflict, to spare Sesto's life, he does not yet know why his former friend tried to kill him. Sesto has not told him the whole truth. So Tito's decision to set aside his just condemnation by not delivering Sesto to the rigour of the law only keeps this monarch true to his character, true to his habitual preference to let others accuse him of ill-inspired pity rather than mistaken rigour. It follows that his final recourse to clemency for all, when publicly stated, does not constitute in itself the climax of the dramatic action. That would leave the audience with no vision of possible political change: the monarch still rules in isolation. The libretto reserves the last scene (Act II, scene 17) for truth-telling alone, the more significant for not having served as the condition of Sesto's deliverance from death. The opera ends with the full clarification that we can call catharsis. This last scene fully vindicates Tito's earlier insistence on frankness (in Servilia's scene), since everyone finally knows the whole truth in a rare moment of transparency for all.

Whatever Metastasio may have lacked in psychological analysis, I suggest, he made up for in penetrating political insights into the psycho-social relationships of monarchy, and in the highly dramatic elaboration of those relationships in the case of Tito himself, who yearns to undo them from within. Jean-Jacques Rousseau spoke of Metastasio with reverence, and in his *Dictionnaire de musique* he regards his genius as inspiring for others.[11] Rousseau entered the Paris theatrical scene in 1749, and in his scandalous *Lettre sur la musique française* (1753) he denounced French opera, set against high praise for the Italian operas, where 'the arias are all in situation and form part of the scenes',[12] which is not the case, he asserts, in French operas. He gives examples of the dramatic relevance of Italian arias, referring to one sung by Tito: 'He is a good-natured ruler who, forced to set an example of severity, asks the gods to take away his empire, or to give him a less sensitive heart'.[13] Rousseau's high esteem for Metastasio's writing acknowledges the poet's gift for dynamising theatrical action long before Mozart's music and Mazzolà's libretto revisions greatly advanced operatic stagecraft. These observations suggest a reading of Metastasio's libretto that transcends the assertion of lack of sensitivity to the human: no one attends more critically to the political dimension's affective reverberations than Rousseau. In the article

'Opéra' Rousseau describes the defining characteristics of the genre *drame lyrique*, that is, the *opera seria*, as consisting in the need to hold the spectator totally under the spell of the musical illusion; 'nothing cold or reasoned' is appropriate in the composition of the *opera seria* libretto.[14] He defines *opera seria* in terms of overwhelming musicality and warm emotion, rather than a happy ending. For Rousseau, beauty, graceful composition and verisimilitude will fill spectators' hearts with pity and fear. We can agree with him when we see the complex depth of Tito's emotions and experience the shock of others' emotions and deeds in *La clemenza di Tito*. The task of dramatic poetry is to make clear that which is deeply unclear, and the clarification can help spectators to live. Racine's heroine Berenice attests this clarification literally; faced with Titus's insistence that they must part, she did not believe he loved her, but when he tells her that if she dies, he will die (Act V, scene 6, lines 1427-36), she knows he still loves her and so she can promise to live. We see the same powerful effect on Vitellia when she learns that Sesto intends to go to his death rather than denounce her. Understanding at last what it is to be loved, and what that means to him and to her, she sacrifices every ambition of her own selflessly to save him from death. Such life-saving effects achieved in a few lines of dramatic writing have a tremendous impact on spectators and readers; such effects are of the essence of *opera seria*.[15] Rousseau reports in his *Lettre à d'Alembert* that when Mlle Gaussin, a great actress in the role of Berenice, stopped weeping in the final scene of the tragedy, having suddenly understood that Titus still loved her, her dry-eyed promise to depart and to live caused the spectators to forget the tragedy's overt lesson of the hero who prefers duty before love. They all left the theatre, writes Rousseau, having 'married Berenice'.[16] His contention that in a contest between love and duty, love will always win, invalidates the notion of theatre as a school for moral improvement and suggests the need for another kind of theatre, of a kind glimpsed in such moments of emotional revelation.

Historical Depth in the Character of Tito

What we learn of Tito's moral character from the defining scene with Servilia constitutes an instance of this opera's important intertextual relations with two great works of the previous century. The first of these, Racine's 1669 tragedy *Britannicus*, portrays Nero when a very young 'nascent monster', as Racine describes him in his preface.[17] In *Bérénice*, Titus will compare his own court favourably to that of Nero. Nero heeds the sinister advice of the corrupt flatterer Narcissus. He envies the young love between Junia and Britannicus; and desiring to possess Junia, he takes her prisoner. Fearing Britannicus as a rival to the empire, Nero then has Narcissus poison the young man. Narcissus is finally killed by the people of Rome; Junia takes refuge in the temple. In *La clemenza di Tito*, the scene in which Tito safeguards the love of Servilia and Annio enacts the most extreme contrast to the plot of *Britannicus*.[18] By contradistinction, Nero's destruction of the couple Junia-Britannicus sheds light on the meaning of Tito's open-hearted response to the love of Annio and Servilia. Tito will not be another Nero; his moral reform from the start of his reign, publicly illustrated by his separation from Berenice, is genuine and all-encompassing, and the vice of flattery has no place in the opera.

I have already referred to Racine's *Bérénice* (1670), the second seventeenth-century tragedy with a deep intertextual relation to *La clemenza di Tito*. The first two scenes of *La clemenza di Tito* clearly establish Tito's identity as being that of the equally fictional character Titus in *Bérénice*. The continuity of the action from the tragedy to the *opera seria* is perfectly precise. In Racine's tragedy, Titus renounces the love of his life, Berenice, in order to be true to his ideal conception of the faultless ruler. Foreshadowing the Tito of the opera, he speaks with bitter sadness of the 'glorious' identity to which he had aspired until he realised that having attained 'la gloire'—the consent of the people—he would have to lose his love. One day later in fictional time, the action of the opera starts with the news of the heartrending separation of the lovers, and of Berenice's departure from Rome, spreading within Tito's court. These two works elaborate on their historical source, the essay on Titus in *The Twelve Caesars* by Suetonius. Suetonius's account was equally familiar to the first audiences of both Racine's tragedy and Mozart's opera.[19] However we cannot fail to take into account the changing political determinants of character construction from Racine's masterpiece to that of Metastasio, and again to that of Mozart and Mazzolà. In the course of the intervening years, social-historical changes impose upon Tito-Titus a new relationship to being a leader despite important persevering effects of the libretto's fidelity to the inaugural sacrifice of love, expressed in Racine's extraordinary poetry:

> Je sens bien que sans vous je ne saurais plus vivre,
> Que mon cœur de moi-même est prêt à s'éloigner.
> Mais il ne s'agit plus de vivre, il faut régner. (Act IV, scene 5, 1100–1102.)

> (I surely feel that without you I could not go on living,
> and that my heart is about to leave me.
> But it is no longer a matter of living, I must reign.)

Tito's decision to exercise clemency, despite Sesto's refusal to explain his motivation for the attempted assassination, does not deny his need for truth. I suggest that at this point in the drama, the poet refers to the deep-level identity, even fusion, of the character of Tito and the hero Titus of Racine's tragedy. With Berenice, Titus has known a relationship extraordinary in its transparent truthfulness. The pain of the lovers' parting is excruciatingly truthful too, as dramatised by the poetic genius of Racine's tragedy and then as stated in a few simple words by the eye-witness, Annio, in the first scenes of the opera. The thought comes to mind of the idea of the 'limit experience', one of whose forms is an experience where nearness to death ('If you die,

I will die...') takes subjects out of life and yet not to literal death.[20] Might we apply the words: 'Mais il ne s'agit plus de vivre, il faut régner', to the entire characterisation of the emperor in the sequel to that parting: *La clemenza di Tito*? Should we not understand that what Tito and his subjects call his heart, 'il cor di Tito' (Act I, scene 8; Act II, scene 5), always bears the wound of the unbearable effort of the previous day? The action of the opera culminates in a collective situation where the truth, unsatisfactory as it is, is clear to all. Tito knows that the clarification does not guarantee an enduring collective acceptance of his principle of truthfulness. In the end, this ruler's freedom to act on his decision to exercise a universal clemency accompanies a complex clarification of the facts to which all the opera's characters contribute in different ways. Admitting his guilt in the attempt on Tito's life, Sesto does not divulge his motivation, but the *coup de théâtre* of Vitellia's profound remorse, and her genuine confession that she had abused Sesto's love for her to make him attempt the crime, enable Tito to absolve Sesto and all the rebels. Audiences needed no explanation that sexual love is involuntary, and so Tito could exonerate Sesto for his abject obedience to Vitellia's command. Her final clarification, despite its brevity and generality, satisfies the need for truth. The fact that the woman is not held to account for the enormity of the crime that she both plotted and made Sesto attempt, must have seemed acceptable to the eighteenth-century audience. The extremism of Tito's decision to absolve the guilt of Vitellia and her co-conspirators universalises the quality of clemency as the ultimate virtue for the rule of one over all.

From Servilia to Vitellia

In this discussion of a libretto focused on the central character's political sensibility and burden of responsibility, the two female characters call for consideration. While both are apparently politically marginal,

I am struck by the fact that each in her own way acts and thinks more independently in relation to the male characters, including the monarch, than do the three male characters in their own situations.[21]

The important characterisation of Servilia and Vitellia, in the immediate aftermath of Tito's traumatic separation from Berenice, would certainly loom large in the imagination of the opera's creators and first audiences. In face of the emotional impossibility of loving any other woman, Tito must marry a daughter of Rome. Unacquainted with any eligible women, he thinks first of his friend Sesto's sister, then, after learning of her love for Annio, he announces his choice of Vitellia, daughter of Vitellius, a former emperor. As discussed above, Tito has perceived in Servilia's frankness a moral maturity superior to all that he has observed at the court: a quality confirmed by the poet's construction of her character. The astonishing character Vitellia, who has desired to be chosen as Tito's consort and has felt that she loved him, disgracefully abuses her young lover Sesto's weakness to make him stir up a popular revolt and assassinate his admired friend, Tito— all in her ill-judged refusal to believe that Berenice has left Rome. When later summoned to Tito's presence with the welcome news that he has in fact chosen her as his empress, Vitellia then needs desperately to revoke the conspiracy that she has set in motion against him.

The libretto balances these strong female characters, not as moral opposites but in a sharply contrasted tension, as two people whose lives have afforded them totally different situations from which their innate characters emerge as radically dissimilar. In an era of writing often marked by feminine stereotypes, we can admire the poet's ability for creating women who are unique, and as real and credible today as his fictional men. We can also admire the poet for creating men in whom emotion, especially love, is no less necessary than it is for the women. It is, however, the character of Vitellia that grows and changes most dramatically and convincingly in the course of the opera.

This colourful character creates the entire intrigue, the plot against Tito's life and the brutal manipulation of the emotions of the young man who attempts to carry it out for love of her, and while doing extreme violence to his own love for Tito. The Age of Enlightenment did not doubt the violence of amorous passion. Rousseau writes in his *Discours sur l'origine de l'inégalité* [*Discourse on the origin of Inequality*]:

> Among the passions that trouble the heart of man, there is one that is ardent, impetuous, which renders one sex necessary to the other, a terrible passion that braves all dangers, overturns all obstacles, and that seems, in its fury, capable of destroying the human species that its purpose is to preserve. What will become of men prey to this frenetic, brutal madness, without decency or restraint, spilling their blood day after day as they fight one another over their loves?[22]

Sesto does not fight Tito over his love for Vitellia, but rather breaks his own heart in his powerlessness to resist both his passion for her beauty and her brutally cruel command that he kill his emperor, the person he loves most after herself. To convince an audience, he would need to be portrayed as very young, barely adult, enslaved by an unrequited and destructive passion and yet fundamentally made for compassion and faithful friendship. After Sesto is exposed as the perpetrator of the attempted crime, when Vitellia cannot believe he will not expose her as its instigator, he begins to see her moral unworthiness of his love but even then, he still loves her, asks only for her pity, and assures her he will not denounce her.

Vitellia heeds only her own understanding of the political events that excite her ambition, even ignoring contrary evidence supplied by eye-witnesses. Perhaps we can accept that she loves or loved Tito, as she tells Sesto and finally tells Tito himself. Her obsession with his life situation and his position of power are perhaps a deflection of thwarted love. When planning Tito's assassination, she believes that since she cannot become empress by marrying him, she will, after his death, inherit her father's power as ruler of Rome. As readers of Suetonius, the audience would know of Vitellius's irresponsible life and might thus infer a history of emotional and social deprivation from this strong-willed, intelligent but wrong-headed woman's grave errors of judgement through her self-centred obsessions and her gross insensitivity to the generosity and intelligence of others. The poet's art excels in making Vitellia so complex that we can interpret her character with a degree of freedom.

The brilliant characterisation of Vitellia makes her total transformation—a veritable conversion—entirely credible. She did not believe for one moment that Sesto would go to his death without denouncing her, and when she learns that he is doing exactly that, the change in her is immediate and all-embracing. She puts away her plans or expectation of empire and marriage, and in her final rondo 23. 'Non più di fiori' she sings of the dream of garlanded nuptials replaced by a horrific death.[23] At last she allows herself to feel sadness about what she has lacked and will never have. But she must save Sesto's life, and does so selflessly. She confronts Tito, and in the presence of everyone, confesses her guilt. Tito's first reaction of rage and despair at learning the depths of guilt of this most treacherous member of his court gives way to his habit of clemency in preference to cruel punishment. He commands that all the miscreants be freed, and absolves everybody, recreating order in his realm.

In the first scenes of *La clemenza di Tito*, members of the court praise Tito's warm generosity of character. At the end, his enacted clemency confirms their faith in him, and yet his feelings are obscure. He has changed, under the impact of shocking events. The opera stages his thunderstruck silence at Vitellia's revelations. Recalling his earlier lament about 'L'insidiata verità' that undermines even his warmest relations at the court, we must conclude that his state of shock contains his grim confrontation with any monarch's irreducible burden—the heavier for his being the best of monarchs—a lonely figure at the top of a pyramid of unknowable subjects. *La clemenza di Tito* enacts the impossibility of monarchical rule, not just for the many who live under the rule of one, but most of all, for the one who, like Racine's Titus, understands that ruling is no longer a matter of living.

The Opera's Burden

Metastasio's dramatic poem *La clemenza di Tito* holds together all the elements of hugely disruptive events without sacrificing any character as morally irrecuperable. Finally, the opera's representation of humanity remains positive even while dramatising the human potential for endangering lives by generating moral and political disaster. It seems that for more than fifty years, the libretto was the stable element, the dimension that was popular with the audiences, while the music was the variable accompaniment; following the libretto's composition in 1734, numerous composers wrote new music for it. We can be sure that Mozart's music at the Prague premiere on 6 September 1791, combined with some text revisions by Mazzolà, created an entirely new experience for the aristocracy and other dignitaries who constituted the first night audience. The reception of the music's originality and beauty, however, may have been affected by Leopold's late arrival and his implicit lack of interest. As some spectators had waited in the auditorium for two and a half hours (see Chapter 1, II Documents 8, 10, 11 and 12), their enthusiasm for a premiere was dampened, and this in turn may have influenced the lacklustre attendance on ensuing nights (see Chapter 1, II Documents 12, 16, 17, 20, 21). The ceremonial occasion of Leopold's coronation would necessarily have predetermined the politics of the celebratory opera so decisively—not only the choice of the 1734 libretto, but also the new music —that we can admire the credible tumult of the human world that its creators nonetheless dared to conjure up, especially in the first finale: a poetic reference (however momentary) to the real revolutions of America and France. But more than that, the opera's portrayal of the Roman ruler himself, with his freely expressed warmth, his private torment about having to rule at all, and his clemency: all that was an audaciously ideal portrait to offer to the new emperor. But Leopold (who was not an illiberal ruler, although somewhat less liberal than Joseph had been) had already endured the pressure of his subjects pleading for his goodwill, he knew the plot of *La clemenza di Tito* as well as everyone else, and it is possible that Mozart's music was not to his taste. The relation of the theatre to authority, always problematic in pre-democratic times, must surely be more intense in the physical presence of the ruler, disturbing the fundamental relation of the spectators to the spectacle. It is as if Leopold set out to ensure the opera's failure, and he might even have succeeded, but that the production was revived three years later to a resounding success (see Chapter 1, II Documents 20 and 21), precisely because it was now independent from its original ceremonial and political setting.

Notes

1. Georges Forestier, editor of Racine, *Théâtre – Poésie* (Paris: Gallimard, 1999), 1457, makes that *rapprochement*, which also applies to Tito in the Mozart opera: 'A l'image d'un roi de France, Titus est présenté comme un monarque absolu'. Forestier goes on to explain that 'absolute', (Latin *solutus a legibus*, 'untied from the laws'), 'does not mean that the king can do what he wants with the existing laws, nor that he can give force of law to all his whims; it indicates that he has full legislative power, that is, he is invested with the right to replace an old law at any moment with a new one (which will be [...] discussed by the sovereign courts). On the other hand, he must respect the natural and divine laws, as well as the "fundamental laws" of the kingdom that established the conditions of the exercise of monarchy [...]. Transgressing those two types of laws means taking the path of tyranny' (1457–8). Forestier's points remain relevant for the Late Enlightenment opera; the fact that Tito's absolute power may be seen by the opera's public as a reference to a modern

European king has a critical function, but at the same time, the location in Antiquity, greatly favoured throughout the centuries of monarchical rule, corresponded to a deep affection for the ancient myths. I owe the latter point to Paul Bénichou, *Morales du grand siècle* (Paris: Gallimard, 1948), 252, note.

2. Stanley Sadie, *The New Grove Mozart* (London: Macmillan, 1980), 161-4.

3. News of the American and French Revolutions travelled fast. In France, major changes before 6 September 1791, relevant to this opera and to the Holy Roman Empire (far ahead of France politically, thanks to Joseph II's liberalising reforms, most of them maintained by his brother Leopold II), include, in August 1789, abolition of the feudal regime based on privileges of nobility and clergy in favour of a new social order based on freedom and equality; *Déclaration des droits de l'homme et du citoyen*. Ensuing changes included: in 1790, women, admitted to some Jacobin clubs, began to learn to talk about politics, to deliberate, speak publicly, sometimes vote. In early 1791: Olympe de Gouges, *Déclaration des droits de la femme et de la citoyenne*. Her historic manifesto was ignored. 20 June: Louis XVI, trying to flee France, is brought back to Paris, watched by a huge silent crowd.

4. John A. Rice, *W. A. Mozart:* La clemenza di Tito. Cambridge Opera Handbooks (Cambridge: Cambridge University Press, 1991). Rice pinpoints precisely the interweaving of the two great works in the emotions of Tito, p. 26: 'Since both Racine and Metastasio follow the classical precept of unity of time, we can conclude that Metastasio's drama takes place on the day following that on which Racine's drama takes place. [...] This would explain much of Tito's resignation, the lack of pleasure he feels in his reign. This would explain too why Metastasio's Tito lacks the passion of Racine's Titus: he has just given up the only thing that aroused his passion'.

5. The Bohemian Estates were the regional government of Bohemia. Consisting of representatives from the nobility, the clergy, the knights and the burghers, the assembly was dominated by the aristocracy.

6. Derek Beales, *Joseph II: II. Against the World, 1780-1790* (Cambridge: Cambridge University Press, 2009), 1, 59, 243, 623-4.

7. From the extensive bibliography for all aspects of restorative justice, I mention three studies that helped me to connect and contrast Tito's negotiation of the crisis in Rome to this modern procedure: Heather Strang and John Braithwaite, *Restorative Justice: Philosophy to Practice* (Dartmouth: Ashgate, 2000); Heather Strang and John Braithwaite, *Restorative Justice and Civil Society* (Cambridge: Cambridge University Press, 2001); and Heather Strang, *Repair or Revenge: Victims and Restorative Justice* (Oxford: Clarendon Press, 2002). My thanks to Heather Strang and to Elizabeth Minchin for valuable discussions of many questions relevant to *La clemenza di Tito*.

8. However, in Paris on 12 July 1791 in the Legislative Assembly, the Marquis de Condorcet had read out a refutation of pro-royalty arguments entitled: 'De la République; ou un roi est-il nécessaire à la conservation de la liberté?' (On the Republic; or, is a king necessary for the preservation of freedom?).

9. For the instance of *La clemenza di Tito*, and more generally, I prefer Martha Nussbaum's analysis of the meaning of *katharsis* in Aristotle's era, for her conclusion that in its general sense it means clarification (as of water). Medical purgation and spiritual purification, which do not fit this *opera seria*, are specialised applications of that general meaning. See Martha Nussbaum, *The Fragility of Goodness: Luck and Ethics in Greek Tragedy and Philosophy*, rev. edn. (Cambridge: Cambridge University Press, 2001), 388–91. *La clemenza di Tito* is not a tragedy, but Sesto's refusal to explain his reason for attempting to murder his beloved emperor creates the dramatic necessity, for all the characters, of clarification.

10. [Pietro Metastasio and Caterino Mazzolà,] *La clemenza di Tito, dramma serio per musica in due atti da rappresentarsi nel Teatro Nazionale di Praga nel settembre 1791* (Prague: Schönfeld, 1791).

11. Jean-Jacques Rousseau, *Dictionnaire de musique* [1767], article 'Génie', *Œuvres complètes*, 5 vols. (Paris: Gallimard, 1995), V, 837–8.

12. 'Dans les opéras italiens, tous les airs sont en situation et font partie des scènes'. Rousseau, *Lettre sur la musique française*, in *Œuvres complètes* (1995), 316.

13. '[...] c'est un prince débonnaire, qui, forcé de donner un exemple de sévérité, demande aux dieux de lui ôter l'empire, ou de lui donner

un cœur moins sensible'. Rousseau, *Lettre sur la musique française,* in *Œuvres complètes* (1995), 316. The aria paraphrased by Rousseau is Tito's aria 20. 'Se all'impero, amici Dei'.

14. '[…] rien de froid et de raisonné'. *Dictionnaire de musique,* 'Opéra', in Rousseau, *Œuvres complètes* V (1995), 948–62.

15. Abbé Prévost's *Manon Lescaut* (1731) represents the same powerful effect when Manon, about to undergo deportation to the New World, finds Des Grieux beside her, determined to accompany her; she then understands what it means to be loved, and becomes a loving and faithful woman. She and Vitellia represent characters blind to love who exploit their lovers until the last extremity opens their eyes and hearts. Berenice does know love but loses faith in it when confronted by total loss of her lover; then she has to attain the extreme understanding that she remains loved despite total separation. I mention these instances here for their powerful resonance in the public; they are sudden, profound conversions and have something of the quality of a *coup de théâtre*. A great performer in the role of Berenice or Vitellia will remain in memory.

16. Jean Rousset, ed. in Rousseau, *Œuvres complètes,* V (1995), 48–50: 'La reine part sans le congé du parterre; l'empereur la renvoie *invitus invitam*, on peut ajouter *invito spectatore*. Titus a beau rester romain; il est seul de son parti; tous les spectateurs ont épousé Bérénice.' (The queen departs without the audience's permission; the emperor, reluctantly, dismisses the reluctant woman; we can add: the spectator is reluctant too. In vain does Titus remain a Roman; he is the only Roman in the theatre: all the spectators have married Berenice). Rousset remarks: 'Rousseau entend prouver que, contrairement à ce que disent les défenseurs du théâtre, l'effet de la pièce sur le spectateur est indépendant du dénouement.' (Rousseau means to prove that, contrary to what the theatre's defenders say, the play's effect on the spectator is independent of the work's conclusion). This editorial comment by Rousset is in 'Notes et variantes' at the back of vol. V of Rousseau *Œuvres complètes,* V (1995), 1339, note 2. As Rousset remarks, Rousseau contends that a play's effect on spectators is independent of its overt moral argument.

17. 'Je l'ai toujours regardé comme un monstre. Mais c'est ici un monstre naissant.' ('I have always regarded him as a monster. But here, he is a nascent monster.') Racine, *Œuvres complètes* I, *Théâtre - Poésie,*

Georges Forestier, ed. (Paris: Gallimard, 1999), Preface, 372–76: Racine explains that his main source for this work is Cornelius Tacitus, *Annals*. All my references to Racine and to the discussions by the editor Georges Forestier are to this edition. As the present article only discusses in detail the characters of *La clemenza di Tito*, I give the Italian form of their names (e.g. Tito), but, for the sake of clarity, I resort to the English (Latin) forms when referring to Racine's characters by name.

18. Historically, the careers of Nero and Titus were not far apart. Nero (born in 37, died in 68) was emperor from 54 to 68; Titus (born in 39, died in 81) ruled from 79 to 81. The historical Titus' dissolute youthful conduct before holding power led the people to fear he would be another Nero. He knew it, and allayed their fears by a genuine reform, hence his legendary status as a good ruler, and his deification. However close the fictional portrayal of historical persons such as Nero and Titus may be, our understanding of characters based on real persons will always depend ultimately on our analysis and understanding of the fictional portrayal in the context of the work of fiction as a whole, since fictionalisation inexorably entails transformation of facts. What interests the literary reader most intensely is the creator's transformation of the 'source'.

19. Gaius Suetonius Tranquillus, *De vita Caesarum* (known in English as *The Twelve Caesars*), 121 CE. Suetonius' account of the life of Titus is largely endorsed by the most recent scholarship, which however benefits from the much more precise historical documentation possible in recent times; see Brian W. Jones, *The Emperor Titus* (London: Croom Helm, 1984). Jones is somewhat sceptical about Titus's enduring reputation for clemency, but his account is not incompatible with that image; rather, he insists on a de-idealisation. He depicts Titus as an astute manager of men and of the empire; a benevolent, paternalistic autocrat. But with all his predecessors, Jones acknowledges the historical reality of the moral reform that Titus undertook after his very dissolute youth.

20. Maurice Blanchot, *L'Entretien infini* (Paris: Gallimard, 1969) II, 119–418, 'L'Expérience-limite', esp. 'L'Indestructible', 180–200. English translation, Susan Hanson, *The Infinite Conversation* (Minneapolis, MN: University of Minnesota Press, 1992).

21. Cf. Immanuel Kant, 'Beantwortung der Frage: Was ist Aufklärung?' [An Answer to the Question: What is Enlightenment?], *Berliner*

Monatsschrift II/12 (December 1784), 481-94. See *Immanuel Kant: Practical Philosophy*, edited and translated by Mary J. Gregor, (Cambridge: Cambridge University Press, 1996), 11–22: 'It is because of laziness and cowardice that so great a part of humankind, after nature has long since emancipated them from other people's direction (*naturaliter maiorennes*), nevertheless gladly remains minors for life, and that it becomes so easy for others to set themselves up as their guardians.' Kant includes in that great part of humankind 'the entire fair sex'. But half a century earlier, Metastasio represented Servilia and Vitellia as autonomous actors of their own lives.

22. Rousseau, *Discours sur l'origine et les fondements de l'inégalité entre les hommes* [1755], *Œuvres complètes*, III (Paris: Gallimard, 1964), 157: 'Parmi les passions qui agitent le cœur de l'homme, il en est une ardente, impétueuse, qui rend un sexe nécessaire à l'autre, passion terrible qui brave tous les dangers, renverse tous les obstacles, et qui dans ses fureurs semble propre à détruire le genre humain qu'elle est destinée à conserver. Que deviendront les hommes en proie à cette rage effrénée et brutale, sans pudeur, sans retenue, et se disputant chaque jour leurs amours au prix de leur sang?'

23 Act II, scene 15. Aria text by Mazzolà: 'No more lovely flower garlands...' refers to her former dreams of both the happiness of brilliant marriage and the grandeur of processing in a garlanded chariot or carriage as empress. Her portrayal, until the final scene, as a rebellious woman eager to become a political actor is not entirely unrealistic, whether we imagine the opera's context as imperial Rome, the aftermath of the Fronde or Revolutionary Europe. It would do less than justice to the poet's representation of Vitellia to interpret the rondo as an avowal that all she had ever really wanted was to marry the man she loved, and yet in the end, that becomes her truth.

5 Mozart as Epideictic Rhetorician: The Representation of Vice and Virtue in *La clemenza di Tito*

Jette Barnholdt Hansen*

* Revised and reproduced with the kind permission of Jette's family.

The following article presents a rhetorical reading of *La clemenza di Tito*, drawing attention to the epideictic elements that we may recognise in the opera and its historical context.[1] According to Aristotle, epideictic or 'occasional' rhetoric is a genre focused on the present, though it also reminds the audience of the past and points towards the future:[2] it centres on the praising of virtues and the condemning of vices, and in this way serves to concretise, evoke, and maintain *doxai*, i.e. the shared opinions and values of a specific culture.[3] Epideictic rhetoric is traditionally associated with ceremonial situations, such as weddings, coronations, and funerals. It requires the rhetorician to create consubstantial space and identification with the audience,[4] frequently by presenting a poetic vision, narrative or allegory to communicate the abstract more clearly with the audience.[5]

Mozart's *La clemenza di Tito* was neglected through much of the nineteenth and twentieth centuries, partly because it is so coloured by its ceremonial circumstances. Its first performance, at the National Theatre in Prague on 6 September 1791, celebrated the coronation of Emperor Leopold II as king of Bohemia. It was the third of Leopold's three coronations in 1790–91, which represented an ideological offensive within the Holy Roman Empire at a time when the social outlook of the French Revolution threatened European monarchies and their underlying foundations of absolutism.[6] Opera and other

How to cite this book chapter:
Hansen, J. B. 2018. Mozart as Epideictic Rhetorician: The Representation of Vice and Virtue in *La clemenza di Tito*. In: Tessing Schneider, M. and Tatlow, R. (eds.) *Mozart's* La clemenza di Tito: *A Reappraisal*. Pp. 120–133. Stockholm: Stockholm University Press. DOI: https://doi.org/10.16993/ban.e. License: CC-BY-NC-ND 4.0

forms of theatre, including courtly celebrations and ceremonies, functioned both as an empowerment of the absolutist monarchies during this period, and as a means of 'rebranding' integrated civic and enlightened values into the representation of monarchy, thus adapting the institution to the new political situation.[7] While on the one hand *La clemenza di Tito* celebrates the orthodoxies of court culture by employing the ritualistic symbolism of the Baroque, on the other it promotes the more recent social structure of enlightened absolutism. A study of the opera in its historical and rhetorical context therefore calls for two pairs of theoretical lenses: firstly, an approach focused on a 'closed' or 'conservative' form of epideictic rhetoric that celebrates existing values;[8] and secondly, an approach focused on an 'open' or 'radical' epideictic rhetoric that introduces new and visionary values.[9] The latter may potentially change the *doxai* and thus generate action on a par with deliberative, or 'legislative', rhetoric.[10] We can see this in *La clemenza di Tito* through obvious changes in the depiction of the relationship between the ruler and the people; and through this we may recognise an underlying attempt to make the receivers favourably disposed to absolutism while reducing the power of possible counterarguments inspired by the Revolution.

Theatrum mundi and *fraternité*

Let us look at Image 5.1, a print by I. C. Berndt, 'Vivat Leopoldus Secundus'. This was made for Leopold's Frankfurt coronation, as Holy Roman emperor, and shares some features with the Mozart/Mazzolà *La clemenza di Tito*, which was created for one of his later coronations.

Seventeenth-century scholars will recognise in the engraving a series of allegories and *topoi* linked to the old emblematic language of the courtly arts. Observe Leopold II—his central placement and majestic appearance, his crown, robe and sceptre, and his imperious

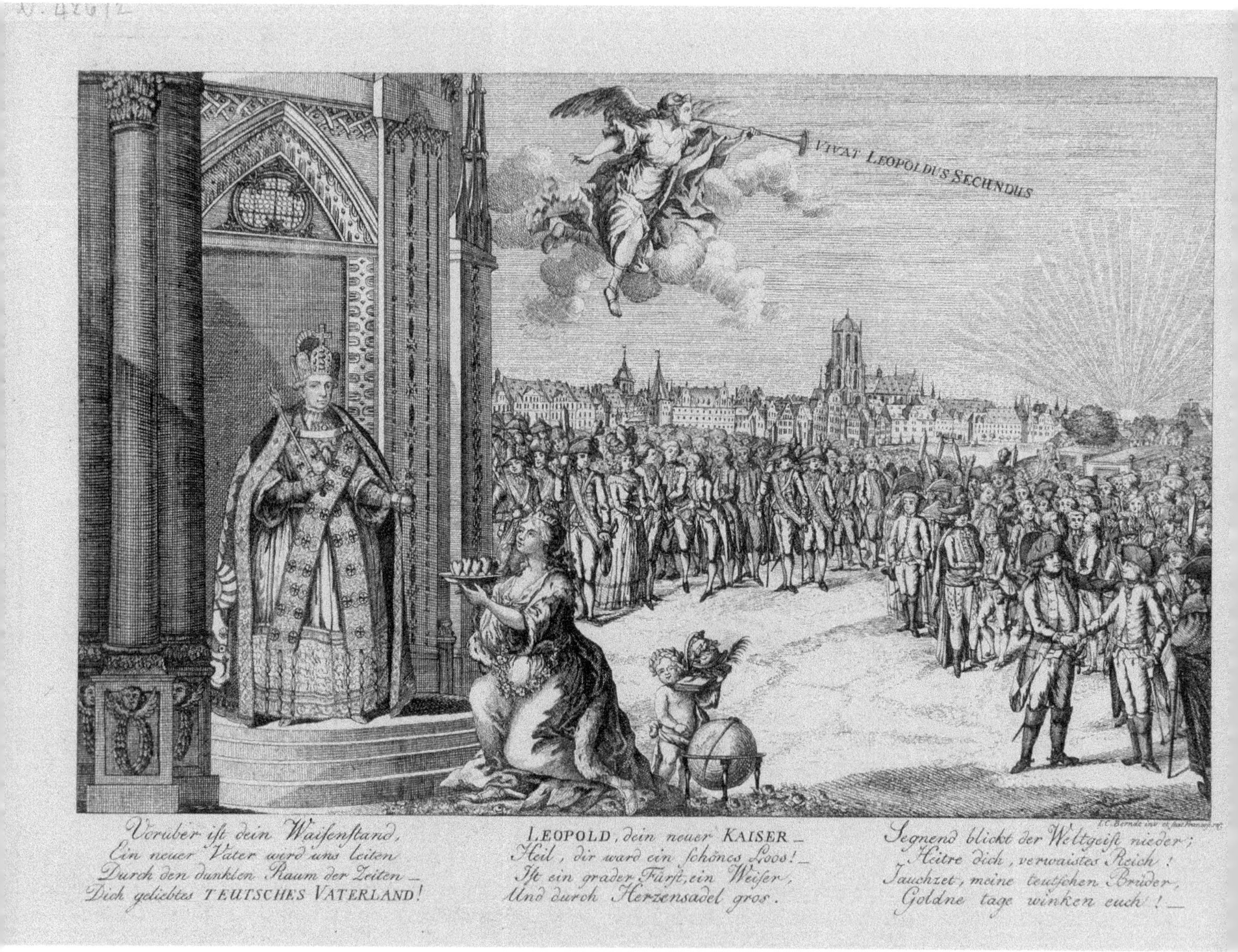
VIVAT LEOPOLDUS SECUNDUS
Vorüber ist dein Waisenstand,
Ein neuer Vater wird uns leiten
Durch den dunklen Raum der Zeiten –
Dich geliebtes TEUTSCHES VATERLAND!
LEOPOLD, dein neuer KAISER –
Heil, dir ward ein schönes Loos! –
Ist ein grader Fürst, ein Weiser,
Und durch Herzensadel gros.
Segnend blickt der Weltgeist nieder;
Heitre dich, verwaistes Reich!
Jauchzet, meine teutschen Brüder,
Goldne tage winken euch! –

Image 5.1. 'Vivat Leopoldus Secundus', coronation of Emperor Leopold II. Engraving by I. C. Berndt, 1790. Reproduced with kind permission from the copyright owner/holder, the Historisches Museum Frankfurt, N42672. On permanent loan from the Städel Museum Frankfurt. Photo: Horst Ziegenfusz. Licence: CC BY-NC-ND 4.0 International use.

and dignified body language—as he receives the hearts of the German people. Germany is represented allegorically as a beautiful young woman. The emperor is placed four steps above the other figures on the print, in front of a heavily ornamented portal framed by columns. This visual divide enhances the political symbolism, as the sovereign appears to be standing on his own platform or stage. The magnificent tableau is an example of the *theatrum mundi* (the world as a stage), understood here as the allegorical staging of a ceremonial event in the manner of a theatrical spectacle. Note also the winged figure of Fame, glorifying the emperor with her trumpet. She is surrounded by clouds, as if the *dea ex machina* of a courtly stage, and turned towards the sun as a metaphor for the absolute ruler.

Some features, however, are not consistent with Baroque *decorum*, unsurprisingly as the print was made shortly after the French Revolution. Observe the people. On the one hand, the populace resembles an audience watching a theatrical performance. On the other hand, in contradiction to the expected *theatrum mundi topos*, the two men in the lower right corner are more focused on each other than on the emperor. They shake hands, which is a gestural expression implying fellowship, and may refer to one of the ideals of the French Revolution, *fraternité*. This important ethical comment, pointing towards enlightened absolutism, depicts the experience of the receivers within the picture itself.[11] It is possible to interpret the populace as a visual expression of the *second persona*, or *implied audience* of the discourse, which, according to Edwin Black, is a synecdochic sign of the rhetorician's own point of view.[12] In other words, the crowd shows us how Berndt intends the viewers of the print to relate specifically to the coronation of Leopold as Holy Roman emperor, and more broadly to absolutism as a social structure. Berndt is suggesting that the Revolution does not have the exclusive rights to the moral and educational ideals of the Enlightenment: if the absolute monarch is enlightened and virtuous, his subjects will be met with kindness and hence thrive as free citizens within his monarchy. In other words, they have no need for a revolution.

The Coronation Opera

Mozart's opera *La clemenza di Tito* represents a dialogue between the old and the new. Not unlike the print, it contains several ritualistic elements that are typical of the emblematic aesthetic of the Baroque. These are indicative of a conservative epideictic rhetoric and continue a long tradition within courtly culture of celebrating and preserving the established order. For example, the overture, in C major, which has the form of a sonata, contains both conservative and radical epideictic features. It opens with a majestic fanfare based on a rising triad with a characteristic dotted rhythm, played by wind and timpani, which is a musical *topos* linking the opera directly to the ceremonial context and that of the surrounding court culture. It is pompous. By contrast, the secondary theme in G major has a lyrical character that seems to evoke the virtue of clemency (*clemenza*), in the sense of compassion.[13] As such it can be seen to represent modern civic culture, hence to function as a radical epideictic element of the overture.

In the recapitulation Mozart ignores the conventional use of repeating the exposition themes, instead reversing the order and beginning the recapitulation with the secondary theme ('civic culture'), and ending with the pompous repeated fanfare ('court culture'). Since such a thematic reversal is rare in Mozart's recapitulations, scholars have suggested that it was due to compositional haste,[14] supported by sources that show that Mozart was under time pressure, and that the overture was one of the last things he wrote (see Chapter I Chronology and II Documents 12, 17, 21 and 22). The case is argued further that by switching the two themes Mozart kept new, transitional material to a minimum, and this may have saved him time and energy. However, I prefer to think that Mozart deliberately composed the overture this way to enhance its emblematic character. By positioning the 'civic' theme at the beginning of the recapitulation, it thus occupies a central position in the overall structure of the overture, which now displays a more traditional Baroque symmetry, with the 'courtly' fanfare serving as a frame repetition or *symploce*. In other words, Mozart chose to adapt the customary and anticipated musical form to its ceremonial context.

The *symploce* frame is used several times in *La clemenza di Tito*, as a means of creating *amplification* to intensify and expand emblematic effects, for example, in other ceremonial numbers, such as the marches and choral eulogies. Mozart also uses *symploce* to characterise allegorical figures in the opera, while other dramatic and musical features reflect enlightened ideals, such as simplicity, naturalness and sensibility, corresponding to the gestural indicator of *fraternité* on Berndt's print.

Rhetoric and Aesthetics

My approach to *La clemenza di Tito* is inspired by the interpretations of intentionality and the dialogic developed within New Rhetoric. I regard Mozart's *opere serie* as sites of transition in which rhetorical and performative musical factors on the one hand, and aesthetic and autonomous factors on the other affect each other reciprocally. They colour each other while enhancing characteristic features of each other's respective ontologies. Though the following concepts have been juxtaposed visually, I do not conceive of them as antitheses, but rather as dynamic and changeable relationships engaging in a dialogue.

Rhetoric	Aesthetics
Mimesis/Imitation	Musical autonomy
Performance	Work
Allegory	Individuality
Affect	*Empfindsamkeit*
Court culture	Civic culture

The aesthetic discourse in the second half of the eighteenth century is often presented as an antithesis, or absolute contrast, to rhetoric, and for good historical reasons. Art is perceived as an end itself and as an independent form of expression. It apparently disengages itself from any rhetorical context, and from one of the central concepts within rhetorical theory, i.e. *persuasion*, which points to the participatory aspects of communication. Many aestheticians at the time therefore rejected rhetoric as a matter of course. Immanuel Kant set a trend when he compared rhetoric unfavourably to poetry in his *Critik der Urtheilskraft [Critique of Judgement]* (1790). Defining poetry as the 'free play of the imagination', in which everything is honest and sincere, he associated rhetoric with the weaker sides of humanity, and hence there was no reason to concern oneself with it.[15] The nineteenth and the first half of the twentieth centuries became dark ages in the history of rhetoric: a period when it almost disappeared as an academic discipline and as a normative theory among artists and scholars.

Although aestheticians of the period rejected rhetoric, however, there are multiple proofs that rhetoric remained very much alive, albeit *incognito*. There are numerous examples in Mozart's operas, where rhetoric has many faces, and is used in very different ways, frequently in conjunction with factors that represent the new aesthetic ideals.

Opera seria and the *da capo* aria

In *Idomeneo* (1781) and *La clemenza di Tito* the emblematic aesthetic of early eighteenth-century *opera seria* interacts with the new Rousseauesque aesthetic, musically as well as dramatically. As a result, the notation in Mozart's score acquires an authority over the performing singers and musicians, which the musical 'work' did not have earlier in the century.[16] We see this most clearly in the contrast between the older *da capo* aria form, which is so characteristic of traditional *opera seria*, and in which the focus was on the performers' vocal improvisation, and the newer aria forms developed by Mozart for purposes of characterisation. With these forms he distinguishes between characters with an allegorical function and characters that reflect the modern ideals of simplicity, sensibility and naturalness.

In the traditional *da capo* aria, the singers were co-creators on an equal standing with the composer, not merely interpreters of his intentions. It was through the performers' vocal and gestural dialogue with the listeners that the character acquired ethos, intentionality and dramatic allure on stage. The demands on the voice were therefore considerable. Apart from possessing vocal beauty, timbre, range, stability, evenness and mobility, which allowed the voice to perform fast runs and improvised cadenzas easily, the singer was required to characterise very different emotions vocally.

The dramatic justification of the *da capo* aria lay specifically in its ability to encapsulate and enhance an affect through repetition. This works because the exterior dramatic narrative is interrupted while the aria is heard, and we experience a shift to an interior lyrical level as the singing character discloses his or her inner affect to the listeners.

A hymn from 1765 by the Danish poet-bishop Hans Adolph Brorson exemplifies this. [The first stanza is given as the dedication to this volume. Eds.] Written in ABA form similar to the *da capo* aria, in translation it reads:

> Here be silent, here be patient,
> Here be patient, O fragile heart!
> Sure of obtaining, just by remaining,
> Just by remaining, our spring thou art.
> Here be silent, here be patient,
> Here be patient, O fragile heart!

Notice how the two opening verses frame the stanza. This repetitive structure (*symploce*) invites the person singing or listening to the hymn to concentrate less on the semantic content when the first lines are repeated. The words here tend to become affective music, transferring the listener's focus to the perception of the sound material. In addition, the fervour, melancholy and slow and slightly restrained rhythm of the poem are underscored by other repetitive structures within the stanza itself: *anaphora* ('here be, here be') and *epanastrophe* ('here be patient, here be patient').

Framed by the conventional repetition, the *da capo* aria acquires its own musical time, its effect depending on the performative dialogue with the listeners, which unfolds here and now in the temporal and oral space of the theatre.[17] In the eighteenth century, the *da capo* section and its vocal improvisations were regarded as the culmination of the aria, which the listeners awaited eagerly, and it was on the basis of the vocal performance that the operatic character finally took shape in their perception,[18] the complete character emerging from the interplay of the affects of the various arias.[19]

We know that Mozart appreciated the Italian vocal tradition, and that he normally only wrote his arias after hearing the voices of the selected singers, which enabled him to shape the music to their advantage (compare with Chapter 1, II Document 24). However, it is also characteristic that the harmonic progression and thematic development inscribed in the score is more important in Mozart's *opere serie* than in earlier traditional *opere serie*. In Mozart harmonic progression and thematic development form the basis of his sophisticated musical characterisation. Mozart uses the external form of the arias to create contrasts between his characters. Hence his choice of a conventional frame repetition (*symploce*, as in the traditional *da capo* aria) for all of Tito's arias, in contrast to the arias for Sesto and Vitellia, which tend to be more integrated into the dramatic action. In this way, Mozart differentiates between the allegorical (Tito) and the non-allegorical (Sesto and Vitellia). Tito's character revolves, musically as well as poetically, around moral values, or virtues, to use terminology made famous by Aristotle:

> We will next speak of virtue and vice, of the noble and the disgraceful, since they constitute the aim of one who praises and of one who blames; for, when speaking of these, we shall incidentally bring to light the means of making us appear of such and such a character, which, as we have said, is a second method of proof; for it is by the same means that we shall be able to inspire confidence in ourselves or others in regard to virtue.[20]

From an epideictic perspective, the main purpose of *La clemenza di Tito* is the creation of an aesthetic vision that introduces an enlightened interpretation of the virtue of clemency into the absolutistic context. Clemency, in the sense of compassion, is embodied in the title role above all, the opera's construction of Tito's ethos emerging as its most open epideictic feature. Indeed, as Gerard Hauser and Cynthia Sheard have both pointed out, epideictic rhetoric may not only celebrate orthodoxy, but may also anticipate political rhetoric by reshaping our values.[21] By integrating the modern ideals of the late eighteenth century, the radical representation of the emperor potentially changes the *doxai* of court culture and attracts broad support for enlightened absolutism as a social structure. Demonstrating the ability to forgive, and setting his own needs aside to accommodate his subjects, Tito is an *enlightened* ruler, who is both morally irreproachable and sensitive. His enlightened virtue is particularly apparent from his interaction with his people on stage, their musical and theatrical representation emerging as an implied audience, similar to the audience in Berndt's print. By forgiving and preserving his subjects, the enlightened ruler allows them to become enlightened themselves.

The Representation of Clemency

The virtue of clemency is represented on many levels in *La clemenza di Tito*, allowing the audience to consider the moral dilemma of the drama on an intellectual level while at the same time perceiving the clemency, or compassion, itself with eyes and ears. In the opera, it is portrayed as a dramatic character, as a pattern of action and as a musical idiom. We see the emperor declining the proposal to have a temple built in his honour, suggesting rather that the gold is used to support the victims of Vesuvius's eruption. And, even though he has offered to marry Servilia, he accepts that she prefers to marry his subject Annio. Furthermore, Mozart supports the emblematic dimensions of the drama by providing Tito with three arias that are all of *mezzo carattere*, i.e. in an intermediate style in terms of melody, harmony and tempo, which can be interpreted as 'clement' or 'benevolent'.[22] All three are given a regular form with a relatively simple tonal structure. Both arias 6. 'Del più sublime soglio' and 20. 'Se all'impero, amici Dei' follow an ABA structure, while aria 8. 'Ah, se fosse intorno al trono' has a bipartite form, the second part clearly functioning as a recapitulation. The reliance on repetition, which encapsulates the emotion, bestows on all three arias a distinctly emblematic quality, and explains why their character seems so similar—they enhance each other as a kind of *amplification*. This is especially the case with Tito's last aria 20. 'Se all'impero, amici Dei', in which he announces that he wants to rule on the basis of love, not fear. In some ways, this aria resembles an old-fashioned *da capo* aria with three sections (allegro–andantino–allegro), the central section providing affective contrast with its slow tempo and by approaching several minor keys, while the repetition of the A section has a hint of *bravura* with its demanding coloraturas and runs. However, the aria's thematic and tonal development points towards the modern sonata form, the central section recalling the development section, and the *da capo* section, featuring a tonal equalisation of the primary and secondary themes, recalling the recapitulation. Here, too, in other words, we can observe the interaction between Baroque and Enlightenment.

My reading of *La clemenza di Tito* continues in the tradition of opera scholars such as Reinhard Strohm, Ellen Rosand and Martha Feldman, all of whom have contributed to the re-evaluation of the long-reviled genre of *opera seria*. As I have tried to show, epideictic rhetoric may help us understand the peculiar ontology of court opera, which is so closely connected to its emblematic function, and political and cultural framework. In the late eighteenth century rhetoric was still an essential part of the *doxai* and cultural preconceptions, and hence epideictic rhetoric enables us to engage with the complex aesthetic, moral and philosophical layers of meaning contained within a work such as *La clemenza di Tito*, with its subtle interplay of the old and the new.

Translated and revised by Magnus Tessing Schneider.

Notes

1. Earlier versions of this article have been published in Danish, both under the title 'Mozart som epideiktisk retor: Dydens og lastens repræsentation i *Titus*'. The first was published in *Musikteater: Opførelse, praksis, publikum: Papers fra kollokvium, december 2003*, ed. Michael Eigtved (Copenhagen: University of Copenhagen, 2004), 8–23; and the second in *Rhetorica Scandinavica*, 36 (2005), 25–37.

2. Aristotle, *Aristotle on Rhetoric: A Theory of Civic Discourse*, ed. and trans. George Kennedy (Oxford: Oxford University Press, 1991), Book 1, IV–V. See also Jette Barnholdt Hansen, 'Values on Stage: Epideictic Rhetoric as a Theoretical Approach to Music Theatre', in *Stage / Page / Play: Interdisciplinary Approaches to Theatre and Theatricality*, eds. Ulla Kallenbach and Anna Lawaetz (Copenhagen: Multivers, 2016), 211–21.

3. I use the Greek concept *doxa* ('opinion') as a general expression of a person's entire conscious worldview and code of opinion, which s/he professes and shares with other people within a particular culture. See Lawrence W. Rosenfield, 'An Autopsy of the Rhetorical Tradition', *The Prospect of Rhetoric*, ed. Lloyd F. Bitzer and Edwin Black (Englewood Cliffs NJ: Prentice-Hall, 1971), 64–77, esp. 65; and also Mats Rosengren, *Doxologi: En essä om kunskap* (Åstorp: Rhetor förlag, 2003).

4. Sullivan associates the concept 'consubstantial space' with the ethos of the epideictic rhetorician: 'It is the experience that occurs during true

epideictic discourse when rhetor and audience enter the timeless, consubstantial space carved out by their mutual contemplation of reality.' See Dale L. Sullivan, 'The Ethos of Epideictic Encounter', *Philosophy and Rhetoric*, XXVI/2 (1993), 113–33, esp. 128.

5. Cf. Sullivan, 'Ethos of Epideictic Encounter'.

6. See also the chapter by John A. Rice in this volume.

7. See John A. Rice, *W. A. Mozart:* La clemenza di Tito (Cambridge: Cambridge University Press, 1991), 1–5; see also his chapter in this volume, Chapter 2, 'Operatic culture at the Court of Leopold II and Mozart's *La clemenza di Tito*'.

8. See e.g. Chaim Perelman and Lucie Olbrecht-Tyteca, *The New Rhetoric* [1969], trans. John Wilkinson and Purcell Weaver (Notre Dame Ind.: University of Notre Dame Press, 1971), 50, in which the aim of epideictic rhetoric is described as the preservation of the values of a particular culture, and Sullivan, 'Ethos of Epideictic Encounter' (1993), 117: 'epideictic rhetoric is the rhetoric of orthodoxies […], its purpose being the creation and maintenance of orthodox opinions within a culture or subculture'.

9. See Cynthia Miecznikowski Sheard, 'The Public Value of Epideictic Rhetoric', *College English*, LVIII/7 (1996), 784–91.

10. See e.g. Sheard, 'The Public Value' (1996), 784: 'The Deliberative and Imaginative Functions of Epideictic'.

11. Here I rely on the definition of ethos in James C. McCroskey, *An Introduction to Rhetorical Communication* [1968] (Boston: Allyn & Bacon, 1997), 87: 'Ethos is the attitude toward a source of communication held at a given time by a receiver'.

12. Edwin Black, 'The Second Persona', *The Quarterly Journal of Speech*, LVI/2 (1970), 109–48.

13. On the relation between clemency and pity, see Magnus Tessing Schneider's chapter in this volume, Chapter 3 'From Metastasio to Mazzolà: Clemency and Pity in *La clemenza di Tito*'.

14. See Rice, *La clemenza* (1991), 69.

15. *Critik der Urtheilskraft* (Berlin, Libau: Lagarde und Friederich, 1790). See Paul Guyer, *Values of Beauty* (Cambridge: Cambridge University Press, 2005).

16. Cf. Jette Barnholdt Hansen, '*Dramma per musica* eller *musica per dramma*? Mozarts *Idomeneo* – en *seria* som musikalsk opus', *Dansk årbog for musikforskning*, XXX (2002), 51–73.

17. See Jette Barnholdt Hansen, 'From Invention to Interpretation: The Prologues of the First Court Operas Where Oral and Written Cultures Meet', *The Journal of Musicology*, XX/4 (2003), 556–596, for an analysis of the relation between orality and literacy in the early court operas.

18. Here I am inspired by the emphasis on the receivers' perception of ethos in McCroskey, *An Introduction* ([1968] 1997).

19. Carl Dahlhaus, 'What is Musical Drama?', *Cambridge Opera Journal*, I/2 (1989), 95–111.

20. Aristotle, *The 'Art' of Rhetoric*, trans. John Henry Freese (Cambridge Mass.: Harvard University Press, 1926), Book 1, Chapter IX, 1.

21. Gerard A. Hauser, 'Aristotle on Epideictic: The Formation of Public Morality', *Rhetoric Society Quarterly*, XXIX/1 (1999), 5–23; and Sheard, 'The Public Value' (1996).

22. In his description of Italian aria types, John Brown describes the *aria di mezzo carattere* as 'serious' and 'pleasing'. John Brown, *Letters upon the Poetry and Music of the Italian Opera Addressed to a Friend* (Edinburgh: Belle and Bradfute, 1789), 40.

6 Stage Directions and Set Design in Mozart's *La clemenza di Tito*

Sergio Durante

In this essay I will examine the mise-en-scène of the 1791 Prague production of *La clemenza di Tito*. Beginning with an examination of the sets and their importance for understanding Mozart's score and his use of the stage, I will then apply the results to a broader discussion of aesthetic dimensions within the opera.[1]

The Stage Sets and their Importance in Prague 1791

It has long been known that the main set designer for the Prague production of *La clemenza di Tito* was the Milanese Pietro Travaglia, a pupil of the famous Galliari brothers, Bernardino and Fabrizio (see Chapter 1, II Document 7). The most important source documenting Travaglia's work is the so-called 'Travaglia sketchbook', preserved today in the National Széchényi Library in Budapest. The book, which had been in private possession before it arrived at the Budapest library in the 1950s, includes a number of scenographic sketches at different stages of completion and many miscellaneous notes.[2] It was a main source for Horányi Mátyás in his book devoted to the theatrical productions of the court of Esterháza.[3] Travaglia, like Joseph Haydn, spent most of his professional life at Esterháza, until the death of Prince Nikolaus I in 1790, when the musical activities at the court were scaled down or discontinued altogether:[4] circumstances which

---

How to cite this book chapter:
Durante, S. 2018. Stage Directions and Set Design in Mozart's *La clemenza di Tito*. In: Tessing Schneider, M. and Tatlow, R. (eds.) *Mozart's* La clemenza di Tito: *A Reappraisal*. Pp. 134–158. Stockholm: Stockholm University Press. DOI: https://doi.org/10.16993/ban.f. License: CC-BY NC-ND 4.0

apparently allowed Travaglia to accept a commission for the 1791 Prague production.[5]

The last two of the twelve sketches in part one of Travaglia's sketchbook can be attributed to the production of *La clemenza di Tito*. Horányi published only one of the two, while the second, which is the one more obviously related to Mozart's opera, remained unpublished until 1994. Travaglia's handwritten caption beneath the sketch reads: 'Sala ter[r]ena destinata per le pubbliche udienze' ('A ground-floor hall intended for public hearings'), which mirrors the caption in the libretto of *La clemenza di Tito* (Act II, scene 5): 'Gran sala destinata alle pubbliche udienze. Trono, sedia, e tavolino' ('A grand hall intended for public hearings. A throne, a chair and a table').[6] This is particularly significant since the libretto caption is not taken from Pietro Metastasio's original: it is unique to the Prague production.[7] Caterino Mazzolà's decision (and/or conceivably Mozart's) to introduce a choral piece at this point, the aria with chorus 11. 'Ah grazie si rendano', called for a change of Metastasio's scenic layout, with its 'closed chamber'. Travaglia's caption marks a contrast between the restricted, private space of Metastasio's original and the grander ceremonial space that will host a crowd scene.

It is necessary to understand the function of such stage designs here. According to the renowned historian of scenography, Mercedes Viale Ferrero, the stage designs in Travaglia's sketchbook are 'disegni esecutivi', i.e. designs made for the scene painters, who would have used them as guidelines when creating the sets, consisting of the *quinte* (flat wings), the *principali* (backdrops), and the *carri* ('carriages', solid set pieces on which it was possible to walk when needed), which together created the illusion of a three-dimensional space. Therefore, Travaglia's images should not be regarded as reproductions documenting the appearance of the actual sets, but rather as directions for the painters. A degree of imagination is required to guess what the scene painting might have actually looked like, because many details are only alluded to, and because modifications would have been made as the production evolved. Many details of the designs are lightly sketched, responsibility for their definition being left to the painters, who usually worked under the supervision of the set designer. While the designs give us a fairly good idea of the intended architectural style, leaning away from the decorative Baroque towards the clarity of neoclassicism, they hold important implications and suggestions about the use of the stage by the actor-singers, and especially by the chorus. Image 6.1 shows Travaglia's sketch for the 'great hall for public hearings' in Act II.

The sketch represents only the left half of a symmetric set. It would not have made sense for Travaglia to duplicate the right side of his design: though easily accomplished today by a computer, it would have been a laborious operation at the time. The complete set would have looked more or less like the reconstruction in Image 6.2, with the appropriate correction of the shadows, which were themselves usually painted on the backdrops.

This image contains the directions for two successive sets, one using approximately half of the stage space towards the proscenium, while the other is a 'long set', occupying the whole stage. The 'long' set would have been used for the second finale, discussed in greater detail below, and therefore, only the front part of the image corresponds to the 'great hall', which uses only half of the stage space. Of course, our imaginations should add a throne in the middle, and, probably laterally, a writing table. The two arches must have been used for the entries and exits of the actors from different sides. While the 'great hall for public hearings' was seen, the rear section of the set must have been curtained off or hidden from view by means of an intermediate backdrop.

Image 6.1. P. Travaglia, *Sala ter[r]ena destinata per le pubbliche udienze*, Pietro Travaglia's Sketchbook, f. 11. Published with permission from the copyright owner/holder, the Collection of Theatre History at the Hungarian National Széchényi Library, Budapest. Access. Nr. 1955/9645. Licence: CC BY-NC-ND 4.0 International use.

Sala Terrena destinata per le Publiche Udienze

Image 6.2. Symmetrical duplication of the design in Image 1 (with corrected shadows). Designed by Paolo Kirschner and Silvia Tinazzo. Reproduced with permission from the copyright owners/holders, Paolo Kirschner and Silvia Tinazzo. Licence: CC BY-NC-ND 4.0 International use.

According to scenography historian Maria Ida Biggi, the technical realisation of the great hall might have included two wings and a single pierced backdrop (*principale traforato*) with *trompe l'oeil* effect, as outlined in Image 6.3.

The next set would have been revealed by raising the main backdrop, and the intermediate element that obscures the view of the rear stage. This corresponds to the final scene change in the opera: Act II, scene 14. Clearly intending a *coup de théâtre*, Mozart devised a musical transition for this, from the end of Vitellia's rondo 23. 'Non più di fiori' into the magnificent chorus 24. 'Che del ciel, che degli Dei'. The caption in the libretto introducing the scene reads:

Image 6.3. Hypothetical realisation of the scenographic elements. Designed by Paolo Kirschner and Silvia Tinazzo. Reproduced with permission from the copyright owners/holders, Paolo Kirschner and Silvia Tinazzo. Licence: CC BY-NC-ND 4.0 International use.

> Luogo magnifico, che introduce a vasto anfiteatro, da cui per diversi archi scuopresi la parte interna. Si vedranno già nell'arena i complici della congiura condannati alle fiere.[8]
>
> (A magnificent site leading into a vast amphitheatre the interior of which can be seen through a number of arches. The conspiratorial accomplices, condemned to the beasts, are already seen standing in the arena.)

Image 6.4 magnifies the rear section of the sketch, revealing the 'magnificent site' and the amphitheatre, which are only lightly defined in the design.

Image 6.4. Detail of the set design, showing the rear of the stage. Designed by Paolo Kirschner and Silvia Tinazzo. Reproduced with permission from the copyright owners/holders Paolo Kirschner and Silvia Tinazzo. Licence: CC BY-NC-ND 4.0 International use.

The amphitheatre in particular is only faintly suggested, meant to be completed by the painters. This scene might have been realised with two wings in the front (possibly keeping those from the previous set), a pierced backdrop in the middle (through which the conspirators may be seen), and a *trompe l'oeil* backdrop in the back. Image 6.5 suggests how this may have been designed.[9]

Image 6.5. Hypothetical realisation of the long set. Designed by Paolo Kirschner and Silvia Tinazzo. Reproduced with permission from the copyright owners/holders, Paolo Kirschner and Silvia Tinazzo. Licence: CC BY-NC-ND 4.0 International use.

This conjectural reconstruction is not without its problems. There is a clear imbalance between the lower space of the set and the empty upper space. Moreover, the illusionistic scenography had to accommodate the actual proportions of the human bodies on stage. It is conceivable therefore that the actual sets were larger in proportion. It is also possible that the upper space was re-balanced through the introduction of decorative elements. Interestingly, Travaglia's solution recalls that of his teachers, Bernardino and Fabrizio Galliari, for *Enea nel Lazio*, which had been produced in Turin thirty years earlier in 1760.[10]

We can never be certain how the stage really looked, but the evidence shows that there was a direct functional relationship between the organisation of the stage and the character of the music. The change of sets between the more restricted half-stage of the 'hall for public hearings' and the full stage of the 'magnificent site leading into a vast amphitheatre', for example, perfectly matches the uninterrupted transition from Vitellia's exit solo, rondo 23., to chorus 24. That is, from the stylised depiction of individualised self-awareness and repentance, to the collective celebration of the Handelian-style chorus, which takes place within a monumental public space. The libretto prescribes what was to happen on stage regarding the movement of soloists, choristers and extras, in words that are almost exactly similar to the ones in the original Metastasio:

> Nel tempo, che si canta il coro, preceduto da' littori, circondato da' senatori, e patrizi romani, e seguito da' pretoriani esce Tito, e dopo Annio, e Servilia da diverse parti.[11]
>
> (While the chorus is sung, Titus enters, preceded by the lictors, surrounded by senators and Roman patricians, and followed by praetorians; later, Annius and Servilia enter from different sides.)

Clearly, in this crucial passage the *coup de théâtre* relies as much on the 'sublimity' of the music as on the visual apparatus.

The conditions of the venue of the original production have a bearing on the next scene. Since 1791, Count Nostitz's National Theatre (the Estates Theatre today) has undergone various renovations, details of which are only partly known to us. Documents from about the same time as the production give an indication of the disposition of the spaces. Prints by Philipp and Franz Heger show the theatre as being very large, and that the depth of the stage was similar to that of the auditorium.[12] Image 6.6, the engraving by Johann Berka after plans by Philipp and Franz Heger, shows that the stage had seven pairs of wings and a back extension.

Stage Directions and Set Design in Mozart's *La clemenza di Tito*

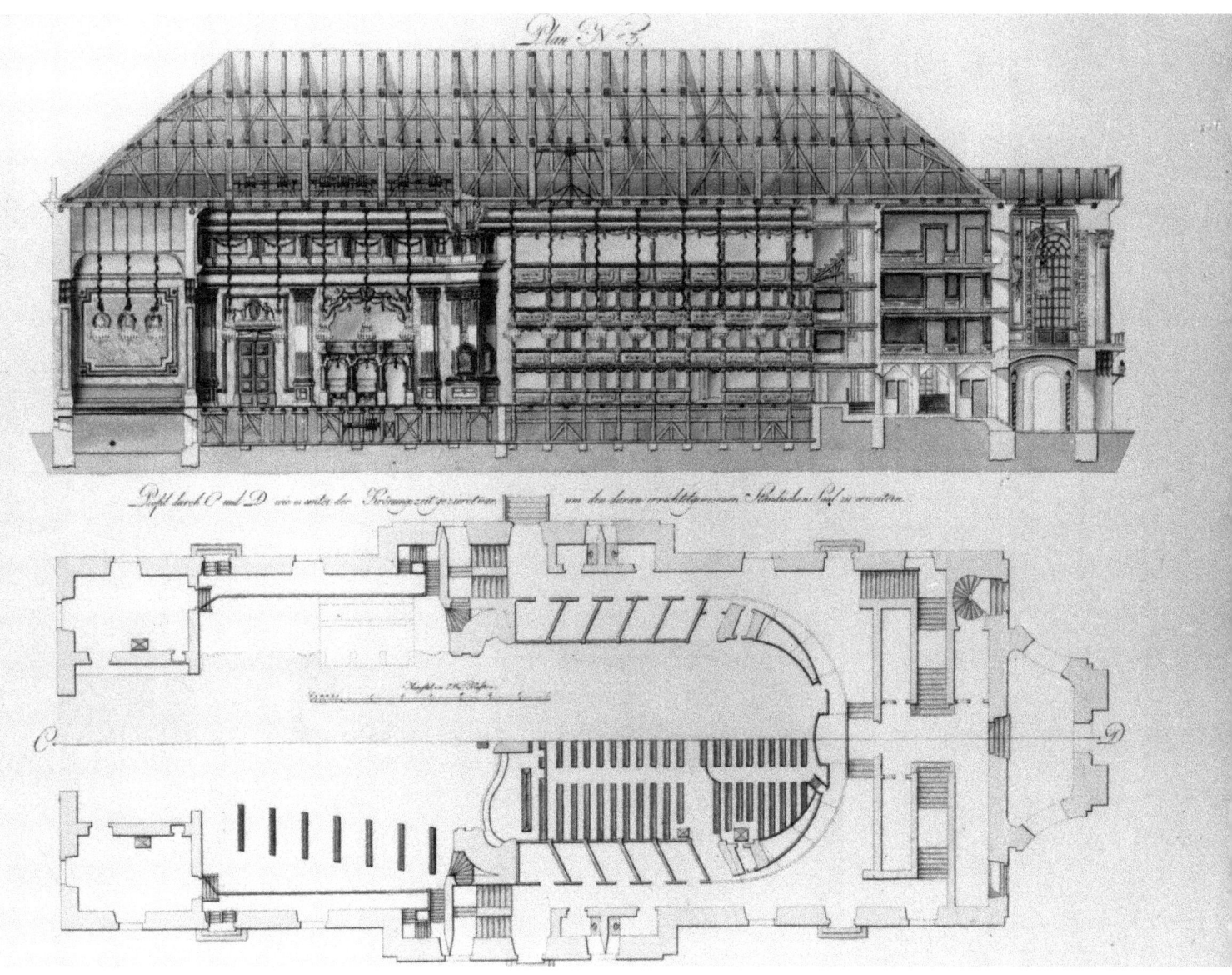

Image 6.6. Section and plan of Count Nostitz's National Theatre, Prague, 1793. Copper plate engraving by Johann Berka, after Philipp and Franz Heger. Reproduced with permission from the copyright owner/holder, AKG images / TT Nyhetsbyrån. Licence: CC BY-NC-ND 4.0 International use.

On 12 September 1791, a week after the premiere of *La clemenza di Tito*, a 'coronation ball' was held in the theatre, which was transformed into a single ballroom of huge dimensions—or at least it was intended to appear so for the occasion, the ball probably being a socially more important event than the coronation opera. The decoration of the space is documented both on the prints of the Hegers and on Caspar Pluth's re-elaborated water-colour version of the print, which includes human images.[13]

Anyone visiting the cosy Estates Theatre in Prague today will realise that the purpose of the prints was to amplify the true dimensions of the space, to enhance the sense of *grandeur* associated with the social and political import of the coronation festivities. Franz Alexander von Kleist—who was one of the few commentators who reported positively on the premiere of *La clemenza di Tito* (see Chapter 1, II Document 13)—also gives a description of both the coronation ball and the lavish ornamentation of the space.[14]

This historical context explains to some degree why the impresario Domenico Guardasoni was faced with extra costs for the new stage sets for *La clemenza di Tito,* and why these expenses were eventually reimbursed (see Chapter 1, II Documents 2 and 16). The show had to meet the expectations of the occasion, whatever the cost.

Travaglia's second design is linked to the first one because of its contiguous position and its decorative detail, the bucranes and metopes being unique to the two designs within the sketchbook. Image 6.7 shows the second design, which is more problematic than the first one because it transmits two overlapping versions: one that is more 'finished', with a flat balcony, and a second one, which is more lightly drafted, with an arch and tympanum.

Image 6.7. P. Travaglia, [parte del foro romano (…)] Campidoglio. Pietro Travaglia's Sketchbook, f. 12. Published with permission from the copyright owners/holders the Collection of Theatre History at the Hungarian National Széchényi Library, Budapest. Access. Nr. 1955/9645. Licence: CC BY-NC-ND 4.0 International use.

Image 6.8. P. Travaglia, [parte del foro romano (…)] Campidoglio, symmetrically expanded. Designed by Paolo Kirschner and Silvia Tinazzo. Reproduced with permission from the copyright owners/holders Paolo Kirschner and Silvia Tinazzo. Licence: CC BY-NC-ND 4.0 International use.

While the implications of the two versions are much the same, I believe it was the second one that was actually realised in Prague, because it offers a better view of the rear space of the stage. This design corresponds to the setting described in the libretto at the beginning of Act I, scene 4, at Tito's first triumphal entry:

> Parte del Foro romano magnificamente adornato d'archi, obelischi, e trofei: in faccia aspetto esteriore del Campidoglio, e magnifica strada, per cui vi si ascende.

> (Part of the Roman Forum, magnificently adorned with arches, obelisks and trophies: opposite, an external view of the Capitol and of the magnificent pathway leading up to it.)

The complete image would have looked approximately as Image 6.8.

Image 6.9. Hypothetical realisation of the scenographic elements. Designed by Paolo Kirschner and Silvia Tinazzo. Reproduced with permission from the copyright owners/holders Paolo Kirschner and Silvia Tinazzo. Licence: CC BY-NC-ND 4.0 International use.

Image 6.9 suggests a possible technical realisation: the set might have included two wings (green), two three-dimensional movable elements and one walkable stairway (*carri*, in red), with a pierced main *trompe l'oeil* backdrop (in yellow, to be placed approximately at centre-stage). A second painted backdrop at the extreme rear of the stage would have shown the image of the Capitol (in light blue, including an enhanced design of the Capitol by Silvia Tinazzo).

The representation of the Capitol must have been a compromise between historical imagination and spectacular requirements. Travaglia's rather rough sketch provides a degree of verisimilitude by including three elements: a steep hill, the pathway leading to it, and the temple, or temples, at the top. The painters' work would have provided a little more detail. Today we know more about the appearance of the first-century Capitol than our ancestors in the late eighteenth century. If Travaglia was concerned about faithfulness to reality, he is most likely to have drawn on representations of contemporary Rome.

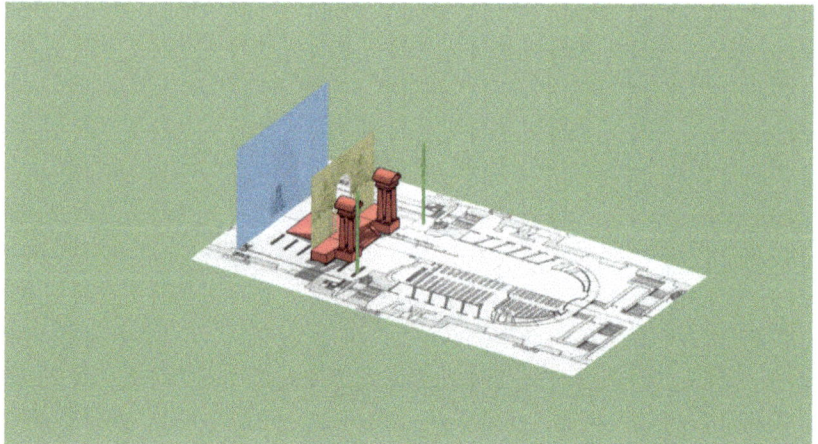

Image 6.10. A rendering of the scenographic elements placed above the map of Count Nostitz's National Theatre. Designed by Paolo Kirschner and Silvia Tinazzo. Reproduced with permission from the copyright owners/holders Paolo Kirschner and Silvia Tinazzo. Licence: CC BY-NC-ND 4.0 International use.

Image 6.10 shows a conjectural 3D rendering of the set, placed above the map of the National Theatre in axonometric projection.

If this is how the stage was laid out (not taking the decorative details into account), we may now ask what the public actually saw on stage in the famous Act I finale. The question does not concern the movements of the principal characters, which are crystal clear from the libretto, but rather the movements of the chorus, and two intriguing captions by Mozart that refer to two different placements of the choristers.

The chorus participates twice in the quintet with chorus 12. 'Deh conservate, oh Dei': the first time at bar 47, when screams are heard ('Ah'), at which point Mozart indicates 'Coro in distanza' ('chorus at a distance'); and later, after Sesto has announced the death of Tito, when the chorus participates in the lament for the emperor (Andante), at which point he writes 'Coro in lontananza'—a different expression, which also means 'chorus at a distance', however.

This is indeed puzzling, as it also seems to have appeared to the editor of the opera's critical edition in the *Neue Mozart-Ausgabe*, who omitted this second indication from the text, as if it had been a mistake on Mozart's part. This editorial decision lacked the evidence of the stage designs, and so it was based on the possibly incorrect assumption that the indication 'in distanza' means that the chorus screams from behind the wings. Both from a dramatic and from a visual point of view, it would not be logical for the chorus to remain out of sight throughout the lament that closes the Act—the editor seems to have reasoned—and so Mozart's second indication must have been a mistake. Therefore it should be omitted.

And yet a different hypothesis may be drawn from the scenic layout suggested in Travaglia's sketchbook, with its distinction between a downstage and an upstage section, divided by the stairway and by the main pierced backdrop.

I do not believe that Mozart made a mistake, but that he intended the stage directions to indicate two different positions for the chorus. The first one suggests that the choristers and extras are placed in the upstage area, within the view of the audience and participating in the action—screaming, possibly running around ('Ah che tumulto orrendo!' ('What a frightful uproar!') Servilia exclaims in scene 12), and trying to extinguish the fire, which must have been ignited in the wings.[15] And the second one, which occurs during the Andante and after the fire has been extinguished, suggests that the chorus is further downstage though still 'in the distance' with respect to the solo singers, who are placed in front of the stairway and the colonnade.

If this is correct, it implies two significant deviations from the prevalent performing tradition: firstly, that the aural impact of the screams is more intense from the rear of the stage than from the wings,[16] and secondly, that the spectacularisation in visual terms is a *coup de théatre* not unlike the one in the second finale, although even more intense and exciting. While there is no definitive proof that this hypothesis reflects what was seen in Prague, it helps us interpret Mozart's indications and points to the importance of establishing a satisfactory coordination between theatre and music.[17]

A further under-investigated scenographical problem concerns the contribution of the second set designer, Johann Breysig, whom the Prague libretto credits with a 'fourth decoration' (see Chapter 1, II Document 7). It is difficult to make sense of this, however, so for our present purposes we may conclude that Travaglia's contribution to the production was the most crucial.

Staging and the Aesthetic of *La clemenza di Tito*

Before discussing the general aesthetic of *La clemenza di Tito*, we must ask: 'whose aesthetic'? The expression 'the aesthetic of *La clemenza di Tito*' appears to assign a compact and well-defined aesthetic integrity to the work itself, whether it is understood as an 'opus' in the classical nineteenth-century sense or as the composite result of the 1791 production. But first we must hypothetically account for a degree of indeterminacy, or even inner contradiction, within such an 'aesthetic' complex, whether it is to be regarded as the sum or stratification of different artistic stances, or as a number of different practical operations carried out by the composer (to whom we traditionally grant the most important position), the librettist (who possibly figured above the composer), the set designer, the costume designer, the singers, and so on. Secondly, the 'aesthetic' of the work is the result of an even broader social and cultural interplay, which suggests that the initial question should be rephrased as 'whose aesthetic for *La clemenza di Tito*?' And it is to this question that I hope to provide a concrete answer.

I would like to represent the aesthetic of *La clemenza di Tito* in the form of a Russian matryoshka doll, the innermost doll being enclosed numerous times by larger matryoshkas, each of which represents a historical time closer to the present.

The first matryoshka represents the culture which generated the concept and historical impersonations of *clementia* in the West—distant in time and yet an immediate ideological context for Metastasio's version of the ancient trope: Lucius Annaeus Seneca's *De clementia* (55–56 CE). This is the earliest theoretical source for the concept of clemency, considered the highest attribute of monarchic sovereignty. It was also the literary source for Pierre Corneille's tragedy *Cinna ou la Clémence d'Auguste* (1643), the immediate precedent of Metastasio's dramatic treatment of the concept in his *dramma per musica*.[18]

Even before the clemency of the ageing Augustus, or of the younger Titus Vespasian, became a subject for the stage, it served as a political justification for absolutism. The possibility of exerting clemency, i.e. of surpassing the law, gave tangible substance to the divine right of the kings because it made the sovereign similar to God. The benevolence of the sovereign, as manifested in his clemency, is a structural function of monarchy, and one of its strongest ideological pillars.

At the time of Metastasio and Mozart, clemency was especially associated with the 'Clementia austriaca' ('Austrian clemency'),[19] although it was applied to a broad array of monarchies. We should not be surprised, for example, that in 1807 Jerôme Bonaparte—a bourgeois king—was celebrated in Westphalia as a new Titus, with the music of Mozart's *La clemenza di Tito*.[20]

While *clementia* as a concept might be dismissed as an irrelevant ideological feature, I believe that it had assumed an aesthetic significance by Mozart's time, which was lost to dramatists and critics of later generations. This seems to have occurred not long after Mozart's death, when Friedrich Rochlitz (ca. 1809) wrote a German version of Metastasio's text in which Sesto is actually acquitted of his crime. Understandably, Otto Jahn criticised the drama in 1856–58 because he could see no reason for Tito's clemency:[21] an understanding of clemency as a deeply-rooted cultural structure is therefore an indispensable preliminary to the aesthetic appreciation of Mozart's opera.

The next matryoshka is Metastasio's *La clemenza di Tito* (1734), i.e. his dramatic text and the aesthetic stances on which his text is based. Harking back to Aristotle's *Poetics*, this kind of music theatre has been defined as 'neoclassical'. When compared to the pre-Arcadian operas, however, Metastasio's libretto represents only a partial rationalisation of the earlier dramatic type, retaining more than a few 'baroque' features, including a taste for relatively intricate plots. Metastasio's view of the solos (arias) as serving a function similar to the one of the chorus in classical drama, leads him to entrust the progress of the action to the recitatives, and to suspend it during the set-pieces that comment on and/or express sentimental states or values, as does—in Metastasio's view—the classical chorus. And finally, Metastasio, and Enlightenment-oriented dramatists in general, avoids any act of violence on stage.

These three points lead us directly to the next matryoshka, which is Mozart and the 1791 Prague production. When Mozart described his *La clemenza di Tito* as a 'vera opera' (see Chapter 1, II Document 6) he must have referred to the coherent complex of modifications imposed upon the Metastasian text, including the acceleration and simplification of the plot (with the omission of an entire subplot and the trimming of many of the recitatives), the reversal of the principle that associates dramatic action with recitatives (introducing a number of action-ensembles), and the spectacular representation of turmoil and fire on the Capitol: an episode which Metastasio represented merely through the intervention of messengers, but which Mozart made visible in Prague, with a staged action-finale. These alterations may be regarded as a significant stylistic progress towards the opera *der Zukunft*[22] and, in the case of the scenic spectacularisation and the expansion of the role of the chorus, as an inclusion of French-inspired elements. The clear striving for *Pracht, grandeur, sublimity*, had to come to terms with the space of Count Nostitz's National Theatre, however, which was anything but grand. In this way the Prague production—if not *La clemenza di Tito* altogether—marked a gap between artistic intention and historical achievement. Other aspects, both musical (such as the use of a castrato voice or the introduction of smaller arias for minor characters) and dramatic (the subject itself), were soon to fall out of fashion in accordance with the spirit of post-Revolutionary Europe.

Yet in today's cult for Mozart, the revised libretto is considered an 'improvement' upon Metastasio's original, though Mazzolà's version, from a purely technical perspective, has both advantages and drawbacks. For example, it is dramatically inconsistent that the subplot of Annio and Servilia ends in the first Act rather than in the second; and the reduction into two Acts, although masterly in many respects, implies a very different dramatic pace in the two parts, with a fast Act I and a much slower Act II. This does not even take minor narrative incongruences into account, furthermore, which are hardly noticed in today's productions.[23] Metastasio would almost certainly have found the visual rendering of the first Act finale—that we today, with good reason, consider a stroke of genius—unnecessary and unstylish.

The next matryoshka accounts for the original reception of *La clemenza di Tito*—a complex phenomenon that has been summarised elsewhere.[24] It is sufficient to recall here that the early reception was highly contradictory, and that the opera was equally praised and criticised by authoritative enthusiasts and detractors, which caused a great deal of critical confusion. For example, in 1802 Franz Horn went as far as to describe *La clemenza di Tito* as 'durchaus Romantisch',[25] and as late as in 1816 Heinrich Marschner wrote music to the libretto of *La clemenza di Tito* that he considered a model of Romanticism. But their idea of Romanticism was far from the mature theorisation established by August Schlegel in his 1808 *Vorlesungen über dramatische Kunst und Literatur*.[26] Both

Horn and Marschner (at least in his early years) refer back to the 1790s and to W. H. Wackenroder's essentialist and non-historicist idea that all music *per se* is intrinsically 'Romantic'. On the other hand, Schlegel develops a more mature and structured theory that connects any high aesthetic achievement to clearly defined historical and national roots, consequently rejecting the neo-Latin (and neo-classical) cultures (be they Italian or French) as models for an authentic Germanic art. It is on this ground particularly that a negative critical attitude towards a Metastasian operatic setting by a 'German' composer, blossomed and bore fruit, no doubt influencing Otto Jahn and the strongly negative image of *La clemenza di Tito* that he presented in his 1856–58 Mozart biography. Deeply rooted in nineteenth-century German national and bourgeois culture, such negative views were repeated and even intensified by Hermann Abert in his revision of Jahn's book from 1921. And these views, albeit not undisputed, have dominated until recent times, and even now they still find authoritative followers, such as Manfred Hermann Schmid, who in his recent guide to Mozart's operas excludes *La clemenza di Tito* from his list of the 'unsterbliche Werke' ('immortal works').[27]

The final matryoshka represents the more recent reception and stagings of *La clemenza di Tito,* which owe a great deal to the musicological reassessments from the second half of the twentieth century, spearheaded by Tomislav Volek's ground-breaking study, and possibly even more to the general reappraisal of eighteenth-century opera, beyond the confines of Mozart studies. *La clemenza di Tito* has made it back onto the stage, and each new production, according to the custom of modern directorial theatre, or *Regietheater*, represents a 'new interpretation'—not necessarily an intelligent one. From this point of view, we face not so much a new aesthetic for *La clemenza di Tito* as the diffraction of its aesthetic kernel in as many diverse inflections (or disfigurations) as there are productions and directors. Such multifariousness is characteristic of postmodern culture, where more or less anything can be sold and bought provided it has a good wrapping—a result of the lack of a prevailing aesthetic model.

More specifically, while I have seen numerous productions of *La clemenza di Tito*, few of which were convincing, I perceive a recurring problem that is caused by the idea of staging it in a quasi-neo-Baroque mid-eighteenth-century style, that emphasises elements of classical Metastasian *opera seria* rather than the forceful innovations introduced by Mozart and Mazzolà (and Travaglia for his part). Moreover, the loss of the original scenographic traditions, which are paramount in terms of the spectacularisation of *La Clemenza di Tito*, endangers the full appreciation of the opera's expressive potentials.

All things considered, this opera must be acknowledged both as an immortal masterpiece and as a problematic one. It encloses different stylistic layers that encourage different readings, and in some unfortunate cases, these confuse both directors and spectators alike. The best we can do as scholars is to try to grasp its theatrical potential, and promote a sensible understanding of the opera as a whole.

Notes

1. Much of the first part of this essay was published in Italian as 'Le scenografie di Pietro Travaglia per *La clemenza di Tito* (Praga, 1791): Problemi di identificazione ed implicazioni', *Mozart Jahrbuch* 1994, 157–169. Since then my work has been more widely known to international readership through John A. Rice's book *Mozart on the Stage* (Cambridge: Cambridge University Press, 2009), particularly Chapter 8.

2. A report on the source is found in *Barokk, klasszicista és romantikus dìszlettervek magyarországon* (Budapest: Magyar Szinházi Intézet, 1976), 14–15.

3. Horányi Mátyás, *Eszterházi vigasságok [The Esterházy Festivities]* (Budapest: Akadémiai Kiadó, 1959). See also Horányi Mátyás, *The Magnificence of Eszterháza* (Budapest: Akadémiai Kiadó, 1962).

4. See the essay by John A. Rice in this volume: Chapter 2 'Operatic Culture at the Court of Leopold II and Mozart's *La clemenza di Tito*.

5. Mátyás, *Eszterházi vigasságok*, 14. Travaglia was in the active service of the Esterházy family until 1798 on different locations, including Vienna and Prague. He moved to Bratislava in 1802 to enter the service of the Grassalkovich family.

6. [Pietro Metastasio and Caterino Mazzolà,] *La clemenza di Tito, dramma serio per musica in due atti da rappresentarsi nel Teatro Nazionale di Praga nel settembre 1791* (Prague: Schönfeld, 1791).

7. In Metastasio, the set for Act III, scene 1 is described as follows: 'Camera chiusa con porte: sedia e tavolino con sopra da scrivere' ('A closed chamber with doors, a chair and a small table with writing utensils'). Pietro Metastasio, *La clemenza di Tito, dramma per musica, da rappresentarsi nella cesarea corte* (Vienna: Gio. Pietro Van Ghelen, 1734).

8. [Metastasio and Mazzolà], *La clemenza di Tito* (1791).

9. Designed for this essay by Paolo Kirschner and Silvia Tinazzo and reproduced with permission.

10. Mercedes Viale Ferrero, *La scenografia del '700 e i fratelli Galliari* (Turin: Pozzo, 1963), 161; Mercedes Viale Ferrero, 'Stage and Set', in *Opera on Stage,* eds. Lorenzo Bianconi and Giorgio Pestelli, (Chicago & London: The University of Chicago Press, 2002), 1–123.

11. [Metastasio and Mazzolà], *La clemenza di Tito* (1791), Act II, scene 16. In addition to the instructions given in the Metastasian caption, all the choristers must be on stage by the end of the instrumental introduction: 11 bars, and no more than 25 seconds on John Eliot Gardiner's recording: Archiv 431806-2.

12. Reproduced in John A. Rice, *Mozart on the Stage* (Cambridge: Cambridge University Press, 2009), 169.

13. For a reproduction of the coloured print, see H.C. Robbins Landon, *Mozart: The Golden Years: 1781–1791* (London: Thames and Hudson, 1989), 218–19.

14. [Franz Alexander von Kleist:] *Fantasien auf einer Reise nach Prag* (Dresden & Leipzig: Richterschen Buchhandlung, 1792), 131–2, 134.

15. According to Mercedes Viale Ferrero, fire on stage was produced by burning alcohol-based liquids in flat trays which guaranteed the possibility of a fast fire extinction.

16. The customary indication for the wings is *dentro* (inside) or *dietro* (behind) although neither form is used in Mozart's scores. In *Idomeneo* (chorus 5. 'Pietà, numi pietà' Mozart specifies 'Coro lontano' and 'Coro vicino').

17. Note also that on 15 March 1795 Constanze Mozart organised a concert performance of *La clemenza di Tito* in Vienna. A libretto has survived from the same year, presumably from this performance: *Arie tirate dall'opera la Clemenza di Tito di Wolfgango Amadeo Mozart* (Vienna: Schönfeld, 1795). Because it was printed for a concert performance the libretto provides some extra captions to supplement the lack of visual action. The following direction is included at the first entry of the chorus: 'Gridi del populo tra le fiamme' ('Screams of the people among the flames'). This is probably a direct recollection of what had been staged and seen in Prague four years earlier.

18. Wilhelm Seidel, 'Seneca – Corneille – Mozart: Ideen und Gattungsgeschichtliches zu *La clemenza di Tito*', *Musik in Antike und Neuzeit*, eds. Michael von Albrecht and Werner Schubert (Frankfurt am Main, New York: Peter Lang, 1987), 109–28. This is included in Italian translation in *Mozart*, ed. Sergio Durante (Bologna: Il Mulino, 1991). While theoretically developed by Seneca, the connection between *clementia* and absolutism dates from the end of the republican era in Rome, and is related to Cicero's so-called 'Caesarean' speeches.

19. Adam Wandruszka, 'Die "clementia austriaca" und der aufgeklärte Absolutismus: Zum politischen und ideellen Hintergrund von *La clemenza di Tito*', *Österreichische Musikzeitschrift*, 31 (1976), 186–93.

20. Emanuele Senici, La clemenza di Tito *di Mozart: I primi trent'anni (1791–1821)* (Thurnout: Brepols, 1992), 249; see also the text, which is preserved in US-Wc, ML48 S6755.

21. Sergio Durante, 'Quando Tito divenne Titus: Le prime traduzioni tedesche della *Clemenza* mozartiana ed il ruolo di Friedrich Rochlitz', *Festschrift Max Lütolf zum 60. Geburtstag*, eds. Bernhard Hangartner and Urs Fischer (Basel: Wiese Verlag, 1994), 247–58, and 'La clemenza

di Jahn, ovvero Le nozze perturbate di Musica e Filologia', *L'edizione critica fra testo musicale e testo letterario*, eds. Renato Borghi and Pietro Zappalà (Lucca: L.I.M., 1995), 345–57. Clemency is more easily understood and internalised within a monarchy-oriented social body than within a democracy, where, despite the institutional recognition of the act of clemency, it belongs to an elected officer, inevitably suspect of expedience.

22. Hans Joachim Kreutzer, 'Mozart's Opera of the Future *La clemenza di Tito*', W.A. Mozart, *La clemenza di Tito K.621: Facsimile of the Autograph Score* (Kassel: Bärenreiter, 2008), 1–15; Sergio Durante, 'Musicological Introduction', in ibid., 17–34) describes the genesis of the opera.

23. For instance, the addition of the aria with chorus 15. 'Ah, grazie si rendano' is incongruent with the following recitative announcing that the people are waiting for Tito at the arena (whereas they have just celebrated the sovereign's well-being).

24. John A. Rice, *W. A. Mozart:* La clemenza di Tito (Cambridge: Cambridge University Press, 1991), 118–33. See also the article by Magnus Tessing Schneider in this volume; Chapter 3, 'From Metastasio to Mazzolà: Clemency and Pity in *La clemenza di Tito*.

25. Franz Horn, 'Musikalische Fragmente', *Allgemeine musikalische Zeitung*, IV/28 (7 April 1802), 452.

26. Sergio Durante, *Mozart and the Idea of "vera opera": A study of* La clemenza di Tito, PhD diss., Harvard University, 1993, Chapter 2, 24–42.

27. Manfred Hermann Schmid, *Mozarts Opern* (Munich: Beck, 2009), back cover. While Schmid might not be responsible for the text of the back cover, it is in itself significant that the notion filtered into his authoritative book.

Select Bibliography

Online reference sources

Edge, Dexter and Black, David, *Mozart: New Documents*, https://sites.google.com/site/mozartdocuments/

Jean-Jacques Rousseau. Collection complète des œuvres. 17 vol. in 4°, Geneva, 1780–88. https://www.rousseauonline.ch/tdm.php

Mozart Briefe und Dokumente – Online-Edition (Mozarteum Foundation Salzburg and The Packard Humanities Institute Salzburg) www.dme.mozarteum.at/DME/main/cms.php?tid=110&sec=briefe&l=1

Søren Kierkegaard Forskningscenteret, Copenhagen 2013: www.sks.dk (accessed 20 April 2017).

Sources pre-1825 — Alphabetical

Albrecht, Johann Friedrich Ernst. *Krönungsjournal für Prag*. Prague, 1791.

Allgemeine musikalische Zeitung (Leipzig, 1798–1848).

Arie tirate dall'opera la Clemenza di Tito di Wolfango Amadeo Mozart. Vienna: Schönfeld, 1795.

Auswahl neuer Lustspiele für das Königliche Hof-Theater in Berlin. Berlin: Schüppelschen Buchhandlung, 1824.

Brown, John. *Letters upon the Poetry and Music of the Italian Opera Addressed to a Friend*. Edinburgh: Belle and Bradfute, 1789.

Chronique de Paris (Paris, 1789-93).

Cramer, Carl Friedrich. *Individualitäten aus und über Paris*. Amsterdam: Kunst- und Industrie-Comptoir, 1806.

Debrois, Johann. Ed., *Aktenmässige Krönungsgeschichte des Königs von Böhmen Leopold des Zweiten und Marie Louisens*. Prague, 1792.

Debrois, Johann. *Urkunde über die vollzogene Krönung Seiner Majestät des Königs von Böhmen Leopold des Zweiten und Ihrer Majestät der Gemahlinn des Königs Maria Louise, gebornen Infantinn von Spanien.* Prague: Gottlieb Haase, 1808.

Dlabacž, Gottfried Johann. Ed. *Allgemeines historisches Künstler-Lexikon für Böhmen und zum Theil auch für Mähren und Schlesien*, 3 vols. Prague: Gottlieb Haase, 1815.

Encyclopédie ou Dictionnaire raisonné des sciences, des arts et des métiers, 28 vols. Paris: Le Breton, Durand, Briasson and Michel-Antoine David, 1751–72.

Gazzetta toscana (Florence, 1766-1811).

Gazzetta universale, o sieno Notizie istoriche, politiche, di scienze, arti, agricoltura ec (Foligno, 1775-98).

Kant, Immanuel. *Critik der Urtheilskraft.* Berlin, Libau: Lagarde und Friederich, 1790.

[Kleist, Franz Alexander von]. *Fantasien auf einer Reise nach Prag.* Dresden, Leipzig: Richterschen Buchhandlung, 1792.

Krönungsjournal für Prag. Prague, 1791.

Kunzen, F[riedrich] Ae[milius] and Reichard, J[ohann] F[riedrich]. Eds. *Studien für Tonkünstler und Musikfreunde: Eine historisch-kritische Zeitschrift fürs Jahr 1792.* Berlin, Verlage der neuen Musikhandlung, 1793. I, *Musikalisches Wochenblatt.*

Lessing, Gotthold Ephraim. *Laokoon: oder über die Grenzen der Mahlerey und Poesie. Mit beyläufigen Erläuterungen verschiedener Punkte der alten Kunstgeschichte.* Berlin: Christian Friedrich Voß, 1766.

Lessing, Gotthold Ephraim. *Sämtliche Werke. Dreyzehnter Band. Zweyter Theil. Hamburgische Dramaturgie.* Vienna: Anton Pichler, 1801.

Löschenkohl, Hieronymus. *Beschreibung der Huldigungsfeyerlichkeiten seiner königlichen apostolischen Majestät Leopolds II. Königs von Ungarn und Böheim, Erzherzogs von Österreich, welche von den Nieder-Oesterreichischen Landständen zu Wien am 6ten April 1790 gehalten wurden.* Vienna, Löschenkohl, 1790.

[Metastasio, Pietro.] *La clemenza di Tito, dramma per musica, da rappresentarsi nella cesarea corte*. Vienna: Gio. Pietro Van Ghelen, 1734.

[Metastasio, Pietro and Mazzolà, Catterino.] *La clemenza di Tito, dramma serio per musica in due atti da rappresentarsi nel Teatro Nazionale di Praga nel settembre 1791. In occasione di sollenizzare il giorno dell' incoronazione di Sua Maestà l'Imperatore Leopoldo II*. Prague: Schönfeld, 1791.

Morgenblatt für gebildete Stände, XII/181 (24 November 1818), Stuttgart, Tübingen, 1807–65.

Mozart, Wolfgang Amadé. *Verzeichnüß aller meiner Werke vom Monath febrario 1784 bis Monath [November] 1[791]*. GB-BL, Zweig MS 63, ff. 28v.

[Franz Xaver Niemetsche]k, 'Einige Nachrichten über den Zustand des Theaters in Prag. Im Dezember 1794', *Allgemeines europäisches Journal*, II/3 (December 1794), 564–70.

Niem[e]tschek, Franz [Xaver]. *Leben des K. K. Kapellmeisters Wolfgang Gottlieb Mozart, nach Originalquellen beschrieben*. Prague: Herrlischen Buchhandlung, 1798.

Němetschek, Franz Xaver. *Lebensbeschreibung des K. K. Kapellmeisters Wolfgang Amadeus Mozart, aus Originalquellen, Zweite vermehrte Auflage*. Prague: Herrlischen Buchhandlung, 1808.

Prager Theater-Almanach auf das Jahr 1808. Prague: Caltreischen Buchhandlung, 1807.

Prévost, Antoine François (Abbé). *Histoire du Chevalier de Grieux et de Manon Lescaut*. Amsterdam, 1731.

Reichard, Heinrich August Ottokar. *Taschenbuch für die Schaubühne, auf das Jahr 1793*. Gotha: Carl Wilhelm Ettinger, [1792].

Rochlitz, Johann Friedrich. 'Verbürgte Anekdoten aus *Wolfgang Gottlieb Mozarts* Leben, ein Beytrag zur richtigern Kenntnis dieses Mannes, als Mensch und Künstler', *Allgemeine musikalische Zeitung*, I/2 (10 October 1798), 17–24; I/4 (24 October 1798), 49–55; I/6 (7 November 1798), 81–86; I/8 (21 November 1798), 113–17; I/10 (5 December 1798), 145–152; I/12 (19 December 1798), 177–83.

Rousseau, Jean-Jacques. *Discours sur l'origine et les fondements de l'inégalité parmi les hommes* (1755), *Collection complète des œuvres*. Geneva, 1780–88.

Rousseau, Jean-Jacques. *Dictionnaire de musique*. Geneva, La Veuve Duchesne, 1767.

Der Sammler, ein Unterhaltungsblatt (Vienna, 1809–46).

Siboni, Joseph. 'Berichtigung', *Originalien aus dem Gebiete der Wahrheit, Kunst, Laune und Phantasie*, V/20 (1821), 159–60.

Tagebuch der böhmischen Königskrönung. Prague: Joseph Walenta, Kunst- und Buchhändler, 1792.

Wiener Zeitung (Vienna, 1703-).

Wismayr, Joseph. Ed. 'Ueber den gegenwärtigen Zustand der Tonkunst in Italien', *Ephemeriden der italiänischen Litteratur, Gesetz-Gebung und Kunst für Deutschland*, IV/6 (1804), 301–9.

Zeitung für die elegante Welt (Leipzig, 1801–59).

Sources post 1825 — Alphabetical

Anderson, Emily. *The Letters of Mozart & His Family: Chronologically Arranged, Translated and Edited with an Introduction, Notes and Indices*. London: Macmillan & Co., 1938.

Angermüller, Rudolph. *Antonio Salieri: Sein Leben und seine Welt unter besonderer Berücksichtigung seiner großen Opern*, 3 vols., Munich: Katzbichler, 1971–74.

Angermüller, Rudolph. 'Zwei Selbstbiographien von Joseph Weigl (1766–1846)'. *Deutsches Jahrbuch der Musikwissenschaft* XVI (1971), 46–85.

Aristotle. *Aristotle on Rhetoric: A Theory of Civic Discourse*. Edited and translated by George Kennedy. Oxford: Oxford University Press, 1991.

Barnholdt Hansen, Jette. 'From Invention to Interpretation: The Prologues of the First Court Operas Where Oral and Written Cultures Meet'. *The Journal of Musicology*, XX/4 (2003), 556–596.

Barnholdt Hansen, Jette. 'Mozart som epideiktisk retor: Dydens og lastens repræsentation i *Titus*'. *Musikteater: Opførelse, praksis, publikum: Papers fra kollokvium, december 2003*, ed. Michael Eigtved. Copenhagen: University of Copenhagen, 2004, 8–23.

Barnholdt Hansen, Jette. 'Mozart som epideiktisk retor: Dydens og lastens repræsentation i *Titus*'. *Rhetorica Scandinavica*, 36 (2005), 25–37.

Barnholdt Hansen, Jette. '*Dramma per musica* eller *musica per dramma*? Mozarts *Idomeneo* – en *seria* som musikalsk opus'. *Dansk årbog for musikforskning*, XXX (2002), 51–73.

Barnholdt Hansen, Jette. 'Values on Stage: Epideictic Rhetoric as a Theoretical Approach to Music Theatre'. *Stage / Page / Play: Interdisciplinary Approaches to Theatre and Theatricality*, eds. Ulla Kallenbach and Anna Lawaetz. Copenhagen: Multivers, 2016, 211–21.

Beales, Derek. *Joseph II: II. Against the World, 1780-1790*. Cambridge: Cambridge University Press, 2009.

Beer, Adolf. Ed. *Joseph II., Leopold II. und Kaunitz: Ihr Briefwechsel*. Vienna, Braumüller, 1873.

Bénichou, Paul. *Morales du grand siècle*. Paris: Gallimard, 1948.

Blanchot, Maurice. *L'Entretien infini*. Paris: Gallimard, 1969.

Börner-Sandrini, Marie. *Erinnerungen einer alten Dresdnerin*. Dresden: Warnatz & Lehmann, 1876.

Dahlhaus, Carl. 'What is Musical Drama?' *Cambridge Opera Journal*, I/2 (1989), 95–111.

Deutsch, Otto Erich. *Mozart: Die Dokumente seines Lebens*. Kassel, Basel: Bärenreiter, 1961.

Durante, Sergio. Ed. *Mozart*. Bologna: Il Mulino, 1991.

Durante, Sergio. *Mozart and the Idea of "vera opera": A Study of* La clemenza di Tito, PhD dissertation, Harvard University, 1993.

Durante, Sergio. 'Quando Tito divenne Titus: Le prime traduzioni tedesche della *Clemenza* mozartiana ed il ruolo di Friedrich Rochlitz'. *Festschrift Max Lütolf zum 60. Geburtstag*, eds. Bernhard Hangartner and Urs Fischer. Basel: Wiese Verlag, 1994, 247–258.

Durante, Sergio. 'La clemenza di Jahn, ovvero Le nozze perturbate di Musica e Filologia'. *L'edizione critica fra testo musicale e testo letterario*, eds. Renato Borghi and Pietro Zappalà. Lucca: L.I.M., 1995, 345–357.

Durante, Sergio. 'The Chronology of Mozart's *La clemenza di Tito* Reconsidered'. *Music and Letters*, LXXX (1999), 560–94.

Durante, Sergio. 'Musicological Introduction', in Wolfgang Amadeus Mozart, *La clemenza di Tito, K. 621: Facsimile of the Autograph Score* (Los Altos CA: The Packard Humanities Institute, 2008), 17–34

Edge, Dexter. 'Mozart's Reception in Vienna, 1787–1791'. *Wolfgang Amadeus Mozart: Essays on His Life and His Music*, ed. Stanley Sadie. Oxford: Clarendon Press, 1996.

Eible, Joseph Heinz. 'Una porcheria tedesca'? Zur Uraufführung von Mozarts *La clemenza di Tito*'. Österreichische *Musikzeitschrift*, 31 (1976), 329–34.

Ferrero, Mercedes Viale. *La scenografia del '700 e i fratelli Galliari*. Turin: Pozzo, 1963.

Freeman, Daniel E. 'Mozart, *La clemenza di Tito*, and Aristocratic Reaction in Bohemia'. *Music in Eighteenth-Century Life: Cities, Courts, Churches*. Ed. Mara E. Parker. Ann Arbor: Steglein Publishing, Inc., 2006, 125–41.

Forestier, Georges. Ed. *Racine: Théâtre – Poésie*. Paris: Gallimard, 1999.

Genast, Eduard. *Aus dem Tagebuche eines alten Schauspielers*, 4 vols. Leipzig: Voigt & Günther, 1862-66.

Guyer, Paul. *Values of Beauty*. Cambridge: Cambridge University Press, 2005.

Hanson, Susan. *The Infinite Conversation*. Minneapolis, MN: University of Minnesota Press, 1992.

Hauser, Gerard A. 'Aristotle on Epideictic: The Formation of Public Morality'. *Rhetoric Society Quarterly*, 29/1 (1999), 5–23.

Horányi, Máthiás. *Eszterházi vigasságok [Das Esterházische Feenreich]*. Budapest: Akadémiai Kiadó, 1959.

Horányi, Máthiás. *The Magnificence of Eszterháza*. Budapest: Akadémiai Kiadó, 1962.

Jahn, Otto. *W. A. Mozart*, 4 vols. Leipzig: Breitkkopf & Härtel, 1856–59.

Jones, Brian W. *The Emperor Titus*. London: Croon Helm, 1984.

Jonášová, Milada. 'Semiramide riconosciuta - opera k pražské korunovaci Marie Terezie 1743'. *Barokní Praha - barokní Čechie 1620-1740. Sborník příspěvků z vědecké konference o fenoménu baroka v Čechách, Praha, Anežský klášter a Clam-Gallasův palác, 24.-27. září 2001*. Prague: Scriptorium, 2004, 19–68.

Kant, Immanuel. *Immanuel Kant: Practical Philosophy*. Translated by Mary J. Gregor. Cambridge, Cambridge University Press, 1996.

Kierkegaard, Søren. *Either/Or: A Fragment of Life*. Translated by Alstai Hannay. London: Penguin Books, 1992/2004.

Kierkegaard, Søren. *Enten–Eller: Et Livs-Fragment*. Copenhagen: C. A. Reitzel, 1843.

Kleist, Franz Alexander von. *Fantasien auf einer Reise nach Prag*. Ed. Anke Tanzer. Heilbronn: Stadtbücherei, Heilbronn, 1996.

Kreutzer, Hans Joachim. '*Mozart's Opera of the Future* La clemenza di Tito'. *W. A. Mozart, La clemenza di Tito K.621. Facsimile of the Autograph Score*. Kassel: Bärenreiter, 2008, 1–15.

Lebrun, Elisabeth Vigée. *Souvenirs*, 3 vols. Paris: H. Fournier, 1835-7.

Lessing, Gotthold Ephraim. *Laocoon: An Essay upon the Limits of Painting and Poetry*. Translated by Ellen Frothingham. Mineola NY: Dover Publications, Inc., 2005 [1898].

Libin, Kathryn L. Ed. *Mozart in Prague: Essays on Performance, Patronage, Sources and Reception*. Prague: Czech Academy of Sciences, 2016.

Link, Dorothea. *The National Court Theatre in Mozart's Vienna: Sources and Documents, 1783–1792*. Oxford: Clarendon Press, 1998.

Lühning, Helga. Titus-*Vertonungen im 18. Jahrhundert: Untersuchungen zur Tradition der* opera seria *von Hasse bis Mozart*. Volkach: Arno Volk – Laaber Verlag, 1983.

Perelman, Chaim and Olbrecht-Tyteca, Lucie. *The New Rhetoric* [1969]. Translated by John Wilkinson and Purcell Weaver. Notre Dame, IN: University of Notre Dame Press, 1971.

McCroskey, James C. *An Introduction to Rhetorical Communication* [1968]. Boston: Allyn & Bacon, 1997.

Meissner, Alfred. *Rococobilder: Nach den Aufzeichnungen meines Grossvaters*. Gumbinnen: Wilhelm Krauseneck, 1871.

Nussbaum, Martha. *The Fragility of Goodness: Luck and Ethics in Greek Tragedy and Philosophy*, rev. ed. Cambridge: Cambridge University Press, 2001.

Racine, Jean. *Œuvres complètes* I, *Théâtre – Poésie*. Edited by Georges Forestier. Paris, Gallimard, 1999.

Rice, John A. *W. A. Mozart:* La clemenza di Tito. Cambridge Opera Handbooks. Cambridge: Cambridge University Press, 1991.

Rice, John A. 'Antonio Baglioni, Mozart's First Don Ottavio and Tito, in Italy and Prague'. *Böhmische Aspekte des Lebens und des Werkes von W. A. Mozart*. Eds. Milada Jonášová and Tomislav Volek. Prague: Institute of Ethnology of the Czech Academy of Sciences, 2012, 295–321.

Rice, John A. 'Emperor and Impresario: Leopold II and the Transformation of Viennese Theater, 1790–1792'. PhD dissertation. Berkeley: University of California, 1987.

Rice, John A. *Antonio Salieri and Viennese Opera*. Chicago: University of Chicago Press, 1998.

Rice, John A. 'From Venice to Warsaw: '*Zenobia di Palmira* by Sertor and Anfossi Performed by Guardasoni's Troupe (1791)'. *Mozart in Prague: Essays on Performance, Patronage, Sources and Reception*. Ed. Kathryn L. Libin. Prague: Czech Academy of Sciences, 2016, 295–310.

Rice, John A. *Mozart on the Stage*. Cambridge: Cambridge University Press, 2009.

Robbins Landon, H. C. *Mozart: The Golden Years, 1781–1791*. London: Thames & Hudson, 1989.

Robbins Landon, H. C. 'Acta Musicalia No. 141', *The Haydn Yearbook* XV (1984), 153–57.

Romilly, Samuel. *Memoirs*, 2nd edition, 3 vols. London: John Murray, 1840.

Rosenfield, Lawrence W. 'An Autopsy of the Rhetorical Tradition'. *The Prospect of Rhetoric*, eds. Lloyd F. Bitzer and Edwin Black. Englewood Cliffs NJ: Prentice-Hall, 1971.

Rosengren, Mats. *Doxologi: En essä om kunskap*. Åstorp: Rhetor förlag, 2003.

Rousseau, Jean-Jacques. *Discourse on the Origin of Inequality*. Translated by Franklin Philip. Oxford: Oxford University Press, 1994/2009.

Sadie, Stanley. *The New Grove Mozart*. London, Macmillan, 1980.

Sadie, Stanley. Ed. *Wolfgang Amadè Mozart: Essays on His Life and His Music*. Oxford: Clarendon Press, 1996.

Schepelern, Gerhard. *Giuseppe Siboni: Sangeren – Syngemesteren: Et Afsnit af Operaens Historie ude og hjemme hovedsagelig paa Grundlag af hidtil ubenyttede trykte og utrykte Kilder*, 2 vols. Copenhagen: Amadeus, 1989.

Schmid, Manfred. *Mozarts Opern*. Munich: Beck, 2009.

Seidel, Wilhelm. 'Seneca – Corneille – Mozart: Ideen und Gattungsgeschichtliches zu *La clemenza di Tito*'. *Musik in Antike und Neuzeit*. Eds. Michael von Albrecht and Werner Schubert. Frankfurt am Main, New York: Peter Lang, 1987, 109–128.

Senici, Emanuele. La clemenza di Tito *di Mozart: I primi trent'anni (1791–1821)*. Thurnout: Brepols, 1992.

Sheard, Cynthia Miecznikowski. 'The Public Value of Epideictic Rhetoric'. *College English*, 58/7 (1996), 784–91.

Sidney, Michael. Ed. *Sources of Dramatic Theory*. Vol. 2: *Voltaire to Hugo*. Cambridge: Cambridge University Press, 1994.

Sullivan, Dale L. 'The Ethos of Epideictic Encounter'. *Philosophy and Rhetoric*, XXVI/2 (1993), 113–33.

Strang, Heather and Braithwaite, John. *Restorative Justice: Philosophy to Practice*. Dartmouth: Ashgate, 2000.

Strang, Heather and Braithwaite, John. *Restorative Justice and Civil Society*. Cambridge: Cambridge University Press, 2001.

Strang, Heather, *Repair or Revenge: Victims and Restorative Justice*. Oxford: Clarendon Press, 2002.

Tessing Schneider, 'Kierkegaard and the Copenhagen Production of Mozart's *Don Giovanni*'. *European Romantic Review*, 29/1 (2018), 43–50.

Volek, Tomislav. 'Über den Ursprung von Mozart's Oper *La clemenza di Tito*'. *Mozart-Jahrbuch* 1959 (Salzburg, 1960), 274–286.

Volek, Tomislav. Ed. *Miscellanea musicologica* vol. 16: *Repertoir Nosticovského divadla v Praze z let 1794, 1796–98*. Prague: Charles University, 1961.

Waldoff, Jessica. *Recognition in Mozart's Operas*. Oxford: Oxford University Press, 2006.

Wandruszka, Adam. 'Die "clementia austriaca" und die aufgeklärte Absolutismus: Zum politischen und ideellen Hintergrund von *La clemenza di Tito*'. *Österreichische Musikzeitschrift*, 31 (1976), 186–193.

Woodfield, Ian. *Performing Operas for Mozart: Impresarios, Singers and Troupes*. Cambridge: Cambridge University Press, 2012.

Žižek, Slavoj. '*La Clemenza di Tito*, or the Ridiculously-Obscene Excess of Mercy'. 2004 www.lacan.com (accessed 8 December 2017).

Index

A

Abert, Hermann 154
Adamberger, Valentin 48, 54n
Anfossi, Pasquale 53
  Il curioso indiscreto 44
Angiolini, Gaspar 35
Antonini, Anna (see Campi, Antonia) 13, 18, 21, 94n
Aristotle 66, 71, 116n, 120, 128, 131n, 133n, 152, 162, 164
Austria 2, 3, 4, 6, 36, 39, 151, 157n, 168

B

Babbini, Cherubino 13
Baglioni, Antonio 5, 6, 13, 21, 43, 53n, 88n, 166
Baker, Felicity xiv, xv, 88n, 91n, 97–119
ballet 5, 7, 35, 38, 47
Barnholdt Hansen, Jette vii, xiv, xvi, 92, 120–133, 162–3
basset horn 26
Bassi, Luigi 21, 175
Bastille, the 2
Bedini, Domenico 5, 13, 18, 21–2, 26, 29, 43, 83–5
Beethoven, Ludwig van 35
Benda, Georg
  Romeo und Julia 3

Benucci, Francesco 40
Berenice (historical person) 69–70, 80, 97, 99–100, 103, 107–8, 110, 117n
Berenice (Racine) 97, 106–8, 117n
Berka, Johann xii, 142, 143
Berlin 38, 57
Berndt, I. C. xi, xv, 122–3, 125, 129
Bertati, Giovanni 4
Biggi, Maria Ida 138
Black, Edwin 53, 123, 131n, 132n, 159, 167
Bohemia xv, 3–5, 9–10, 15, 18, 22, 34, 36–7, 41, 43, 56–7, 83, 87n, 94n, 98, 100, 120
Bohemian Estates 3, 4, 7, 10–11, 14, 16–17, 19–20, 22, 24, 27, 56, 83, 100, 115n
Bonaparte, Jerôme 115
Bratislava 3, 36, 156n
Breysig, Johann 13, 150
Brorson, Hans Adolph, 127
Budapest xi, xii, 30n, 134, 136, 144, 155n
Bussani, Dorothea 48, 54n

C

Caldara, Antonio
  La clemenza di Tito 2

Calvesi, Vincenzo 44, 45, 48, 54n
Campi, Antonia 6, 13, 84, 85, 94n, 95n
Candeille, Pierre-Joseph 50
Capitol, the 67–8, 70, 146–7, 152
Casti, Giovanni Battista 47, 48, 50, 54n, 55n
Charles VI, Emperor 33, 41
Cimarosa, Domenico
  Il matrimonio segreto 68
clemency ix, x, 34, 56, 59–60, 63–4, 76, 88n, 92n, 98, 105, 108–9, 112, 114, 118n, 124, 129, 132n, 151, 158n
compassion 59–61, 63–6, 72–3, 75, 77–8, 80, 111, 124, 129
Copenhagen 29, 86, 96n, 175
Corneille, Pierre
  Cinna ou la Clémence d'Auguste 2, 33, 51n, 151, 157n
Coronation xiii
  King Leopold II of Hungary: 3, 36
  Holy Roman Emperor Leopold II: 3, 36, 37, 40, 121–4
  King Leopold II of Bohemia: 4, 5, 7, 9, 10, 14–16, 22, 36, 37, 41, 56, 57, 80, 98, 100, 120, 144
court poet 37, 57, 87n
Crescentini, Girolamo 7, 45

D

da capo aria 126–8, 130
D'Alembert, Jean-Baptiste 60, 106
Da Ponte, Lorenzo 4, 35, 39, 99
Debrois, Johann 18, 30n, 31n, 92n, 160
Diderot, Denis 60, 81
Ditters von Dittersdorf, Carl
  Betrug durch Aberglauben 3
  Der Apotheker und der Doktor 3, 40
drame lyrique
dramma giocoso 85
dramma per musica 49, 151
dramma sacro 42
dramma serio 21, 31
Durante, Sergio x, xiv, xv, 30n, 32, 27, 43, 51n, 57, 59, 87n, 88n, 89n, 92n, 134–58, 163–4

E

Elisabeth of Württemberg 38
Enlightenment xiv, 59, 64, 66, 87, 92n, 98, 111, 114n, 118n, 123, 130, 152
Estates Theatre, see Prague
Esterháza 47, 48, 49, 134
Esterházy, Prince Anton 46, 47, 48
Esterházy, Prince Nicholas 46

F

Feldman, Martha 130
Ferdinand III, grand duke of Tuscany 42
Ferdinand IV, king of Naples 3
Ferrarese del Bene, Adriana 45
Florence 41–3, 45, 48, 83

Francis (II), Archduke (later
    Emperor) 36, 38, 39, 47
Freeman, Daniel E. 56, 59, 87n,
    88n, 164
fraternité x 72, 121, 123, 125
Fux, Johann Joseph
    Costanza e fortezza 41

G

Gallieri, Bernardino 134, 141,
    156n, 164
Gallieri, Fabrizio 134, 141,
    156n, 164
Gaussin, Jeanne-Catherine 106
Giuliani, Cecilia 4, 41–9,
    54n 55n
Giuliani, Francesco 49
Gluck, Christoph Willibald
    23, 175
Guardasoni, Domenico 5–9, 16,
    19, 21–3, 29, 37, 43, 46, 53n,
    56, 58–9, 85–6, 95n, 144, 166
Guglielmi, Pietro
    Debora e Sisara 42

H

Hauser, Gerard 129, 133n, 164
Haydn, Josef 4, 6, 35 46, 47, 54n,
    94n, 134
    Arianna a Naxos 94n
    Die Schöpfung 94n
Heger, Franz xii 142, 143, 144
Heger, Philipp xii 142, 143, 144
Hennet, Baron Johannes von 9
Holy Roman Empire 3, 11, 36,
    115n, 120

Horace 24
Horn, Franz 153, 154, 158n
Huldigung (oath of allegiance) 3,
    7, 36, 37, 51n, 160

J

Jahn, Otto 93, 151, 154, 158n,
    164, 165
Jaucourt, Louis de 60
Joseph II, Emperor 2, 3, 34, 35,
    38, 41, 52n, 115n, 163
justice 68, 88n, 101, 102

K

Kant, Immanuel 118n, 119n, 126,
    160, 165
Kaunitz, Prince Wenzel Anton
    von 38, 52n, 163
Kierkegaard, Søren 86, 96n, 168
Kinigl, Count Kasper Hermann 9
Kleist, Franz Alexander von 17,
    31n, 82, 144, 156n, 160
Koželuch, Leopold 20, 57

L

Lange, Aloisia 44, 45
Leopold II, Emperor
    see Coronation
Lessing, Gotthold Ephraim 64–6,
    71, 90n, 91n, 160
    Emilia Galotti 66
    Laocoön 64, 65, 71, 90n, 165
libretto xiii, xiv, 2, 4, 8, 13,
    33–49, 56–80, 88n, 89n, 94,
    97–113, 135, 138, 142, 146,
    148, 150, 152–3, 157n, 160

Lolli, Giuseppe 21
London 6, 35, 38, 42, 46, 47, 54n
Löschenkohl, Hieronymus 36, 51n, 160
Louis XVI, king of France 4, 5, 6, 33, 50, 97, 115n

M
MacNeven, Baron Wilhelm Hugo 7
Maffoli, Vincenzo 4, 41–3, 46,
Marat, Jean-Paul 6
Marchesi, Luigi 7, 43,
Marchesini (see Marchesi, Luigi)
Marchetti Fantozzi, Maria 5, 13, 14, 18, 21, 23, 26, 29, 43, 83–5, 92n
Maria Carolina, queen of Naples 3, 39
Maria Luisa, Empress 5, 14, 18, 41, 43
Maria Theresa, Empress 34, 36, 41
Maria Theresa, Archduchess (Princess of Naples) 3, 39
Maria Theresa, Archduchess (Princess of Tuscany) 14, 38
Marie Antoinette, queen of France 2, 4, 5, 6, 33, 34, 50–51
Marschner, Heinrich 153, 154
Martín y Soler, Vicente
  L'arbore di Diana 38
Mazzolà, Caterino 50, 56–89, 97–8, 105, 108, 113, 116n, 119n, 121, 132n, 135, 153, 155, 156n, 158n, 161

Meissner, August Gottlieb 20, 57, mercy 60, 91n, 92n, 102, 168
Metastasio 37, 38, 99, 102, 105, 108, 151
La clemenza di Tito xiii, xiv, 2, 8, 10, 16, 27, 28, 29, 33, 37, 38, 56–92, 97–99, 103, 105, 108, 113, 115n, 119n, 135, 142, 151–3, 156n,
  Semiramide 41,
mezzo carattere 130, 133n
Micelli, Caterina 21
Miklaszewicz, Antonina (see Campi, Antonia)
Milan 42, 134
Montesquieu, Charles-Louis 60
Mozart, Constanze 18, 157n
Mozart, Wolfgang Amadeus
  Clemenza di Tito, La, K.621
    Annio 61–3, 67, 71–3, 102–4, 107, 108, 110, 130, 142, 153
    Publio 67, 73, 74, 80,
    Servilia 62, 63, 71–2, 94, 102–5, 107, 109, 119n, 130, 142, 149, 153
    Sesto 6, 23, 29, 43, 60–96, 101, 104–112, 116, 128, 148, 151,
    Tito 5, 6, 23, 29, 33, 34, 43, 60–62, 64, 67, 69–87, 98–119, 128–130, 142, 146, 148, 151,
    Vitellia 6, 29, 43, 60, 62–79, 81, 84–95, 100–101, 106, 109–112, 117n, 119n, 128, 138, 142

1. 'Come ti piace imponi' (duet) 66, 78,
3. 'Deh prendi un dolce amplesso' (duettino) 72
6. 'Del più sublime soglio' (aria) 130
7. 'Ah perdona al primo affetto' (duet) 18, 72,
8. 'Ah, se fosse intorno al trono' (aria) 104, 130
9. 'Parto, ma tu ben mio' (aria) 68,
10. 'Vengo...aspettate... Sesto' (trio) 23, 67, 78, 86
11. 'Oh Dei, che smania è questa' (recitativo accompagnato) 68, 79
12. 'Deh conservate, o Dei' (quintet with chorus) 23, 28, 68, 86, 148
13. 'Torna di Tito a lato' (aria) 73
14. 'Se al volto mai ti senti' (trio) 73
15. 'Ah grazie si rendano' (aria with chorus) 80, 158
17. 'Tu fosti tradito' (aria) 61
18. 'Quello di Tito è il volto' (trio) 74, 76
19. 'Deh per questo instante solo' (rondo) 75, 76, 80,
20. 'Se all'impero, amici Dei' (aria) 117, 130,
21. 'S'altro che lagrime' (aria) 62
23. 'Non più di fiori' (rondo) 18, 77, 79, 85, 86, 112, 138
24. 'Che del ciel, che degli Dei' (chorus) 138
26. 'Tu è ver, m'assolvi, Augusto' (sextet with chorus) 26, 86,
Così fan tutte, K.588 3, 92, 95
Dissoluto punito, Il (see also *Don Giovanni*) 21
Don Giovanni, K.527 5, 23, 24, 28, 38, 82, 86, 87, 91n, 92n, 94n, 95n, 96n, 168
Entführung aus dem Serail, Die, K.384 25, 65,
   3. 'Solche hergelaufne Laffen' (aria) 65
Idomeneo, K.366 25, 28, 126, 133n, 157n, 163
'No, che non sei capace', K.419 44
Nozze di Figaro, Le, K.492 4, 38, 40, 53, 94n, 95n
Requiem K.626 35
Zauberflöte, Die, K.620 5, 18, 22, 34, 99
Muzzarelli, Antonio 5

N

Nasolini, Sebastiano
   Teseo a Stige 5, 42, 43, 44, 43
Nencini, Santi 44, 45
Nero 107, 118,
Netherlands, The 2
Niemetschek, Franz Xaver 5, 22, 24, 32n, 82, 84–7, 93n

Nostitz-Rieneck, Count Franz Anton 21, 142, 143, 148, 153
Noverre, Jean-Georges 35

O

opera buffa 25, 35, 38, 39, 41, 43
opera seria x, xiv, 4, 5, 7, 10, 13, 28, 35–38, 41–5, 49, 50, 83–85, 92n, 98, 99, 103, 106, 107, 116n, 126–9, 131, 155, 165

P

Pacchierotti, Gasparo 43
Paisiello, Giovanni
   Fedra 44–5, 47, 48
Pasticcio 41
Paulinus (Racine) 103
Perini, Angiola 21
Perini, Carolina 13, 18, 21
Perini, Caterina 21
Pietà 59–62, 67, 70, 73, 74, 75, 77, 78, 79, 92n, 157n,
Pillnitz, Declaration of 5
pity 56–96, 105, 106, 111, 132n, 158n
Pluth, Caspar 144
Ponziani, Felice 21
Prague
   Estates Theatre (see National)
   Gubernatorial House 11
   National Theatre xii, xv, 5, 7, 10, 12, 15, 18, 21, 66, 91n, 120, 142, 143, 148, 153
Prati, Alessio
   La vendetta di Nino 6, 42, 43

prima donna 7, 16, 21, 22, 43, 83, 84, 92n, 95n
primo uomo 45, 48
propaganda 56, 59, 81, 83
Prussia 3, 5, 82,

R

Racine, Jean
   Bérénice 97, 106, 107, 117n
   Britannicus 107
   Phèdre [Phaedra] 44,
rage 65, 67, 68, 70, 71, 72, 78, 112, 119n,
Rameau, Jean-Philippe
   Castor et Pollux 5, 50
Regicide 50, 55n, 101
Regietheater 154
Reichard, Heinrich August
   Ottokar 22, 32n, 52n, 161
Reichenbach, Treaty of 3
restorative justice 101, 106n, 168
Revolution,
   American 114, 115n,
   French xv, 2, 34, 36, 55n, 114, 115n, 120, 121, 123,
Rice, John A. ix, xiv, xv, 2, 33–55, 59, 88n, 92n, 99, 115n, 132n, 155n, 156n, 158n
Robespierre, Maximilien 6
Rochlitz, Friedrich 57, 58, 151, 157n, 161, 163
Rome 24, 33, 42, 62, 80, 82, 100, 103, 107, 110, 112, 116n, 119n, 147, 157n
Romilly, Sir Samuel 55n, 167

Rosand, Ellen 130
Rottenhan, Count Heinrich Franz von 8, 9, 19, 83
Rousseau, Jean-Jacques 63, 64, 66, 89n, 105, 106, 111, 116n, 117n, 119n, 126, 159, 162
Rubinelli, Giovanni Battista 7
Russia 38, 150

S

Sadie, Stanley 99, 167
Salieri, Antonio 4, 9, 46, 51n, 54n, 162, 166
    Axur re d'Ormus 3, 21, 39, 40, 52n,
    Il talismano 3
Saxony 13, 38
Schlegel, August 153, 154
Seneca 151, 157n, 167n
Shakespeare, William 28, 175
Sheart, Cynthia 129, 132n, 167
Siboni, Giuseppe 29, 32n, 58, 84, 86, 88n, 93n, 162, 167
singspiel 7, 18, 38, 41
Sistova, Treaty of 4
Stadler, Anton 18, 82
Staël-Holstein, Anne Louise Germaine de (Madame de Staël) 50, 55n
Strinasacchi, Teresa 6, 23, 85, 95n
Strohm, Reinhard 130
Süssmayr, Franz Xaver 5
Sweerth, Count Johann von 9

T

Tarchi, Angelo
    Virginia 42

Tatlow, Ruth xiii–xvi, 1–32, 175,
Tessing Schneider, Magnus xiii–xvi, 1–32, 56–96, 120–133, 158n, 168, 175
Testori, Angelo 5, 42, 43, 45, 46,
theatrum mundi 121, 123,
Tinazzo, Silvia xi, xii, 138, 139, 140, 141, 146, 147, 148, 156n
Titus (historical person) 64, 97, 98, 108, 118n, 151
Titus (Racine) 97, 103, 106–8, 113, 114n, 115n, 117n
tragédie lyrique 37
tragedy 44, 66, 97, 102, 106–8, 116n, 151,
Travaglia, Pietro xi, xii, xv, 13, 47, 48, 49, 134–6, 141, 144, 146, 147, 149, 150, 155
Trompe l'oeil 138, 140, 147
Truth 29, 79, 102, 103, 104, 105, 108, 109, 119n,
Tuileries 50
Turkey 4, 36
Tuscany 41, 42

U

Ugarte, Count Johann Wenzel 4
Unwerth, Count Johannes 9

V

Varennes 4, 50
Vienna,
    Burgtheater 38, 40, 44, 45
    Court Chapel (Hofkapelle) 36
    Kärntnertortheater 2
    St Stephen's Cathedral 36
    Tonkünstler-Societät 44, 45

Violani, Violano 7
Virtue x, 56, 60, 63, 73, 77, 109, 120–133,
Vittelius 110, 112,
Volek, Tomislav 30n, 32n, 53n, 88n, 93n, 96n, 154, 166, 168,

W

Wackenroder, Wilhelm Heinrich 154
Waldorff, Jessica 59, 88n, 168

Weigl, Joseph 46, 47, 48, 50, 52n, 54n
 La caffettiera bizzarra 3, 39, 40, 47, 52n,
 Venere e Adone 4, 46, 47, 48, 49, 54n, 55n
Wranitzky, Paul
 Oberon 3, 40

Z

Zinzendorf, Count Karl von 14, 29, 40, 83

Editors of *La clemenza di Tito*

Magnus Tessing Schneider (b. 1975) is a Danish theatre and opera scholar. His PhD thesis concerned the original production of *Don Giovanni* (Aarhus University, 2009). From 2013 to 2017 he was a member of the interdisciplinary research group Performing Premodernity, funded by the Swedish Foundation for Humanities and Social Sciences and based at Stockholm University. In the spring of 2018 he was a research fellow of the Italian Academy for Advanced Studies in America at Columbia University. He specialises in the relation between dramaturgical criticism, aesthetic theory and vocal and scenic performance practice in Italian seventeenth- and eighteenth-century opera. He has published various articles on the operas of Cavalli, Monteverdi, Gluck, Mozart, Paisiello and Verdi, and has research interests in the librettos of Giovan Francesco Busenello and Ranieri Calzabigi, and in historical singers such as Anna Renzi (the original Ottavia/Drusilla in *L'incoronazione di Poppea*) and Luigi Bassi (the original Don Giovanni). Outside the field of opera, he has published on Shakespeare, and from 2010 to 2013 he was editor-in-chief of *Nordic Theatre Studies*. He has been active as a stage director in Copenhagen, and is a founding member of the Nordic Network for Early Opera. https://orcid.org/0000-0001-8903-7739

British-Swedish musicologist **Ruth Tatlow** is a widely published independent scholar and editor with a research base in Stockholm, Sweden, and a performance background as a prize-winning clarinettist (as Ruth Ballard). Her examination of compositional theory and practice in the works of J. S. Bach began with her doctoral thesis *Lusus musicus vel poëticus* (King's College, London University, 1987) and produced ground-breaking results reflected in her publications that include two classic monographs, *Bach and the Riddle of the Number Alphabet* (Cambridge, 1991) and *Bach's Numbers: Compositional Proportion and Significance* (Cambridge, 2015), the latter awarded Choice 'Outstanding Academic Title 2016'. Her current research interests include tracing the origins and transmission of proportional parallelism 1650–1850, and the theory and practice of emblematic techniques in early eighteenth century music collections. She co-founded Bach Network in 2004 and its journal *Understanding Bach* in 2006. She currently serves as chair of the Bach Network Council and is a member of the Editorial Board of the American Bach Society. https://orcid.org/0000-0003-3367-9921